A Borough-by-Borough Tour of the City's
Most Infamous Crime Scenes

New York Notorious

PAUL SCHWARTZMAN AND ROB POLNER

Maps by Barbara Glauber

Crown Publishers, Inc., New York

Published by Crown Publishers, Inc., 201 East 50th Street, New York, New York 10022.
Member of the Crown Publishing Group.

CROWN is a trademark of Crown Publishers, Inc.

Manufactured in the United States of America

Library of Congress Cataloging-in-Publication Data
Schwartzman, Paul.
    New York notorious : a borough-by-borough tour of the city's most infamous crime
scenes / by Paul Schwartzman and Rob Polner.
        p.   cm.
    1. Crime—New York (N.Y.)—Case studies.   2. New York (N.Y.)—
Description and travel.   I. Polner, Rob.   II. Title.
HV6795.N5S38   1992
364.1'09747'1—dc20   92-3692
                                                                     CIP

ISBN 0-517-58670-3

10   9   8   7   6   5   4   3   2   1

First Edition

New York Notorious

To our parents,
who've never been mugged . . . except once,
and to the memory of
John Cotter, our friend and editor,
who put us on the map

Contents

Introduction

Fun City

WELCOME TO NEW YORK, HOME OF THE stray bullet, birthplace of Al Capone, city of the ever-screaming police siren. The sightseeing opportunities are endless: a mob hit in Manhattan, perhaps, a bank robbery in Brooklyn, or a killing spree in Queens.

New York is a monument to mayhem, its streets and boroughs a thrilling trip down larceny lane. Name a block or a neighborhood where a serious crime hasn't been committed in the last four hundred years. Now name two.

Crime and scandal are as much a part of the city's history as the Empire State Building, the Brooklyn Bridge, and the Statue of Liberty. The city's original sin dates back to 1626, when Dutch settlers, perhaps setting the tone for future generations of local leaders, practically stole Manhattan from the Indians for $24.

New York doesn't have the ancient pyramids, the Sistine Chapel, or the Roman ruins, but the city's streets did inspire the early formation of marauding street gangs, as well as the world's most famous mobsters—Al Capone, Dutch Schultz, and Lucky Luciano, among them.

Gang slayings were a form of popular entertainment in the twenties, thirties, and forties, when it seemed as though every other day a well-dressed mobster with a nickname was being fished out of the East River. You could read all about it in the next day's newspaper—KID TWIST IN DEATH FALL screamed one headline—and still stroll through Central Park at night without fearing for your life.

Today, though, Fun City has become Gun City. Crime has lost its innocence. New York in the nineties is the city where you never have to say you're sorry: "Please don't shoot!" will suffice. Still, New Yorkers take the danger in stride, even as they duck or dash for cover. Survival is a matter of pride. After all, it's not everyone who can live in a city where there are six murders a day and a robbery, mugging, or car theft every forty-five seconds.

part one

Tourist
Trap

MANHATTAN

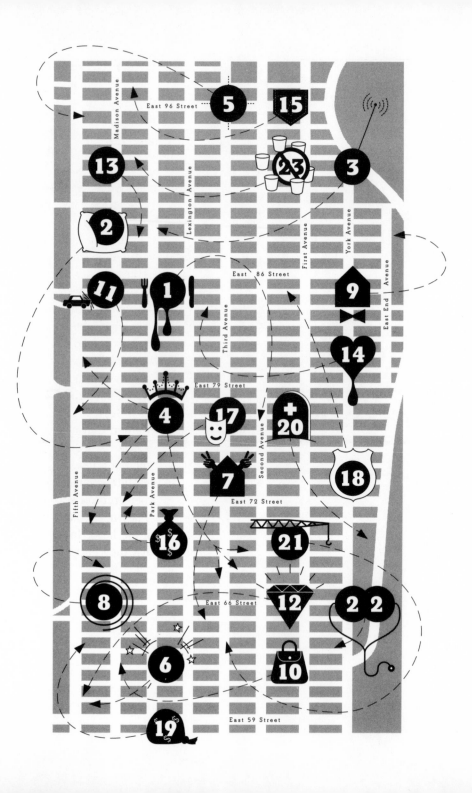

1

Crimestyles of the Rich and Famous

The Upper East Side

(Fifth Avenue to the East River, 60th to 97th Streets)

OH, TO BE SHOT ON THE UPPER EAST Side!

Or even mugged.

The cops respond in a jiff. So do the ambulances. Nothing beats Lenox Hill or Mount Sinai hospitals for comfort. On the way to the emergency room, swing by Elaine's for a drink with Woody and Mia. Or the Met, for a peek at your favorite Rembrandt.

If you're an unknown, an assault on the Upper East Side can do wonders for your career. Think of the publicity. Packs of reporters crashing your luxury condo, your elegant hotel, even your funeral, salivating for the really important details of your life—everything from who you're sleeping with to what color shoes you were wearing when you were shot.

Of course, some don't need the publicity—the Kennedys, Bess Myerson, Richard Nixon, Dan Rather, Calvin Klein, Dutch Schultz, Thomas Dewey, and Andy Warhol, to name but a few.

They'd all had their fifteen minutes— or years—of fame when crime or scandal snuck up on them. They needed the attention like a hole in the head. In some cases, that's just what they got: a one-way ticket to stardom.

1

Dinner Ain't Over 'Til the Fat Man Is Dead
1452 Second Avenue

The mob has a history of making personnel decisions over dinner. In the case of Irwin "The Fat Man" Schiff, the bullets were served just after the *rigatoni*.

Schiff was a charmer who conned his way from the tenements of Brooklyn's Brighton Beach to the fancy high-rises of the Upper East Side. He weighed four hundred pounds, talked tough, and liked to hang out with tough guys. But the tough guys thought Irwin was nothing more than a glorified groupie, a wise guy wannabe.

Mainly, Schiff wrote bad checks, didn't pay taxes, and toured the town in any one of three sparkling cruisers—a Rolls, a stretch Mercedes, and a Stutz Bearcat. He rented a $13,000-a-month apartment on East 54th Street and liked to hand out $30 tips to the doorman just for opening the door.

No one knows where he got all the cash, but some say Irwin stole from the mob, which could explain why on August 8, 1987, he exited the Bravo Sergio restaurant with a sheet over his face.

Schiff's killer didn't bother hanging around after the shooting, but he had been polite enough to wait until the Fat Man finished his meal before blasting him in the head with two shots. That's saying a lot considering the size of Irwin's feast—a salad, two appetizers, two main courses, and two desserts.

Schiff's companion that night, a woman later referred to as a "mystery blonde," excused herself from the table and fled to the street, as did the rest of the diners. They were no fools: a mob hit may upset one's appetite, but it's a terrific excuse for skipping out on the tab.

Bravo Sergio changed owners in 1991 and is now called Boccaccio. We still like it for fine cuisine. Indeed, we recommend the Irwin Schiff Memorial Dinner. Start off, as the Fat Man did, with two orders of shrimp cocktail and a Caesar salad. The *rigatoni amatrigiani* is a perfect entree, but don't stop there. Irwin didn't. Try the veal *rollatini*. For dessert, order the strawberries and bananas *flambé*.

No need for fine wine. Take it from Irwin, diet soda is the way to go. A cup of hot tea and a slice of melon make a nice kicker.

2

JFK and Marilyn at the Carlyle
35 East 76th Street

The White House, the limo, the private airplane—John Kennedy loved the perks of power.

But nothing beat the babes.

In May of 1962, just three months before she would die, Marilyn Monroe was sewn into a skintight beaded dress to sing "Happy Birthday" to the President in front of fifteen thousand people at Madison Square Garden. Kennedy described Marilyn's performance as "sweet and wholesome." His pal Adlai Stevenson had a different observation. He said it looked as though Marilyn wasn't wearing any clothes.

Later that night, JFK brought Marilyn back to the Hotel Carlyle. Kennedy's biographers claim he invited many women to the duplex suite on the hotel's 34th floor. As far as pickup lines go, "I'm the President of the United States" isn't bad. Kennedy didn't have to worry about Jackie, who was watching John-John and Caroline back at the White House. Sometimes, JFK would sneak out of the Carlyle through underground tunnels and meet his mistresses at their apartments in the neighborhood.

The Carlyle suite, 34A, still exists in case you have a hankering to live out your own presidential fantasy. But you may have to break in: the love nest has been turned into an apartment with a full-time tenant.

JFK, of course, wasn't the only Kennedy who made memories on the Upper East Side. One January night in 1989, Teddy Kennedy was hoisting a few with a young woman at American Trash, a bar on First Avenue near 76th Street. Dennis McKenna, 32, downing a few nearby, said he thought the senator was being crude as he listened to Kennedy flirt with several women at the bar. He told Teddy he was an embarrassment to the Kennedys and that he didn't measure up to his brothers John and Bobby. Teddy's answer, McKenna later claimed, was very simple. The senator threw his drink in McKenna's face and, after unleashing a barrage of cuss words, went home.

3

Dan, What's the Frequency?
1075 Park Avenue

On a fall night in 1986, Dan Rather looked into the camera and told millions of viewers that he was feeling fine. It was an interesting admission, considering that Dan had limped into the studio with the help of a cane. He had bruises all over his body.

In other words, America's most famous television anchorman, a journalist paid to tell the truth, the whole truth, and nothing but the truth, was telling a fib. Or so it seemed.

Only hours before, two men had accosted Rather at the corner of Park Avenue and 88th Street. The men wore raincoats and asked a rather bizarre question: "Kenneth, what's the frequency? Kenneth, what's the frequency?"

Dan, normally the one asking the questions, didn't know the answer. Not to worry, the men weren't interested. They had other plans, namely feeding Dan a knuckle sandwich. They hit him in the face and kicked him in the ribs, all the while repeating that same strange refrain, "Kenneth, what's the frequency?"

Dan managed to escape the beating by dashing into the lobby of 1075 Park Avenue. As sanctuaries go, this one wasn't too bad. The tasteful decor was highlighted by English paintings of hunting scenes, and the carpet—Dan saw a lot of that from ground zero—was a deep forest green. The men followed Dan inside, but a doorman chased them away.

Dan went home to nurse his battered body. Within hours, reporters swarmed to his East 74th Street apartment. Oh, the pain of having a bruised but famous face. All those questions, cameras, all that speculation. Some gossiped that Dan was beat up for having an affair with a married man's wife.

Dan, ever eager to help fellow journalists, said he did not know why he was attacked, that perhaps it was a case of mistaken identity. He was unable, however, to explain who he was supposed to be.

Bessville
3 East 71st Street

In 1986, a scandal of soap-operatic proportions teased New Yorkers with tales of sex and seduction, bribery and political betrayal. Still, the drama was not without convenience: all the players, everyone from Bess Myerson to Sukhreet Gabel to Andy and Nancy Capasso, lived in a ten-block radius on the Upper East Side.

Welcome to Bessville, where political connections are everything and links to the mob don't hurt, where rich women shoplift, married men cheat, and divorce lawyers are as common as face-lifts.

Start the Bessville tour at 3 East 71st Street, home to the scandal's star and self-proclaimed "Queen of the Jews." For years, Bess Myerson was the city's princess, a former Miss America who helped Ed Koch become mayor, only to help get him voted out of office.

Next stop, 990 Fifth Avenue, where Andy and Nancy Capasso lived in a luxurious 13-room duplex. Andy had it all—a sewer contracting business worth millions, gangster pals, a pretty wife, and two children. But that could never be enough, not in Bessville. Andy needed Bess as well, and so, late at night and on early mornings while Nancy slept, he slipped away and dashed nine blocks south to 3 East 71st just to be close to the Queen of Bessville.

Bess and Andy's romance began in 1980, when she was running for senator and just after she had ended an affair with a prominent financier. Bess and the financier spent many candle-lit nights at the Carlyle, but when he left her for another woman Bess apparently got revenge. She harassed him with crank telephone calls and he suspected her of having deposited a goodbye gift on his doorstep, a shopping bag filled with human excrement. No doubt this would have endeared her to Andy, who, of course, specialized in raw sewage.

For two years, Nancy Capasso knew nothing about Andy and Bess's affair, until the night in 1982 she spotted them eating dinner at Fortune Gardens, a Chinese restaurant at 68th and Third Avenue. Just a friend, Andy told her. Sure, said Nancy. Within months, she was calling Raoul Felder, Bessville's favorite divorce lawyer.

Which brings us to our next stop, 210 East 68th Street, home of Hortense Gabel, the venerable 74-year-old judge who presided over the Capassos' divorce. Judge Gabel had a long and distinguished career on the bench, but in 1983, the year the Capasso case reached her desk, she was worried about her daughter Sukhreet, then 34, who was depressed, unemployed, and who lived nearby at 219 East 69th Street. No one would hire Sukhreet—no one, that is, except the city's Department of Cultural Affairs, whose commissioner just happened to be Bess Myerson.

In the summer of 1983, Sukhreet became Bess's special assistant, after her mother made Bess happy by reducing Andy Capasso's monthly alimony payments to Nancy from $1,850 to $680. It wasn't too long before people were buzzing about the deals being made in Bessville. A small item on the *New York Post's* gossip page about Sukhreet's job turned into a front-page scandal in 1986, when it seemed that all of Ed Koch's political pals were turning up corrupt.

For a while, Koch stood by Bess. After all, she was a longtime ally, having helped him win the mayoralty in 1977 by posing as his girlfriend to deflect rumors that he was gay. At first, Koch blasted the attacks on Bess as "McCarthyism" but then called her hiring of Sukhreet "deplorable" after a mayoral commission concluded that she had abused her office. As 1986 ended, Bess resigned.

The soap opera offered still more titillation. First Bess, Andy, and the judge were indicted for conspiracy, mail fraud, and attempted bribery. Bess was also hit with an obstruction of justice charge. As if that wasn't bad enough, Myerson, who was worth about $10 million, managed to get herself splashed across the front pages again by stealing $44 worth of nail polish, film, and batteries from a department store in Pennsylvania.

The corruption trial was the hottest show in town in 1988, drawing SRO crowds, including Koch, who testified, and the 1957 Miss Detroit, who came by to lend moral support to Bess. Sukhreet took the stand against her mother, a small price for her newfound fame, which she said was as delightful as "dancing with Fred Astaire."

The prosecution talked big but had no proof that any deal had been struck between Judge Gabel, Bess, and Andy. Not surprisingly, the jury acquitted the threesome of all charges. "I'm grateful for the American judicial system," said a smiling Bess, leaving court for the last time as hundreds of reporters and photographers followed her back to Bessville.

The Plot Against Dewey
1148 Fifth Avenue

Dutch Schultz, the gangster, never taught speech to school kids, but we think he had a real gift for the language. Note, for example, the way he once described his plans for then–special prosecutor Thomas Dewey. "Dewey's gotta go," Dutch growled in 1935. "He's gotta be hit in the head."

We're quite sure that Dutch was not forecasting a moment of affection between himself and Dewey. In fact, it is widely held among some mobophiles, or mobologists as we like to call them, that Schultz planned to assassinate the prosecutor.

Death certainly would have dampened Dewey's ambition, a fire which eventually helped him grab the Republican Party presidential nomination in 1952. At the time of Schultz's pronouncement, Dewey's goal was to run the mob out of New York. He chose to focus on Dutch, who lorded over a $20-million-a-year numbers racket.

Schultz, not pleased with Dewey's plans, apparently went before the mob's ruling board of directors, otherwise known as the Commission, a body that included Lucky Luciano, Meyer Lansky, Louis Lepke, and Frank Costello. Dutch asked that the Commission approve Dewey's murder. Luciano, who lived at the Waldorf Astoria (suite 39D), was the boss of bosses at the time and wasn't interested in killing prosecutors, cops, or others whose deaths would provoke a massive crackdown on his criminal empire.

But Dutch was furious and announced he would kill Dewey on his own. He dispatched a hood to trace Dewey's steps each morning as he left 1148 Fifth Avenue, where he lived in an eight-room apartment with his wife and son. Dutch had a plan just so Dewey wouldn't catch on: the hood disguised himself as the "perfect parent," bringing along a little boy, who rode at his side on a tricycle.

Luciano found out about Dutch's plans and pronounced that it was time to save Dewey's life. On October 23, 1935, Lucky sent a team of assassins, including one nicknamed "The Bug," to the Palace Chophouse across the Hudson River in Newark, where they shot Schultz and three of his cohorts. For two days tough guy Dutch held on to life, mumbling from his hospital bed about everything from his mother to murder. "A boy has never wept, nor dashed a thousand kim," he mumbled incoherently at one point, a phrase that inspired at least one English professor to ponder whether the Dutchman spent his spare time reading James Joyce. No one was happier when he died than the court stenographer assigned to record his final ramblings. Dutch's last words: "Let them leave me alone."

6

Billy, Mickey, and Yogi: Those Crazy Nights at the Copa
10 East 60th Street

Midnight show at the Copacabana, May 16, 1957: Sammy Davis Jr. belting tunes from the stage, gorgeous blondes blowing smoke rings through red lips, waiters in maroon jackets serving drinks, ice cubes clinking delicately against glass.

It was a scene too delicious, too glamorous to last, especially with brawling Yankee Billy Martin in the joint. Billy was celebrating his 29th birthday that night with fellow pinstripers Mickey Mantle, Yogi Berra, and Hank Bauer.

Suddenly, Sammy's show was interrupted by a brawl in front of the stage between the Yanks and members of the "Republicans," a nineteen-member bowling team from New Jersey. A body went flying into the coat room as Sammy put down his mike and the cops flooded into the Copa.

The Yanks accused the Republicans of calling Davis a "Little Black Sambo." The bowlers charged that Bauer, the rightfielder nicknamed "The Bruiser," had thrown the first punch.

The next morning the headlines screamed YANKS IN BRAWL AT COPA and Bauer was arrested for assault. The Yanks were hauled before a grand jury, which prompted Mantle, known more for his skill with the bat than with the history books, to compare the ordeal to "the Nuremberg Trial."

The charge against Bauer was dropped after no one could say they saw who started the fight. The Yank's owner, though, had his own verdict: Billy Martin was a bad influence, particularly on Mantle, who, of course, had just led the league in hitting, runs batted in, and home runs. Martin was traded a month later to Kansas City. He would eventually return to New York, but we can't say for sure if he ever went back to the Copa, where you can still sit on the spot where the Yankees brawled in 1957. Just ask for table 11.

Four years later, on an October night in 1961, two New York City police detectives, Eddie Egan and Sonny Grosso, went to the Copa for a few drinks after work. The cops' attention became riveted on a little man in a silk suit, with a diamond stickpin in his tie, flashing a huge bankroll.

Something about this little guy didn't sit right with Egan and Grosso. They decided to follow him when he left the Copa that night. Good thing: the chase lasted eighteen months and turned into "The French Connection," in which Egan and Grosso made nine arrests and confiscated 112 pounds of heroin worth $32 million.

Dick
142 East 65th Street

New York City, home to the Statue of Liberty and millions of suspected crooks, was the perfect refuge for Richard Nixon after he departed Washington under a Watergate cloud in 1974.

Nixon—or Dick, as we like to call him—had an easier time getting into the White House than he did buying an apartment on the Upper East Side. After he resigned from office, he zeroed in on a six-figure pad in the neighborhood, only to get rejected by the building's tenants.

It wasn't Dick's politics that made the residents nervous at 817 Fifth Avenue, or even the fact that he no longer had a steady job. In fact, they believed him when he said he was not a crook. The tenants just didn't want a lot of reporters hanging around the lobby, not to mention protesters and Secret Service agents with those unseemly wires plugged into their ears.

No matter, Tricky Dick got into New York anyway. He simply bought an entire building, a 12-room town house at 142 East 65th Street for $750,000 that he would sell in 1982 for $2.6 million. The century-old home featured three bedrooms, seven bathrooms, a study, two living rooms, two kitchens, two fireplaces, a paneled library, and an elevator.

Best of all, there were no hostile neighbors—none, that is, except for the historian Arthur Schlesinger Jr., a crony of John Kennedy. Schlesinger, who lived across the backyard, once made Nixon's famed enemy list, so he wasn't exactly dashing over to borrow a cup of sugar. "He's a very luck man," Schlesinger said of his new neighbor, "living out his days in luxury when he ought to be in the federal penitentiary."

8

Bad Day for a Bureaucrat
36 East 68th Street

Peter Franconeri could take stock of his life on April 26, 1990, and count his blessings. He had an attractive wife, an $80,000-a-year job with the city, and an apartment in the richest, most sophisticated neighborhood on Earth. Just saying the address gave him goosebumps: Thirty-Six East Sixty-Eighth. Between Madison and Fifth. New York, New York 10021.

Franconeri had just one problem that April 26 and it had something to do with the young blonde dead on his living room floor. This was no ordinary woman. This was his 29-year-old mistress. She was enough to turn his pretty good life into a shambles.

Franconeri met Laurie Sue Rosenthal a year earlier while she was applying for a waitress job at a restaurant where he was a regular. She found him intelligent and charming, unlike the men she met in Jamaica, Queens, where she lived with her Orthodox Jewish parents. Laurie Sue was also impressed by the extremely crisp fifty-dollar bills Franconeri kept removing from his wallet. Before long, he was buying her dinner. Then lingerie. Soon, she was sleeping over at his apartment when Mrs. Franconeri was out of town.

Hours before she died, Laurie Sue phoned her parents from Franconeri's apartment and said she wasn't feeling well. Sobbing, she told them Franconeri had beaten her. Laurie Sue's parents insisted she take a cab home right away. For some reason, she never did. Soon she was dead, apparently from a lethal combination of alcohol and painkillers.

Alone with Laurie Sue's corpse, Franconeri panicked. What would the police say? And his wife? In one moment of desperation, Peter Franconeri found the solution: he rolled Laurie Sue's body in a carpet, went downstairs, and put her out on the street with the trash.

But then, perhaps, came the self-doubt. How would anyone know her body was there? What about her parents? Wouldn't they want a proper burial? Ever the gentleman, Franconeri made sure to place Rosenthal's handbag and ID next to her body. He also phoned in an anonymous tip to 911 that a corpse had been dropped on 68th Street. All in all, it was a rough morning for Peter Franconeri, but after a shower and shave he managed to get to work on time.

The cops, not surprisingly, found his name scribbled in Rosenthal's address book, next to his beeper number. He became the prime suspect in her death. Within a month, he surrendered, but not without a high-priced lawyer at his side. Franconeri eventually pleaded guilty to a misdemeanor, the "unlawful removal of a dead body without notifying local authorities." The punishment: seventy-five hours of community service.

9

Gracie Mansion
Carl Schurz Park, 88th Street and York Avenue

Back in the days when New York was more country than city, a wealthy Scottish merchant made himself a home on the banks of the East River. Archibald Gracie, who built Gracie Mansion in 1799, loved to sit on the porch of his country manor and gaze out at the water. He invited kings and queens for the weekends, along with presidents, bankers, and so-cialites. John Quincy Adams dropped by, as did Washington Irving and Alexander Hamilton.

Nearly two hundred years later, Gracie Mansion, with armed guards and bulletproof windows in every room, including the bathrooms, is only steps away from poverty, crime, and a polluted river.

Now that's progress.

The mansion became the official residence of the city's mayors in 1942. That meant, of course, that shenanigans would also move in—even into the mayor's bedroom. David Dinkins faced heat in 1990 over the headboard attached to his bed. The piece was hand-carved by city workers normally assigned to repair homeless shelters. Their bill to the taxpayers: $11,000.

Dinkins raised private funds to pay for the headboard, but it wasn't the first time there had been chicanery at the mansion. A few years earlier, city workers custom-built $600 dinner trays for Dinkins' predecessor, Ed Koch. Speaking of dinner, Koch's chef was caught running a private catering business out of the Gracie Mansion kitchen.

Koch received dozens of death threats as mayor and took steps to protect himself from intruders. For one, he converted his bathroom at the mansion into a bunker, installing a combination lock, bulletproof windows, and a direct phone line to police headquarters. There was even a rope ladder for a quick, mayoral escape to the lawn.

If all else failed, Koch could always look for comfort to Peewee, the three-foot-high pink papiér-mâché rabbit sculpture that occupied his bedroom floor while he was mayor. A bachelor, Koch said he enjoyed the late-night company. "When you get up to go to the bathroom in the middle of the night," Koch once told a writer, "it's nice to see a familiar face like Peewee's."

10

Next Time, Take the Limo: The Mugging of Felix and Elizabeth Rohatyn
62nd Street and Madison Avenue

Wall Street financier Felix Rohatyn, who helped save the city from fiscal bankruptcy in the mid-1970s, is a Park Avenue kind of guy, but he has always considered himself a man of the people. Translation: he's worth mega-millions, but he doesn't feel it's necessary to take a limo fifty yards to visit a friend.

Maybe he should.

On April 10, 1990, Felix and wife Elizabeth ate Passover seder on the East Side with some VIP pals. At 11 P.M., the socially acceptable moment to say goodnight, everyone went home. Some couples took cabs. Others called their drivers. Not the Rohatyns. They decided to walk. They lived only four blocks away.

Strolling south on Madison Avenue, the Rohatyns stepped gingerly over a homeless couple sprawled on the sidewalk. Imagine the dialogue:

"Oh, the plight of the underclass," Felix perhaps mused. "A tragedy," Elizabeth might have replied. That's the kind of people the Rohatyns are. They notice the people they walk over.

Suddenly, their little odyssey took a turn for the worse. As they reached the corner of East 62nd Street, a thief snatched Mrs. Rohatyn's Hermès leather purse and ran off. It happened so quickly that Felix didn't have a chance to chase the man. "When she screamed, I thought she had been stabbed," he later told the *New York Times*.

Elizabeth wasn't harmed, but the couple was disturbed by the incident for weeks. The very next day, Felix vented his anger before a group of young executives. One MBA, in a white shirt and suspenders, asked Rohatyn to describe life in contemporary New York.

"What you feel is the constant threat that something is going to happen to you," Felix said. "It's not civilized to consider yourself lucky when you've been mugged but haven't been killed."

Crossing the Street with Churchill
Fifth Avenue, near 77th Street

In December of 1931, Winston Churchill arrived in New York City to see the sights, give a speech, and meet with local dignitaries like Governor Al Smith and Mayor Jimmy Walker. Before he could get out of town, Churchill also met up with the front end of a car driven by one Mario Constasino, an unemployed mechanic from Yonkers.

Churchill, in a bow tie and a tweed overcoat, had just climbed out of a taxi that December 16th on the park side of Fifth, between 76th and 77th streets. He looked to his right as he stepped off the curb, the direction from which the traffic would have been approaching had he been in England and not on the Upper East Side. Too bad. A moment later, Churchill was flat on his duff and Mario Constasino was rushing him to Lenox Hill Hospital. Churchill was treated for a concussion, many bruises, and a nasty chest ailment.

Churchill was picky about who could visit him at the hospital, but found time to see Governor Smith, who slipped him a "little medicine," a bottle of Scotch. Churchill also invited Constasino in for a chat and, finding him to be a well-meaning chap, confessed that the accident had been his own fault. Churchill offered the mechanic some money to help him through hard times. When Constasino declined the gesture, Winston handed him a copy of his latest book, *The Unknown War*.

On New Year's Eve, Churchill decided to go to the Caribbean for a vacation less hazardous to his health. A small crowd collected at the foot of the *Majestic* oceanliner on the West Side to see him off, but he looked drawn-out, too weak even to stand without his new cane. Taking a puff on his cigar, Churchill doffed his hat and hobbled to his cabin.

Robbery at the Pierre
795 Fifth Avenue

Sure, we'll meet you at the Pierre. Lovely hotel, really. We especially adore the silk-draped Sapphire Room, with its shirred eggs so delicate and the $27 lobster salad. Do visit the Yellowbird Room, the peach tablecloths are such a nice touch.

Yes, the Pierre is a fine place to visit, but you may not want to stash your cash or jewels there. History tells us the hotel's safe-deposit boxes haven't been so safe after all. On the second day of 1972, five bandits stopped by the Pierre and pulled off the greatest jewel heist of all time.

The thieves arrived at 4 A.M., four men dressed in tuxedos accompanied by a chauffeur, a limousine, and luggage. It was late and the Pierre's front door was locked, but the security guard let the men inside, anyway. Why not? They looked like they were born at the Pierre.

Popping their bags open, the men whipped out guns, handcuffs, and reams of masking tape and manacled the wrists and wrapped the eyes of nineteen hotel employees and two guests. For the next two and a half hours, the intruders cracked open forty-seven safe-deposit boxes, stealing $8 million in jewelry, cash, and securities. It was a daring heist, but not without a sense of humor. After the thieves were long gone, the police found rubber noses on the lobby floor.

That was about all the men left behind. Certainly no fingerprints. But in a week, with the help of an FBI informant, the police got to the bottom of the heist. Detectives were led to a balding, 41-year-old Detroit man known as Sammy Nalo, who was staying in an apartment at 946 Anderson Avenue in the Bronx, where the cops found jewelry settings, a crowbar, and a hammer.

All five bandits were sentenced within a year. Nalo and his No. 1 sidekick, Robert Comfort, got the stiffest sentences—seven years apiece—but the terms were eventually reduced to two and a half years. "Let this be a lesson that crime does not pay—except for criminal lawyers," Judge Andrew Tyler said. Perhaps for criminals as well. It's believed that several million dollars' worth of jewels were never recovered.

Criminal Justice: The Career Girl Murders
57 East 88th Street

The slaying of two young women in their Upper East Side apartment in 1963 showed the city's criminal justice system at its worst. The police department, for one, was caught torturing a murder confession out of a penniless man. The district attorney's office, not to be outdone, was found to have deliberately ignored evidence that would have set the suspect free.

The victims, Janice Wylie, a 21-year-old research assistant at *Newsweek,* and Emily Hoffert, a 23-year-old studying to become a teacher, were discovered in their apartment at 57 East 88th Street (now a parking garage), tied back-to-back with torn bedsheet. Emily's throat was cut and her body bloodied from a number of stab wounds. Wylie, naked, had been sexually assaulted and also stabbed with a kitchen knife. Police officers found the murder weapon in the kitchen, stained with fingerprints. Neighbors told of seeing a baby-faced Hispanic man in the courtyard outside the building. Other than that, the cops had few clues.

The public was horrified by the double murder. Politicians promised execution for the killer, whoever he was. Wylie's father, Max, published a series of magazine articles entitled "Career Girl—Watch Your Step!" which suggested safety tips for women living in the city.

Eight months passed before the police arrested George Whitmore Jr., a poor 19-year-old black man described in the press the next day as a "Brooklyn drifter." The cops charged Whitmore with trying to rape a woman not related to the Wylie and Hoffert case. But during the interrogation, Whitmore "admitted" killing the so-called career girls. Of course, his confession occurred forty-eight hours after a group of police officers threatened to kill him, punching and stomping him with the heels of their heavy black shoes and refusing him food and drink.

The truth was that on the morning of the murders, Whitmore was in the lobby of a hotel in southern New Jersey, watching Martin Luther King Jr.'s "I Have a Dream" speech. But District Attorney Frank Hogan's office was not interested in summoning the witnesses who could testify to Whitmore's innocence. Nor did Hogan's staff talk in court about a heroin dealer who had told police that one of his addicts, Richard Robles, had confessed to killing the women. Robles, the baby-faced stranger spotted by neighbors, had been heard asking the dealer whether the sperm left in one of the victims' throats could be traced back to him.

All the same, Hogan's office convinced a jury that Whitmore was the killer. The district attorney won praise all around after Whitmore was sentenced to the electric chair. It was only when Robles later told the police on videotape that he was the murderer that prosecutors went ahead and convicted the right man. Robles was sentenced to life, and twenty-four years later, while in prison, he confessed his guilt to parole officers.

Whitmore had served nine years before he convinced prosecutors to drop the attempted rape conviction and release him. He sued the district attorney's office for $10 million in 1973, contending that prosecutors had ignored evidence that would have cleared him. Whitmore settled for $400,000 in damages, nearly all of which paid his legal fees.

Whitmore's ordeal inspired the "Kojak" television series and formed part of the basis for the U.S. Supreme Court's Miranda ruling in 1966, which forced police officers to advise suspects of their right to remain silent and their right to an attorney. The cops who battered Whitmore and the prosecutors accused of covering up evidence in his case were never punished.

14

Breaking Up Is Hard To Do
155 East 84th Street

Howard "Buddy" Jacobson, a renowned horse trainer, was terrific with thoroughbreds, but no one ever bet on his relationships with women. Listen to a dialogue he once had with his girlfriend Melanie Cain, a blonde model who lived with him in a building he owned at 155 East 84th Street. "You deal with me as if I were a piece of meat," Melanie said in 1978. Answered Buddy the Ladies' Man: "No, I believe you're the greatest broad in the world."

That was Buddy's tone when he was in a good mood. Imagine how sweet he was after learning Melanie was sleeping with another man—a man who lived in Buddy's building, no less. It didn't take long for Jacobson to decide that Melanie's lover, Jack Tupper, had to go. Buddy would take care of it, though not simply by putting a gun to Tupper's head and telling him to get lost. Too easy, even for a betting man.

Instead, Buddy and a friend went to Tupper's apartment, where they stabbed him first and shot him second. They packed Jack's body into a crate and drove to a junkyard in the Bronx where they set him on fire.

The cops arrested the killers within days and Buddy became the star of one of the 1970s' most sensational trials, a titillating concoction of stunning models, mob influence, and revenge. The jury didn't buy Jacobson's claim that Tupper, a restaurant owner with unsavory connections, was killed by the underworld. Buddy was sentenced to twenty-five years to life. In jail, he got cancer and died in 1989 while waiting to appeal the verdict.

15

Calvin Klein's Bad Day
60 East 97th Street

Calvin Klein was awakened by the telephone early one morning in 1978. The caller, a man, didn't say much, but he did mention that he had kidnapped the designer's 11-year-old daughter. The price for her return: $100,000.

At that moment, Marci Klein was sitting bound, gagged, and blindfolded in an apartment at 60 East 97th Street. She had been traveling to the prestigious Dalton School that February 3, 1979, when her former babysitter lured her off a school bus with a tale about Calvin being ill.

Calvin, a divorcé, always seemed to have more time for health spas and fashion runways than for fatherhood. He was one of the glamour kids who made the seventies so meaningless, partying nightly with other celebrity hedonists—you know, Bianca, Mick, and Halston—at Studio 54.

Calvin managed to clear most of the day to secure Marci's return. He bounced among midtown phone booths negotiating with the kidnappers. As instructed, he left a bag with $100,000 on an escalator in the Pan Am building. The kidnappers told him where to find Marci.

It was late in the day when he arrived at the apartment building on East 97th Street. Just one mixup: as he carried his daughter to freedom, dozens of cops and FBI agents staked outside thought Calvin was the kidnapper. It was only when Marci shouted, "Daddy, Daddy, Daddy!" that the authorities realized Calvin was actually Calvin. Three were arrested for the kidnapping and the cops recovered all but $100 of Calvin's $100,000 dropoff.

Did the experience provoke any revelations for Calvin? Did it make him think about spending more time with family? Not a chance. "It's just amazing," Calvin said. "You go through something like this and you just want to get back to work."

16

Creative Financing
52 East 72nd Street

Maybe it was because he was short and his acne-covered face made him look like a prune. A rotten prune, at that. We don't mean to play Monday morning psychiatrist (a popular game in New York), but David Bloom obviously had something to prove in 1986—even if it meant lying and stealing some $10 million from his family and friends.

And why not? It was the Greed Decade and everyone seemed to be ripping off somebody. Bloom, then 23 years old and a recent college graduate, was a little younger than most of the financial felons of his time. But he lived just as well: a three-bedroom condo at 52 East 72nd Street and a $1.9 million beach house in East Hampton. He owned a $139,000 Aston Martin convertible and a $60,000 Mercedes. His art collection, including originals by Hopper and de Kooning, was worth $4.7 million.

Perhaps David's proudest moment was seeing himself featured as "one of Wall Street's new breed of private investors" in *The New York Times Magazine.* David aspired to have an important art collection. "First I decide what I want to buy," he said. "Then I worry about how I'm going to pay for it."

He was a freshly minted Duke University graduate when he began his big-money scam. It started with a power tie, an office on 57th Street, and a business name: Greater Sutton Investors Corporation. The idea was to invest other people's money in the stock market. But David was cleverer than that: he put the cash in his own bank account.

Of course, Bloom didn't know squat about finance. But he made sure to feature in his office a stock-quote machine, a secretary, and other investment banker paraphernalia. He talked big and dropped names. Big names. He assured prospective clients that he managed investments for the Rockefellers, Bill Cosby, and, oh yes, the Sultan of Brunei. Questions from nervous investors? David had the answers. He printed fictitious stock portfolios and trading histories to convince clients—his neighbors and friends—he was making a killing.

The Securities and Exchange Commission caught on in 1989 and David packed his bags for an eight-year stay at Allenwood federal prison camp. Perfect. The minimum-security prison, replete with tennis courts for inmates, is known as Club Fed.

Guess Who Came to Dinner?
36 East 72nd Street

David Hampton has never much cared much for life as David Hampton. So in 1983, at the age of 23, he decided to become the son of Sidney Poitier. Trouble was, he never told anyone his true identity, at least not until after he was caught conning several elite New Yorkers out of cash and hospitality.

Tops on the sucker list was Osborn Elliot, or Oz, as the former *Newsweek* editor liked to be called. Hampton telephoned Elliot out of the blue on a Saturday night at his 36 East 72nd Street town house, saying he was David Poitier and a friend of Oz's daughter, a student at Yale. Hampton spun a tale about being robbed and without money or a place to stay.

Generous guy that he is, Oz not only urged him to come over but offered to pay for his taxi. The Elliots treated David to a lovely home-cooked meal and chatted through the night about movies, books, and what it's like being the son of Sidney Poitier. Oz offered Hampton a bed for the night, a change of clothing, and $50.

Mrs. Elliot was in for quite a surprise when she went to wake David the next morning. She found him in bed with another young man, both of them naked. Mrs. Elliot ran to fetch Oz, who was furious. "What do you think you're doing?" he demanded. David didn't blink. "Oh," he said, still *lying* between the sheets with his friend, "this is Malcolm Forbes' nephew."

Before meeting the Elliots, Hampton had charmed and hoodwinked at least four other well-to-do Manhattan couples, including Jay Iselin, then the president of WNET Channel 13. Hampton was eventually arrested at a Greenwich Village telephone booth as he talked on the phone with Oz's wife. He pleaded guilty to attempted burglary and went to prison for twenty-one months. A judge ordered him to repay $4,000 to fourteen people and businesses he had ripped off.

His exploits inspired John Guare's successful 1990 play, *Six Degrees of Separation*. During the show's run at Lincoln Center, Hampton threatened to harm the author if he didn't pay him royalties, but no one paid him a nickel, not even a wooden one.

The Cop Killer
308 East 85th Street

Steroids and movie videos. Spaghetti and shotguns. Strange combinations, perhaps, but not for a cop-killer hiding out on the Upper East Side. Everyone was looking for Gus Farace in 1989. Five hundred FBI agents wanted him for the February killing of federal drug agent Everett Hatcher. The mob wanted him for provoking too much police heat to their rackets.

Farace spent nine months on the lam. He could have written a survival guide for fugitives: dye your hair blond, grow a beard, and rent plenty of videos. Pop steroids for your muscle tone and snack on home-cooked meatballs. Stay home. Always have a shotgun within reach. Maybe two.

Perhaps Farace's shrewdest move was to the East Side, the last place the police would think to look for a cop-killer from Staten Island. Farace rented a fifth-floor studio at 308 East 85th Street, but after two months he got sick of the neighborhood and missed his wife and newborn baby. Gus decided he would move and celebrated his last night on 85th Street by watching *The Godfather*.

The next morning, November 17, 1989, Farace climbed into a car with a friend, who drove him to the Bensonhurst section of Brooklyn. He thought he was on his way to a safe refuge, but two men who the police believe were dispatched by the mob were waiting for him with guns in front of 1803 81st Street. Before you could say "Sonny Corleone," Gus Farace was on his way to the morgue.

Serge Rubinstein
814 Fifth Avenue

Classy guy, Serge Rubinstein. When a woman resisted joining him between the sheets, he pulled out his money clip and peeled off crisp hundred-dollar bills until she said yes. Serge was very patient. He could afford to be. In the 1940s and 1950s, he was one of the world's most powerful—and hated—financiers.

Serge was born in Russia and liked to say that his earliest dream was to become a duke—"because they had the longest limousines and blondest women." Serge never became a duke, but he got everything else, mostly by buying and selling corporations while putting thousands of workers on the street. "My technique in finance is to figure out how much a company is worth dead, not living," said Serge, whose empire was valued in excess of $10 million.

Rubinstein bought a 30-room mansion at 814 Fifth Avenue, where he lived with his mother, aunt, and butler. He filled the house with pictures of himself and portraits of his hero, Napoleon. Just in case anyone missed the connection, Serge hung over his bed a picture of himself dressed as the Little Corporal. He was a fixture on the social scene, often parading around town with several beauties on his arm, wining, dining, and eventually discarding them with ease.

Of course, a guy can make a lot of enemies burning business partners and spurning lovers. So, few were surprised—or heartbroken—when Serge, dressed in black and blue silk pajamas, turned up dead from strangulation on his bedroom floor on the morning of January 27, 1955. The police never figured out who killed Rubinstein, but detectives liked to joke that they could fill Yankee Stadium with all the suspects.

20

New York Hospital
1300 York Avenue

With its white stone facade and towering bullet-shaped windows, New York Hospital evokes a bank and a cathedral, a monied church of medical science in one of America's richest neighborhoods. Here is a world-famous medical center, first class all the way: $1,225-a-day private rooms, brilliant surgeons, and the latest in medical technology.

Sound better than the Waldorf? Perhaps not.

Consider the fate of two of the hospital's more famous patients, Andy Warhol and Libby Zion, both of whom died while under hospital care. Warhol died after routine surgery, Zion after being treated for a fever. Their deaths cast a long shadow on the hospital's stellar reputation.

Zion, 18, arrived at the emergency room with a fever on March 4, 1984. She had become sick after having a tooth pulled earlier that week. Her father, Sidney Zion, a writer and former journalist, took her to New York Hospital after consulting with the family's physician. Doctors on duty told Sidney not to worry, it was a passing fever. He left Libby at the hospital and went home.

It was the last time Sid Zion saw his daughter. She died during the night. Zion, who once worked for the *New York Times,* bullhorned his outrage to the world, demanding that those entrusted with Libby's care be sent to prison. "I sent them a daughter with a fever," he said. "They sent me back a girl in a box."

A state grand jury condemned the hospital three years later after learning that unsupervised trainees had given Libby a potentially fatal mix of medications. But Zion learned that it's difficult to punish a hospital. No criminal charges were filed; the hospital was fined a meager $13,000.

Five weeks after the grand jury handed up its scathing Zion report, Andy Warhol arranged to have gall bladder surgery at the hospital.

The February 21, 1987, operation, all agree, went perfectly. But early the next morning, Warhol died at 58 of cardiac arrhythmia, or an irregular heartbeat. A public furor ensued, and the state health department fined the hospital $6,000 for "serious deficiencies" in Warhol's care. Later, his estate received an undisclosed settlement from the hospital.

21

The Great Crane Accident
Third Avenue Between 63rd and 64th Streets

A travel tip: when crossing the street in New York, don't just watch the traffic. Crazy cabbies aren't all that are dangerous to your health. We suggest looking up. It could save you a visit from the mayor, two thousand cops, and a priest ready to hear your final confession.

Just ask Brigitte Gerney.

A chaplain was called to listen to Gerney's last words on that sunny May 30th afternoon in 1985. Gerney, then a 45-year-old widow and mother of two, happened to be pinned beneath a thirty-five-ton crane that had toppled on her at Third Avenue between 63rd and 64th streets. Both her legs were partially severed below the knee.

More than two thousand emergency workers, along with Mayor Koch, raced to the scene. New Yorkers crowded around televisions and radios, listening to accounts of how paramedics were trying to keep Brigitte alive, pumping plasma into her body and feeding her painkillers. Brigitte's courage was especially impressive: at one point, she asked her rescuers to leave, lest they die trying to save her.

Five hours later, after the chaplain had passed her a Communion wafer in a silver case, workers managed to pry Gerney from the concrete jumble. They rushed her to Bellevue Hospital, where doctors reattached her legs. Ten operations later, she can almost walk normally.

It was a tragic accident, but Brigitte came out of it healthy, not to mention wealthy. She won a $10 million lawsuit against the company responsible for the crane. As for the developer, the Tishman Construction Corporation got a mess of bad publicity, but of course they made their money. The site is now a 42-story apartment building called "The Royale."

22

Dead Ringers
450 East 63rd Street

In the city's long and illustrious gallery of gore, there may be no incident more bizarre than the deaths of identical twins Stewart and Cyril Marcus. Born two minutes apart, the twins lived forty-five years—until their bodies were discovered in a garbage-strewn apartment at 450 East 63rd Street.

The Marcus brothers were prominent gynecologists who shared a successful practice on East 72nd Street. Women from across the country flocked to them with fertility woes. One writer speculated that because of the Marcus brothers' expertise, hundreds of children in this world are named Stewart and Cyril.

It was not unusual for the brothers to do things together. They attended the same college and medical school. Both were captains in the army. They held prestigious jobs at New York Hospital. They wrote for the same medical journals. Sometimes they even switched patients without telling anyone.

From afar, they seemed to be on top of the world—handsome, wealthy, well known. But there was a dark side to their success, namely their addiction to barbiturates. They were also emotional Siamese twins, habitually co-dependent. The brothers parted twice in their lives and then only because of outsiders. In the first case, a medical professor who worried that they spent too much time together insisted that they take internships in separate states. In the second instance, Cyril got married— but that didn't last. Before long, the brothers were back together again.

Stewart and Cyril were being investigated by New York Hospital for malpractice—there were allegations that they worked while on drugs— when their decomposed bodies were found in 1975 amid half-eaten sandwiches and empty bottles of pills. Investigators ruled out murder because the front door and windows were locked from the inside. The city's medical examiner said they were killed by withdrawal from barbiturate addiction. Whatever the case, it was clear the brothers couldn't live, or die, without each other.

The tale of the Marcus twins was eventually turned into a chilling movie, *Dead Ringers,* starring Jeremy Irons as both of them.

23

Cold Turkey in Style
56 East 93rd Street

If you happen to develop a cocaine or booze addiction while visiting the city, we recommend the Smithers Alcohol and Drug Treatment Center at 56 East 93rd Street. Rehab may be tough on the psyche, but at Smithers it means a nice room in a fancy neighborhood. That's nothing to sniff at in this town.

The clinic is ensconced in a classic, 40-room mansion between Madison and Park avenues that was once the home of the Broadway producer Billy Rose. The Corinthian columns are impressive, as are the black marble and elegant spiral staircase. There's even a landscaped garden in the backyard.

Ask to see Doc's old room—as in New York Mets pitching star Dwight "Doc" Gooden. He was treated for cocaine cravings at Smithers for a month in 1987. Doc's pal Darryl Strawberry also was admitted, in 1990 after a drinking binge. Truman Capote, Joan Kennedy, and John Cheever are some of the less athletic but equally famous patients who have checked into the rehab palace.

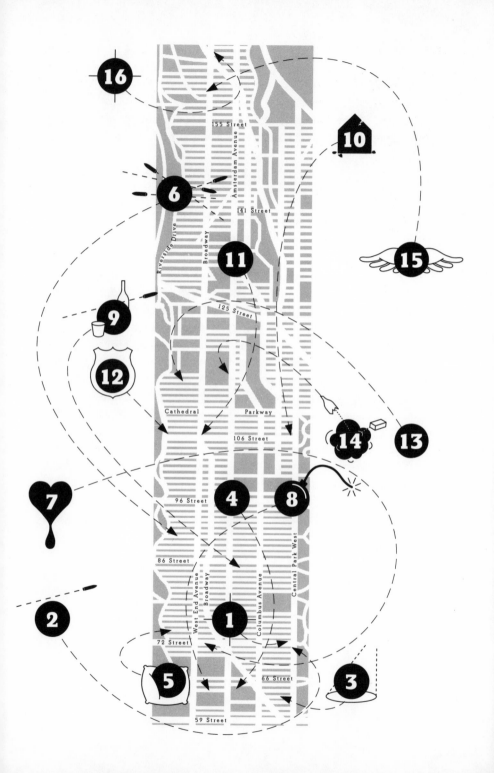

2

Wild, Wild West

The Upper West Side

THE UPPER WEST SIDE IS A GRAZER'S paradise. Check out the boutiques. Stop in the bookstores. Walk Broadway. Remember: no matter where you are, a Chinese restaurant isn't far away. Neither is a shrink. Maybe that's why the neighborhood has that sweatshirted, messy-haired charm. The natives spend so much time on the couch, they don't have time to kill.

Or do they? Some of the city's most famous crimes have occurred on the Upper West Side. John Lennon died here. So did Malcolm X. Even gangsters aren't safe: a mob chief survived a bullet aimed for his head inside a regal apartment house on Central Park West. The Upper West Side is also where a quite proper lady turned into the quite prosperous Mayflower Madame.

So don't let those tweed jackets or those anti-everything petition tables fool you. Better to keep alert. In this neighborhood, the blood is never far from the surface.

Lennon
1 West 72nd Street

Mark David Chapman seemed harmless, almost goofy, standing outside John Lennon's Dakota residence December 8, 1980. Fat face. Short hair. Silly grin. In his hands, Chapman held a pen and John and Yoko's latest album, *Double Fantasy*.

A nowhere man. A nobody who wanted to be a somebody in the worst way. A nerd fatale. By morning, Chapman would become, at the age of 25, as famous as his hero.

Mark had flown to New York from his Hawaii home two days before. He spent $82 to stay at the Sheraton Centre in midtown. Dectectives would later find in his room a Bible. Where it said "Book of John," Chapman hand-wrote "Lennon." Mark ordered room service that night. He also ordered a prostitute. No sex, though. Mark wasn't interested. He just wanted a massage.

On December 8, Chapman took a cab to the Dakota, where Lennon owned five sprawling apartments, each of them worth $1 million. A small crowd was gathered outside, many of them carrying Beatles albums and pens, just like Mark.

John and Yoko left the Dakota at 5 P.M. They were heading for the Hit Factory, a recording studio in Times Square. With the limousine waiting, John paused to sign autographs. The last fan on line was Chapman. "Do you want me to sign this?" Lennon asked, taking Mark's copy of *Double Fantasy*. Chapman grinned—that same silly grin—and John scribbled his name.

John and Yoko returned six hours later. The fans were gone, or so it seemed. As the couple ambled up the carriageway, Chapman leaped from the shadows of the building's courtyard and fell into a combat crouch. "Hey, John!" Chapman yelled, and fired a .38 special. Two bullets tore into Lennon's back, spinning him around. Two more shots struck him in the torso. As Yoko screamed, John crashed to the ground, dead at 42.

Minutes later, the cops arrived and found Chapman leaning against the building reading a crisp copy of *Catcher in the Rye*. Holden Caulfield, another nobody who wanted to be somebody, was Chapman's hero.

"Please don't hurt me," Mark said as the officers slapped handcuffs on his wrists. Before climbing into the squad car, Chapman leaned his autographed Lennon album against the outside of the Dakota's guard booth. A passing fan found the record and later turned it over to prosecutors. From prison, Chapman asked for the record back. He even promised to auction it for a worthy cause, gun control, but the authorities refused.

Today, you can still find photographs of Lennon in store windows throughout the neighborhood. Many of the merchants like to say they knew John. It's good for business. Yoko spent $1 million landscaping what is now called Strawberry Fields, in the park across from the Dakota. She also put up a plaque—twice stolen, twice replaced—listing the countries that donated plants and trees. Fans gather every October 9th and December 8th to celebrate the anniversaries of Lennon's birth and death.

One fan who won't be attending until some time next century is Mark David Chapman. He's not eligible for parole from Attica state prison until 2001.

2

The Gangster of Central Park West
115 Central Park West

Frank Costello was no ordinary mob boss. For one thing, he visited a psychiatrist several times a week (all that blood can get to a guy). For another, Costello lived on Central Park West. He disliked the marble and chrome palaces his thug cronies preferred in Queens and Staten Island. No knee-high statues of Mary in the front yard for Frank.

Costello was the target of an assassination attempt in 1957 in the lobby of his apartment building, the Majestic, at 115 Central Park West. Frank and his wife shared seven rooms in the elegant Art Deco landmark with their poodle and Doberman pinscher. The Costellos fed their dogs toast and butter for breakfast.

Costello liked the Majestic because it was respectable, and respectability was something Frank coveted, whether it was by wearing conservative suits or getting his hair trimmed and face shaved daily at the barber shop at the Waldorf-Astoria. Sure, crime had made Frank a rich man. But by the late 1940s, after three decades of blood and guts, he was sick of the bad guys. He told his shrink he wanted to be a good guy, but no matter what he did—hosting fundraisers for the Salvation Army, for example—everyone thought he was still a thug. A thug with manners, but a thug all the same.

The mob tired of Frank by 1957. The ambush at the Majestic occurred as he arrived home at 11 P.M. on May 2nd. A plump gunman jumped out from behind a pillar in the lobby and yelled, "Hey, Frank, this is for you." Luckily for Costello, the gunman wasn't much of a shot. The bullet passed through the hatband of Frank's fedora and nicked his scalp.

Spots of blood on his collar, a cucumber-cool Costello refused to identify the shooter. "I didn't see nothin'; I feel fine," he told reporters. Vincent "The Chin" Gigante was the suspected culprit. Thirty years later, The Chin would stroll Sullivan Street in his bathrobe, apparently to make cops think he was insane and not a mob boss.

Some mobologists say Gigante never intended to kill Costello. The shooting was meant as an early retirement party, a warning to Frank to stay home with his wife and dogs. He did, until 1973, when he died of a mere heart attack.

Busted: Mae West's Brush with the Law
22–26 West 63rd Street

Mae West, a veritable Shakespeare with hips, took up play writing in the early 1920s. It was a far cry from her usual shimmy across a stage, but Mae had a surefire way of guaranteeing success. She called the play *Sex*.

It was a powerfully drawn tale of despair turned to hope, of passion and love. But mostly it featured a scantily clad prostitute (played by Mae) hanging around with a bunch of sailors. A police officer would later testify that in one scene West performed a belly dance, moving "her navel up and down and from side to side."

Needless to say, tickets for *Sex* sold like hotcakes after the play opened in April 1926 at the old Daley's Theatre, a 900-seat hall on West 63rd Street. But not everyone approved. The theater critic for the *New York Times* called the play "crude" and "inept," while the Society for the Suppression of Vice blasted it as immoral.

After eleven months of performances, District Attorney Job Banton declared that *Sex* was threatening the city's so-called moral fiber. On March 19, 1927, in the play's forty-first week, the police closed the show down, arresting West and the show's producer and stage manager.

The trial was front-page news and Mae seemed to enjoy the attention. One reporter wrote that upon her arrival one day she "swaggered past a courtroom full of spectators, a perverse smile quivering on her lower lip."

Nevertheless, a jury found West and her cohorts guilty; the judge called the play "filth," levying a $500 fine and sending her to prison for ten days for corrupting "the morals of youth and others." The jail sentence was especially inconvenient for Mae since she was about to go into rehearsal for another play, a comedy, entitled *The Hussy*.

Fiddler Off the Roof
Lincoln Center

Murder at the Met or *Phantom of the Opera* could be the title of a mystery best-seller. In New York, it could only be the headline announcing the death of concert violinist Helen Hagnes Mintiks.

Mintiks vanished in 1980 during an intermission at the Metropolitan Opera House in Lincoln Center. Her body was found the following morning bound, gagged, and naked at the bottom of a sixty-foot air shaft near 64th Street and Amsterdam Avenue. Initially, the cops had few clues and no suspects.

Mintiks, 30 when she died, was as innocent as they come, a child prodigy who began playing violin at age four. She grew up in British Columbia and moved to the big city to play professionally. At her funeral, friends described Helen as beautiful and generous. One recalled that after a performance, she took out a homemade cheesecake and offered slices to the rest of the orchestra.

Fifty detectives, at the time the largest team ever assembled for a murder case, set up headquarters inside Lincoln Center. They began the difficult task of interviewing two thousand performers and stagehands as well as tracing Mintiks' final steps through the opera house's 10-story maze of halls, staircases, and elevators. Each day that passed, the detectives knew the killer could strike again.

Mintiks had placed her violin on her chair in the orchestra pit at 9:30 P.M. for intermission. She was performing with the Berlin Opera Ballet and was expected back in forty minutes to accompany "Miss Julia," a dance about an emotionally repressed woman with scenes of rape and seduction. She never returned.

The detectives knew she'd been on a third-floor staircase—they'd found her pen and a hair clip there the night of the murder. Later, a ballerina said she saw Mintiks on an elevator with a young man but couldn't remember what he looked like. The cops called in a hypnotist, and soon the dancer recalled enough to describe the man to a police sketch artist. The composite sketch closely resembled Craig Crimmins, a 21-year-old stage carpenter from the Bronx.

The cops were sure Crimmins was guilty, but they needed proof. Five weeks after the murder, they found the stagehand's fingerprint on the roof. Confronted with the evidence, Crimmins admitted that he had tried to rape Mintiks in the Met's basement after a chance encounter with her on the elevator. Drunk, he forced her to the roof, where he ripped her clothes off and tied her to the ledge. He kicked her down the airshaft when she tried to escape.

Crimmins was locked in a cell at Rikers Island next to Mark David Chapman. He went on trial a year later and got his own well-deserved taste of hell: a minimum twenty-year prison sentence.

5

The Mayflower Madam
307 West 74th Street

Sydney Biddle Barrows' parents, bluebloods listed in the Social Register, had certain expectations for their daughter when she was born. She would attend the best schools. She would marry into a fine family. She would learn to hold a tea cup just so.

Oh, did Sydney surprise them. She made a big splash, but in a way that would permanently unlock her parents' jaws. From 1979 to 1984, she ran a $1-million-a-year prostitution ring out of a brownstone at 307 West 74th Street. Cachet Escorts, as the service was called, wasn't cheap: the ladies cost up to $1,000 a night.

The police raided Sydney's place October 11, 1984. Instantly, she became a star, referred to in the papers as the "Mayflower Madam," a descendent of the original colonists who sailed here on the *Mayflower* and landed at Plymouth Rock.

The courts could have sent Sydney to jail for many years, but something happened on the way to trial: a plea bargain. A judge slapped Sydney with a $5,000 fine and sent her home.

There are theories about why this happened, the most compelling of which has to do with what was known as the "black book," Sydney's list of clients, many of whom were rich, famous, and, yes, married. Perhaps, the theory goes, the johns got on the phone (they network so well, you know) and pressured the DA's office into keeping the matter out of court. Otherwise, their names would be read—heaven forbid!—to a public courtroom and, therefore, the entire world.

Ten months after being arrested, Sydney waltzed out of court a free woman. She was shunned by high society and no longer invited to the Mayflower Ball, an annual gala for America's first families. But her scarlet letter quickly turned into a big fat dollar sign. Who needs the lockjaws when Hollywood is calling? Candice Bergen was hired by CBS to play Sydney in a movie called *Mayflower Madam*.

Sydney later taught a class that dealt with the subject of arousing men as well as wrote her autobiography and an etiquette book, which, among other things, decrees that it's okay to invite people who hate each other to the same dinner party. Nowhere in Sydney's book is there advice on whether it's okay to invite a convicted madam.

"Two Gun" Crowley
303 West 90th Street

The residents of West 90th Street never saw a more calamitous day than the afternoon in 1931 when a fugitive known as "Two Gun" Crowley visited their block and shot it out with 150 cops.

It was a drama fraught with danger, but that didn't stop an estimated fifteen thousand people from watching from rooftops, windows, and the street as Two Gun and the cops traded more than four hundred shots.

The baby-faced killer, only 19 years old, had James Cagney good looks and great success when it came to guns. His aim was terrific, his hand steady, his trigger finger never hesitant. Two Gun might have been an ordinary thug the cops didn't have time for, had it not been for one fact: his victims were often police officers.

Crowley's troubles began in February of 1931 when he got angry at a detective trying to confiscate his gun during a frisking. Two Gun reached down to his ankle holster and whipped out a second automatic, firing and critically wounding the officer.

Two months later, Crowley fatally wounded a Long Island patrolman seven times after the officer had the audacity to ask for a look at Two Gun's driver's license. "It's Crowley!" the shot cop yelled to his partner as Two Gun sped away.

The next day, Crowley's jilted girlfriend told the police that the gunman was hiding out at 303 West 90th. More than a hundred officers descended on the building at 4 P.M. They ordered Crowley, along with his partner, Rudolph "Tough Guy" Duringer, to surrender. Clinging to Two Gun's side was his new valentine, Helen, a 16-year-old butterscotch-haired beauty.

Two Gun and Tough Guy tried to keep the police back, firing more than two hundred shots from their windows and receiving an equally fierce barrage in return. Two hours later, the cops were fed up. A half-dozen broke down Crowley's door with pickaxes. Detective John "The Boffer" Broderick burst in and floored Crowley with a right to the jaw.

Two Gun and Tough Guy went to the electric chair. "Tell my mother I love her," Crowley said as he was buckled into the hot seat at Sing Sing on January 21, 1932. "I appreciate everything she did for me." A minister told reporters Two Gun went to his death "like a scared kid."

Looking for Mr. Goodbar
253 West 72nd Street

Murder is never very pleasant for the victims, but it has helped many an author avoid writer's block, not to mention starvation. The killing of Roseanne Quinn in 1973 was the inspiration for Judith Rossner's *Looking for Mr. Goodbar,* a novel about a lonely teacher's descent into New York's singles scene. The best-seller became a smash movie, starring Diane Keaton as the victim and Richard Gere as her killer.

In real life, Quinn, 28, met her murderer, John Wayne Williams, 23, on New Year's Eve at a tavern called H. M. Tweed's at 250 West 72nd Street. Quinn, who taught deaf children, and Williams, a psychopath from Indiana, knew nothing about each other. No matter. For hours, they danced and drank champagne as if they had known each other for a lifetime.

Long after midnight, the couple walked across the street to Quinn's studio apartment at 253 West 72nd Street. There, Williams stabbed Quinn to death in her bed.

Williams fled to Indiana, where the New York City police tracked him down. Five months later, he killed himself in jail. H. M. Tweed's is now the All-State Cafe, a dimly lit bar with a soulful jukebox and fresh vegetables.

8

The Mad Bomber
170 West 64th Street

He'd rise early each morning and put on a gray business suit. George Metesky, balding and bespectacled, had a meticulous manner, reserved, precise, polite. Only his nickname suggested lunatic: The Mad Bomber.

During a sixteen-year span, Metesky detonated at least thirty-two time bombs throughout Manhattan before a massive police hunt caught up with him in 1957. George's first target was a Consolidated Edison substation at 170 West 64th Street, where he planted a dud. George, a former Con Ed employee, was enraged at the company's firing him after a gas explosion made him too sick to work. In George's less than stable mind, not only Con Ed but the whole city was responsible for his dismissal.

Over the years, George's bombs, all of them home-made contraptions neatly wrapped in socks, ripped through Penn Station, the New York Public Library, Grand Central Terminal, and Radio City Music Hall, among other places. Sometimes the bombs didn't go off, but that meant little to the fifteen people who were injured when explosions did occur.

Editors at the *New York Journal-American,* trying to help a stumped police department, if not boost their own paper's circulation, invited The Mad Bomber to explain his attacks in letters to the newspaper. George obliged, submitting anonymous handwritten missives. In one of the letters, which he cryptically signed "F.P.," he mentioned that he once worked for Con Ed.

Detectives finally had a clue. They combed through sixty thousand Con Ed files until they matched the handwriting in the letters with notes found in George's personnel file. On a January day in 1957, police officers surrounded his Connecticut home, which the 54-year-old bachelor shared with his sisters.

Dressed in a nightshirt, Metesky stepped outside to the porch. "I assume you're all here because of The Mad Bomber," he said. Clasping the handcuffs on his wrists and leading him to a police car, an officer asked him about those cryptic initials "F.P." George smiled and answered, "Fair Play. That stands for Fair Play."

A judge declared Metesky criminally insane and sent him to a mental hospital for sixteen years.

9

Shootout at the Red Carpet Lounge
173 West 85th Street

In the 1960s, H. Rap Brown was a tough-talking civil rights leader who urged blacks to use violence to achieve equality. "We must wage guerrilla war on the honkie white man," he once said.

Brown practiced what he preached, but it wasn't always for equal rights. In 1971, he and three men robbed what was then the Red Carpet Lounge, at 173 West 85th Street. The men ordered the bar's customers to lie on the floor and hand over their wallets and jewelry. As Brown collected the valuables, he thanked the patrons, most of whom were black, and called them "brothers."

Someone outside the bar called the police and soon three patrolmen arrived. Shots were fired, injuring two officers, and the gunmen escaped. Three hours later, Brown was found wounded on the roof of 102 West 85th Street, bleeding from three bullet holes in his stomach.

Famed radical lawyer William Kunstler couldn't keep Brown out of jail, but Rap did beat an attempted murder charge. He spent nearly five years in prison for robbery and assault. Today, Brown calls himself Jamil Abdullah Al-Amin and lives in Atlanta, Georgia, where he is married and has three kids. He owns a Muslim food store that sells, among other things, Kosher pickles.

10

Tender Loving Abuse: Rabbi Bergman's Nursing Homes
Central Park West and 106th Street

Rabbi Bernard Bergman contributed generously to charities in the 1960s and won a trophy case full of citizenship awards. The rabbi had many powerful friends, men who delivered long superlative-laced speeches at black-tie dinners in his honor.

When he wasn't taking bows, Bergman ran an empire of nursing homes, including Towers, a now-vacant chateau on Central Park West at 106th Street. The business made Bernard quite prosperous, until the day a *Times* reporter decided to see what it was the Bergman homes had to offer.

The news was not good: the reporter saw elderly patients sleeping on urine-soaked sheets in grimy rooms crawling with cockroaches. The nurses had a shorthand phrase for the many patients who had bedsores and suffered from malnutrition and dehydration. They called it "Bergman's Syndrome."

Others told of Bergman's habit of stealing government medical insurance money and paying off lawyers, political lobbyists, and state legislators. One Bergman crony got a yacht, while another received a Rolls.

Bergman fought to save his reputation, hiring celebrity lawyer Alan Dershowitz. The rabbi insisted he was a victim of anti-Semitism, even though many of the journalists and investigators tracking him down were Jewish.

Bergman was fined $2.5 million and in 1978 spent eight months in jail on state and federal theft convictions. As a result, nursing home nightmares around the country came to light, and scores of homes were shut down. Many states enacted legislative reforms to improve care of the elderly.

Released from prison, Bergman tried to stay in the nursing home business but was forced to retire after facing a hostile outcry. He was then 65, but he would never check into a nursing home. Worth a reported

$100 million, the rabbi settled for his palatial apartment with a view of Central Park.

11

Death on a Rooftop
920 West End Avenue

In the morning she served cappuccino and croissants at a cafe around the corner from her Upper West Side apartment. In the afternoon she read for an acting role, and that night she saw the Broadway play *Hurlyburly*.

Caroline Isenberg, 23, led a busy life. A slender, reddish-haired Harvard graduate, she'd moved to the city from Boston to study acting. Her resumé included a small part in a 1983 CBS-TV movie, *Freshman Year*. She enrolled in an acting school whose alumni include Diane Keaton and Joanne Woodward.

Isenberg wanted success. Instead, she became a tragic symbol of hopes and dreams cut short.

She returned home alone to 920 West End Avenue after midnight on December 2, 1984. Emmanuel Torres was waiting in the elevator. Torres, the son of the building's superintendent, was known on the street as "Peanut." His ambition in life was to be like his older brother, "Wolfman," who was prominent in a neighborhood drug and extortion gang. But the gang wouldn't include Torres. They thought he was a loser.

As the elevator door opened, Torres grabbed Isenberg and forced her to the roof. He tried to rape her, but she fended him off. Furious, he stabbed her several times in the chest and stole $12 from her purse. He left her bleeding on the rooftop.

Neighbors heard Isenberg's screams and called 911. Minutes later, the police found her, semiconscious. Before she died, Isenberg managed to whisper a description of her attacker. The cops caught Torres after a four-day manhunt.

A year later, a judge told Torres, "No punishment fits this crime," a crime he said had "marred the soul of this city." The judge sent Torres to jail for no less than twenty-five years. The city cheered. Isenberg's shattered family said they were satisfied. Only one person in the world seemed to believe in Torres's innocence: his weeping mother.

12

Cops Shot at the DA's House
106th Street and Riverside Drive

The Black Panthers were the bad boys of the 1960s' radical left. They favored revolution to sit-ins and blowing up government buildings to peace and love. The Panthers also talked about killing white cops.

On May 19, 1971, two police officers were shot and critically wounded as they guarded District Attorney Frank Hogan's 404 West 112th Street apartment. A car sped by the building and the officers, Nicholas Binetti and Thomas Curry, chased the driver to 106th Street and Riverside Drive. The car pulled over and the officers stopped alongside. Suddenly, the officers were hit by a spray of bullets.

At a time when the country was being ripped apart by civil strife, the shooting outraged officials from New York to Washington. The men running the FBI and the White House didn't like it that the Panthers and affiliated splinter groups were bragging about cutting down cops. Someone had to pay.

Three weeks later, Panther Richard Moore and another man were arrested for the shooting after they were caught holding up a Bronx social club. Moore was among the Panthers who had recently been acquitted of charges that they conspired to kill police officers and bomb department stores. Investigators were sure they would nail Moore this time. The machine gun used in the social club holdup apparently matched the gun used to shoot the cops.

Moore was convicted and a judge sentenced him to life in prison "for the good of society and for his own sake." Moore claimed he was framed and that his arrest was part of the government's effort to dismantle the Panthers.

No one took him seriously, but from prison, Moore, under the Freedom of Information Act, acquired FBI documents that seemed to back up his claim. One document was a memo from FBI Director J. Edgar Hoover to his troops ordering them "not to pull any punches" in their investigation of the shooting. Moore's lawyers also discovered that prosecutors had suppressed testimony from a woman who told them Moore had nothing to do with the shooting.

In 1990, State Supreme Court Judge Peter McQuillan overturned the conviction. After nineteen years behind bars, Moore—now known as Dhoruba al-Mujahid bin Wahad—was free to go.

13

The Killer Building
601 West 115th Street

Never mind the muggers, rapists, and psychopaths. Even the buildings can kill in this town.

Grace Gold, a Barnard College freshman, died on May 16, 1979, when she was crushed by a falling chunk of masonry while walking past 601 West 115th Street.

"This is like a ten-million-to-one possibility," a police detective said at the time.

Perhaps, but the odds improve when buildings erected before World War II age without repair. In this case, a four-pound slab of window lintel fell because years of rain had caused cracks in the building's facade—cracks hidden by decorative masonry.

Gold's death prompted the city to pass stricter building inspection laws. Some landlords, including Columbia University, which owned the building, weren't taking any more chances. They simply removed ornamentation from their buildings.

Gold's parents, meanwhile, sued Columbia for $10 million. They settled out of court for $153,000.

Columbia University Riots
116th Street and Amsterdam Avenue

It may always be known simply as "The Bust"—that bitter, bloody day in 1968 when the city sent cops to school.

Columbia University, like many campuses across the country, was caught that year in the angry grasp of student demonstrations against the Vietnam War. During the last week of April, hundreds of protesters crippled the ivy-covered campus with sit-ins and marches.

The center of the storm was Hamilton Hall, near 116th Street and Amsterdam Avenue, where three hundred students held a college dean hostage for nearly twenty-four hours. Another group took over University President Grayson Kirk's Low Library office.

The students went through his drawers and left him a note: "If we win," they wrote, "we will take control of your world."

It never got that far. On April 30th, Kirk called the police. More than one thousand cops, all of them wearing riot gear and swinging billy clubs, swept away the demonstrators and anyone else caught in their path. More than seven hundred students were arrested and one hundred were injured. Instead of ending the protests, the crackdown stoked the fires of campus radicalism.

Rudy and the Fonz
160th Street and Broadway

Politicians do the darndest things, especially if there is a remote possibility of scoring big with the voters. For Alfonse D'Amato, the unabashed senator from New York, that meant dressing up like a cool guy and buying crack.

In July of 1986, D'Amato, facing a reelection campaign, donned sunglasses and military fatigues and journeyed to one of the city's meccas for drug dealing, Washington Heights. Al was even big enough to invite along dozens of camera-toting journalists so they could see how easy it is—even for a senator—to purchase crack in New York City.

Joining in the costume party was Rudolph Giuliani, then the mob-conquering federal prosecutor, a man with visions of becoming mayor. Rudy also slipped into what he considered drug-buy wear, a Hell's Angels leather vest decorated with swastikas.

D'Amato's vehicle slowed at 160th and Broadway. The senator lowered his window, flicked a finger across his nose like a pro, and handed over $20. Around the corner, Rudy bagged a couple of vials.

Afterward, television cameras rolled and photographers clicked away as Al and Rudy turned their thumbs up and claimed victory. Since no one was arrested, some called the whole affair free advertising for the dealers.

The Assassination of Malcolm X
166th Street and Broadway

The Audubon Ballroom on 166th Street and Broadway is faded and falling down now, but its place in history is secure. It was here, on a wintry night in 1965, that assassins cut down civil rights leader Malcolm X.

Malcolm was delivering a speech that February 21st to an audience of four hundred supporters. Suddenly, there was a commotion in the middle of the auditorium, three men pushing each other and arguing. Malcolm's bodyguards, standing in front of the stage, moved in to break it up. Stepping out from behind the speaker's rostrum, Malcolm said, "Now, brothers, let's cool it."

Malcolm stood alone on the stage, a perfect target, his left hand raised. One man holding a shotgun raced down the aisle toward him. At that moment, two other assassins fired a fusillade of bullets.

Malcolm fell to the hardwood floor, dead at the age of 39. The auditorium, for a moment silent, reverberated with screams. Few screamed louder than Malcolm's wife, Betty Shabazz. His assassins, all convicted, were members of the Nation of Islam, with which Malcolm had been quarreling.

Today, his message of black pride and defiance still endures among blacks struggling against racism. If you doubt it, consider the fate of the Audubon. In the summer of 1990, Columbia University tried to turn the site into a medical complex but then modified the proposal after angry protests by community activists. The university promised to preserve a substantial part of the ballroom as a memorial to Malcolm X. In 1991, a thief took the matter into his own hands, stealing the wooden panels where the bullets aimed for Malcolm struck.

3

When Bad Things Happen in Nice Places

The Crimes of Central Park

IT IS 843 ACRES OF PASTORAL BEAUTY IN the center of a concrete jungle. The fifty-eight miles of winding paths are lovely. So are the hundreds of elm trees, the rowboats, and the ballfields. Nothing beats the Great Lawn, the Children's Zoo, or Belvedere Castle.

Central Park offers something else out-of-towners just can't get at home: sheer terror—the kind that makes your knees knock and turns your knuckles white. The kind you won't find on Main Street or in most suburban shopping malls. The kind you won't find in New York City's most dangerous neighborhoods.

Don't believe us? Try strolling the park at night. After midnight. Alone. Stand out there—anywhere will do—and listen to your heart sound like the beat of a snare drum. Strain your eyes to spot muggers lurking in the bushes. Chances are no one's there. But you don't know that. Before long, you'll be sprinting back to the hotel. Or back to Main Street.

Of course, the truth is that Central Park is safer—relatively speaking—than the rest of New York City. So safe, in fact, that when a crime does occur in the park, the entire world hears about it, over and over again.

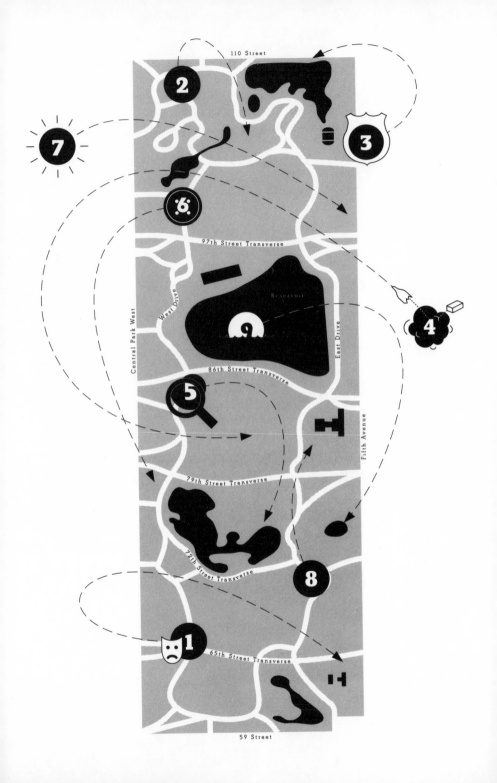

1

The Reward
65th Street, near Fifth Avenue

George Delacorte loved Central Park with his heart and his wallet. The publishing tycoon spent millions funding a myriad of whimsical treasures in the park, including the Delacorte Theater, a colorful, animated clock in the Children's Zoo, and a bronze statue of Alice in Wonderland.

George's reward for all that philanthropy came New York–style on the morning of December 11, 1985: two thugs mugged him and his wife, then 92 and 66 years old, respectively, as they walked—where else?—in their beloved Central Park.

The thugs pounced on the couple as they walked through a tunnel leading to the Children's Zoo, just off 65th Street and Fifth Avenue. It was about 10 A.M. and the park was deserted. The muggers stole George's wallet along with his wife's $5,500 mink coat. They even slashed Mrs. Delacorte's hand.

It was the first time the Delacortes were crime victims, but George refused to give up on his city. "I've walked five miles in the park every day of my life," he said at the time. "This will not stop me. Only death will."

Indeed, George kept on walking until he died of old age in 1991.

2

The Jogger
102nd Street Transverse

In the cool of a spring night, the 29-year-old woman went jogging in the park. It was an odd hour for exercise, nearly 10 P.M., but she had worked late at the office, the Wall Street–based Salomon Brothers, where she was an investment banker. She always made time for a jog, even if it meant entering the park after dark. It was part of her routine, a routine that would end before the night was over.

Most people still don't know the jogger's name. But they know what happened on that April 19, 1989, in the park. She was running along the Transverse, a dimly lit road connecting the East and West drives at 102nd Street, when she encountered a gang of teenagers. The gang had been roaming the park, engaged in an activity that would add a new word to the city's crime vocabulary: "wilding"—robbing and beating people at random.

Already that night, the gang had attacked a pedestrian, a couple riding a bicycle, a homeless man, and a male jogger. The gang, at least six boys, ambushed the jogger as she ran west on the Transverse. They dragged her through a thicket of trees, down a dark ravine into a section of the park known as the Loch. Here, she was stoned, beaten, and raped. The teenagers then fled, leaving the woman in the darkness at the edge of death.

The jogger awoke from a coma two weeks later. After another eighteen months, she achieved what her doctors called a miraculous recovery. Six of her attackers were arrested and prosecuted in tumultuous trials. Fights broke out in the courtroom. Friends and relatives of the accused charged that the gang was being prosecuted by racists. They berated the jogger when she limped into court to testify. One of the accused, Yusuf Salaam, took the stand and read a poem in which he compared himself to Martin Luther King Jr.

The six defendants eventually went to jail. Investigators believe that up to two dozen more youths may have been involved in the rampage but were never caught. The woman who came to be known as the Central Park Jogger is back at work, promoted to vice president. As a rape victim, the police have never released her identity. Doctors say she faces a lifetime of pain, partial memory loss, and recuperation.

She still jogs, but not in Central Park.

3

A Cop Is Shot; A Hero Is Born
Harlem Lake Boathouse

The three teenagers were about to rob a bicyclist at the northern end of the park on the afternoon of June 12, 1986. Police Officer Steven McDonald, dressed in civilian clothes, saw the crime unfolding and, without hesitating, moved in. He was unafraid, coming from a family that spawned seven cops over several generations. His great-aunt had been a police officer in the 1920s, and his grandfather, also a patrolman, was shot in the chest breaking up a robbery in the 1930s.

Questioning the boys, McDonald, 29, called for his partner standing a few hundred feet away. In the next moment, one of the teens turned his back on McDonald, reached into his coat for a gun, then spun around firing. The first bullet hit McDonald in the left side of the neck, just above the spine. The second struck his left wrist and the third grazed his right eye.

Doctors said McDonald was lucky he didn't die, even if he was now paralyzed from the neck down. He would spend the rest of his life in a wheelchair. Most people in his condition would have been bitter. The police commissioner at the time, Benjamin Ward, was furious. Ward said the shooting was another reason to restore the death penalty—even for minors like Shavod Jones, 15, who fired at McDonald. "I'd pull the switch myself," Ward said.

McDonald, whose wife, Patty Ann, was four months pregnant, would have none of it. He spoke from his hospital bed of love for his family and hope for the future. He became a kind of saint, a soft-spoken symbol of courage and dignity. Politicians—Mayor Ed Koch and Governor Mario Cuomo among them—rushed to his bedside. John Cardinal O'Connor sent an autographed picture. Ronald Reagan telephoned from Air Force One.

Perhaps McDonald's most stunning moment came when he forgave Shavod Jones for paralyzing him. McDonald said society had to treat its young better or more kids would grow up to shoot cops. He befriended

Jones's family, and Shavod's grandmother had a special ramp built at her Bronx church so McDonald could attend services.

Four years later, Shavod Jones, then 19 and serving a ten-year prison term, called McDonald from prison. He apologized for the shooting.

Diana Ross Concert
Great Lawn

She burst onstage like a purple flame, her arms reaching for the sea of 500,000 fans stretched across the Great Lawn. Diana Ross, dressed in a sequined jumpsuit, proclaimed, "It's a new day!"

Maybe it was a new day. But it was still the same city.

Hundreds of teenagers terrorized the crowds leaving the park after the show that July 22, 1983. The gangs stole necklaces and pocketbooks and sent dozens to the hospital with cuts and bruises. They even stormed Tavern on the Green, flipping over tables and assaulting diners who got in their way.

The police arrested forty-seven teens. Two hundred people registered formal complaints with the cops, including a French woman who lost her jewelry and vowed never to return to the city. Even Ed Koch, the mayor of all this, ducked three flying bottles.

It got worse: the city had to scrap plans to build a new children's playground with money raised from the concert. Instead, the earnings paid $650,000 in police overtime and cleanup services. No rock superstar was ever allowed to play in Central Park until 1991 when Paul Simon appeared without incident.

5

Dead Professor
72nd Street Boat Basin

Central Park in the early 1960s was still safe enough that New Yorkers could walk there at night without fearing for their lives. It was so safe, in fact, that the police were actually surprised to find a dead body in the bushes near the 72nd Street Boat Basin one morning in 1964.

Charles Gallagher, 31, was a nuclear physicist at Columbia University. He had a seat on the Atomic Energy Commission, which at the time— those paranoid days of the Cold War—was a prestigious position. Three weeks before his death, which occurred on April 15, Gallagher had attended a scientific conference in the Soviet Union.

Was it possible, the newspapers asked in huge headlines, that this birdwatching, stamp-collecting bookworm was at the center of international intrigue? Could Russian spies have chosen Central Park as center stage for a top-secret assassination?

Or was there a love interest? Detectives speculated about the significance of a blue high-heeled shoe found fifty feet from Gallagher's body. Perhaps, some reasoned, Gallagher was the fall guy in a deadly sexual tryst.

Not a chance. This was a crime as simple as they come, a mere mugging that ended with a bullet hole in the professor's heart. The killers, two unemployed ex-cons, were sentenced to life in prison.

Even after he died, Gallagher couldn't escape one of the city's chronic annoyances. His car, parked several blocks from where he was killed, was slapped with a parking ticket as he was being carted to the morgue.

Holiday on Ice
The Ramble

Dick Button epitomized grace when he was an Olympic figure skater in the 1950s and 1960s. He was thin and trim, a Fred Astaire on ice. By 1978, though, Button hardly looked himself. He was 49 years old and had ballooned to two hundred pounds. Time to go on a diet. Time to exercise. A three-mile run in the park in 1978 nearly killed him.

A gang of white punks from the East Side clubbed Button on the head with baseball bats, chair legs, and branches as he ended his jog in the Ramble, the densely wooded grounds just south of 79th Street. The thugs had been terrorizing anyone they thought was a homosexual on that July 5th night.

Button and four other men suffered skull fractures and were hospitalized. As they were arrested, the teens made obscene gestures and imitated the sounds of monkeys. Three of the thugs went to jail for eight years.

A Bullet and a Suntan
North Meadow, near 99th Street and Fifth Avenue

Catching a few rays without risking one's life shouldn't be too much to ask—except in New York City.

A bullet tore through Dr. Amy Rosen's chest as she sat on a Central Park bench enjoying a sunny afternoon in 1990. The Mount Sinai Hospital doctor had been talking to her brother a hundred feet inside the park at 99th Street and Fifth Avenue. It was 3:30 P.M. on March 13th. School children were playing nearby. Suddenly, Rosen, 28, felt something hit her torso. Looking down, she saw blood oozing from her chest.

Rosen, who survived the shooting, never heard the sound of a gun exploding. Police said the bullet may have traveled twelve hundred yards across the park from the top of any one of several buildings between 103rd and 105th streets and Central Park West.

In other words, the cops had no clue who pulled the trigger. There was no one to blame, except the entire city.

8

Preppy Murder
81st Street, off the East Drive

Robert Chambers was tired as the sun rose on August 26, 1986. He was too tired to bother with the cluster of cops gathered a hundred feet away by a large elm tree behind the Metropolitan Museum of Art. The officers were talking among themselves and crouched over the body of a dead girl.

Chambers knew the girl. In fact, he had killed her only hours before as they had sex under the tree. But he didn't bother to tell that to the cops. Instead, he walked home to his mother's apartment at 11 East 90th Street and went to bed. Eight hours later, detectives knocked at his door. They had questions for him about the murder of Jennifer Dawn Levin.

Levin's death ignited the city. Here was a crime with everything—sex, drugs, and money, all on the Upper East Side. Here was a pretty victim and a dashingly handsome suspect. Here was Romeo and Juliet—with credit cards.

Jennifer, 18, was a prep school graduate, spending her last summer in the city before starting college. Her parents were divorced, but she had plenty of friends—many of them boys with whom she sometimes had sex. Those who sympathized with Chambers would try to use this against her. They called her a slut and said she got what she deserved.

It's true that Jennifer was no saint. Her idea of a good time often involved alcohol, drugs, and boys. In other words, she had a lot in common with millions of other teenagers. Robert, on the other hand, was as bad as they come—no matter how innocent his blue eyes and flashing white smile seemed. Sure, he was a former altar boy and his mother, who idolized the Kennedys, worked hard as a nurse to put him through school. But Robert was hardly a model citizen: he spent time in drug clinics for a cocaine habit and robbed apartments on the Upper East Side.

All these details, of course, made Hollywood froth at the mouth after Jennifer died. Agents clamored for the movie rights, with some even promising that Robert could star as himself. "Oh, to be young and under arrest in New York," one agent told the *New York Times*.

The night Jennifer died, she and Robert had been drinking at Dorrian's Red Hand, a rich kids' playpen at 84th Street and Second Avenue. At 4:30 A.M., Robert and Jennifer left Dorrian's and walked into the park. Fifty yards north of Cleopatra's Needle, they had sex—"rough sex," as Robert would eventually confess. Very rough. An autopsy later showed that Jennifer had been strangled.

During the trial at Manhattan Criminal Court, Chambers' attorney Jack Litman argued that his client had been raped, that he had killed Levin in self-defense. Prosecutors found that hard to believe. Chambers weighed 220 pounds, after all. Jennifer weighed 120.

After thirteen weeks, the jury went behind closed doors to deliberate. Eight days passed without a verdict. On the ninth day, the jury declared that it was at an impasse. Several jurors scribbled notes to the judge saying they couldn't go on because of the "mental and emotional strain."

A plea bargain was worked out: on March 26, 1988, Chambers pleaded guilty to manslaughter. He was sent to prison for a maximum of fifteen years. He would be eligible for parole in 1993. At his sentencing, Chambers apologized to the Levins. "Jennifer's looking down on us now at this circus arena, looking and wondering why it all happened, and I don't know," he said. "I never wanted any of this to happen."

The Levins didn't care what Robert wanted. They hoped he would rot in prison. "There is not a day that is not spent forcing down overwhelming feelings of despair, anger, and horror," said Steven Levin, Jennifer's father, two years after her death.

9

The Floater
Conservatory Water, 74th Street near Fifth Avenue

Twenty-two hundred people were murdered in the New York of 1990, but only one dead body turned up during a television interview with the city parks commissioner.

It happened at the Conservatory Water as Betsy Gotbaum was telling a television news reporter of the need in the park for more monuments dedicated to famous women.

In the middle of the interview, the bloated body of a homeless man floated to the top of the pond. Gotbaum's jaw dropped. So did the reporter's. Together they looked like a couple of hooked trout. Only the cameraman knew what to do: he turned his lens away from Gotbaum and zoomed in on the floater.

Police soon took the body away on a stretcher, making the park esthetically safe again. Scenes of the dead man, whose case was classified as a homicide, didn't show up on the tastefully edited piece about Gotbaum that aired on the news.

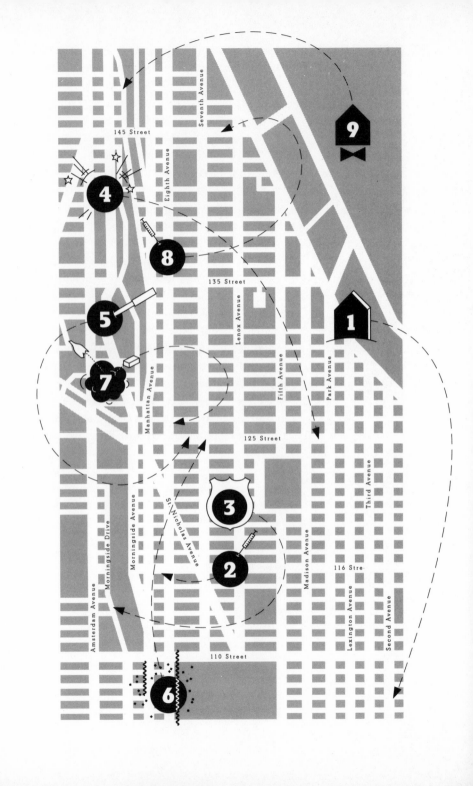

4

Harlem

Take the A Train (Or a Tank)

YES, WE'VE HEARD ALL ABOUT HARLEM'S risky reputation. Don't go there at night, people say. Don't even go there during the day. We're here to tell you different. Go—at night and during the day. Spend a night at the Apollo Theater, stop at Sylvia's for the ribs. Visit the beautiful brownstones of Striver's Row, or the impressive Abyssinian Baptist Church.

Just remember that crime is the great equalizer. All the cash and muscle in the world can't protect you from violence in this city, Harlem included. Ask Mike Tyson. He saw trouble on 125th Street. So did Martin Luther King Jr. Robert Kennedy's son David was mugged on 116th Street.

Which brings us to a travel tip: forget the A train. Try an armored car. Or a tank. Maybe even a bulletproof vest (under "B" in the Yellow Pages).

The Murder Stable
323 East 107th Street

Most people think of apartment buildings as places to live. Lupo "The Wolf" Saietta, a gangster who ruled New York with brass knuckles and a shotgun, was never so conventional. He turned an East Harlem tenement into a burial ground for his enemies.

Lupo the Wolf got rich in the early 1900s charging immigrant shopkeepers a lot of money for protection against thieves. Of course, the only thief the merchants had to fear was Lupo. Those who didn't pay ended up taking a ride to 323 East 107th Street, where Lupo would chop them up with an axe or shoot them in the head.

The cops called the building the "Murder Stable." During a raid, they found sixty corpses buried in the basement. Lupo told the cops he didn't know anything about the bodies. "I'm only the landlord," he said, suggesting they question the building's tenants. Simple, except no one lived in the building.

The "Murder Stable" was eventually razed and a housing project now stands in its place.

Camelot Comes to Harlem—And Gets Mugged
300 West 116th Street

Harlem was a pit stop on the road to ruin for David Kennedy, the tragedy-prone son of Robert F. Kennedy. When he wasn't playing touch football with other Camelot kids in Hyannisport, David lived on East 72nd Street and was a regular at Manhattan discos. He also liked to visit the Shelton Plaza, 300 West 116th Street, a seedy hotel frequented by junkies and prostitutes.

Few knew about David's trips to the Shelton or his drug problems until September 5, 1979, when he was robbed of $30 by three muggers in the hotel lobby. David, then 24, claimed two men standing on the corner of 116th Street flagged him down as he drove by the Shelton in his $15,000 BMW sports coupe. He said he followed the men inside the hotel, where they brandished knives and stole his money.

David claimed he had never been to the hotel before. Shelton residents begged to differ, saying he was a habitual visitor. A week after the mugging, David entered a Boston hospital for drug treatment. Apparently, it didn't help. Less than five years later, his body was found in a classier hotel in Palm Beach, Florida. David died from an overdose of cocaine, Demerol, and Mellaril.

The Shelton, meanwhile, became known among cops as the "Kennedy Arms." It closed in 1988 and was replaced by a homeless shelter. A sign in the lobby advises: JUST SAY NO TO DRUGS.

3

Death of an Honor Student
113th Street and Morningside Drive

Where Eddie Perry grew up—in the heart of Harlem—Columbia University loomed on a hill like the distant capital of another country, all backpacks and bookstores, statues and students.

Down in the valley, below the treacherous no-man's-land known as Morningside Park, Perry, 17, was raised by his mother at 265 West 114th Street. It's a neighborhood of broken sidewalks and burnt-out tenements, where you can hear babies and police sirens wailing through the night.

The night of June 13, 1985, was hot and sticky. Edmund—his six-foot one-inch frame mismatched to his baby face—was going to the movies with his brother Jonah, 19. Short on cash, the brothers apparently went looking for someone to mug.

His name was Lee Van Houten. He was 24, white, and so young-looking that his friends called him "The Kid." He seemed like an easy victim, walking south on Morningside Drive between 114th and 113th streets, dressed in a sweatshirt, blue jeans, and sneakers.

Jonah was the first to leap, grabbing Van Houten around the neck and yanking him backwards. Eddie jumped in, punching and stomping Van Houten until he tumbled to the ground. "Give it up!" the brothers screamed.

"I'm a police officer," Van Houten cried.

He was, in fact, a plainclothes cop looking for car vandals. Van Houten, at five foot ten, was no match for the Perrys. His police radio, hidden in a paper bag, went flying out of his hand. He got up but fell again as the blows kept coming. He felt someone going through his pockets. He began to lose consciousness.

Before blacking out, Van Houten pulled a pistol from his ankle holster and fired three shots. Jonah dashed away, but Eddie collapsed bleeding on the sidewalk, a bullet in his stomach. Eddie was barely conscious, but arriving police officers handcuffed his wrists anyway. Within minutes, he was taken to the emergency room at St. Luke's Hospital, where he died three hours later.

Most of the killings in New York don't make the papers. Eddie Perry's death wasn't made for headlines, either. He was a black teenager from Harlem. He wasn't rich, famous, or an attractive blonde. But his story had a twist: ten days earlier, he had graduated with honors and a full scholarship from a prestigious boarding school, Phillips Exeter Academy. As a result, his death was big news and prompted anger about what some believed was a shooting—and a police department—motivated by racism.

A grand jury thought otherwise, clearing Van Houten of any wrongdoing. Jonah, on the other hand, was indicted for assault and attempted robbery. Later, he was acquitted of those charges, leaving the question of what really happened that night unresolved. A Cornell University sophomore at the time, Jonah went on to graduate and work for the City of New York.

4

Shopping with Tyson at 5 A.M.
41 East 125th Street

We believe Mike Tyson when he says he's the best. We believe him because we are not fools. Iron Mike may not be a rocket scientist, but let's face it: he could break a guy in half.

In other words, we believe Iron Mike when he claims that Mitch

"Blood" Green provoked their 1988 sidewalk brawl outside the now-closed Dapper Dan's Boutique, 41 East 125th Street. As Iron Mike tells it, he punched Green in the face after—not before—Mitch ripped his shirt and slapped him as they were leaving Dapper Dan's. The punch left Mitch with a swollen eye and Mike with a broken hand.

Mitch, of course, offered a different version. He says Tyson sucker-punched him that August 23rd during an argument about who was the better boxer.

Mike Tyson throw a sucker punch? Not a chance. He might get frisky with the ladies, but he would never, ever cheap-shot a fellow heavyweight.

Some people think Mike was really hanging out on 125th Street that night to party at an unmarked nightclub. Mike says he was there to buy clothes, plain and simple. He says he had an appointment with Dapper Dan himself.

Again, we believe him. We realize 5 A.M. is an unusual time to shop, but Mike's the champ—and champs go shopping anytime they choose.

The day after the scrap, Tyson showed off his purchase to reporters: a custom-made, $850 white leather jacket. On the back was scripted, DON'T BELIEVE THE HYPE.

5

A Cross over His Heart
250 West 125th Street

Martin Luther King Jr. became a national figure when he led the 1955 bus boycott in Montgomery, Alabama. He survived 381 dramatic days without injury, even as black churches were bombed and white mobs rioted in the streets.

But King wasn't so lucky when he visited New York City. He was the guest of honor at a book-signing party at the now-closed Blumstein's department store, 250 West 125th Street. Izola Ware Curry, a 42-year-old loner from Harlem, approached King that September 20, 1958, as he signed autographs. "Is this Martin Luther King?" she asked. "Yes, it is," he answered.

Opening her pocketbook, Curry removed a seven-inch letter opener and stabbed King in the chest. The blade lodged a hair's breadth from his aorta. He kept his cool, which probably saved his life. His doctor said he came within a sneeze of death.

Three weeks later, King was released from the hospital and told reporters he forgave Curry. She was locked in a mental hospital, a "deranged Negro domestic," as the newspapers called her. Detectives searching her apartment found a loaded pistol and threatening letters to President Eisenhower and the FBI. Some of the letters, the police said, reflected a phobia about Southern preachers.

King, for his part, spent his remaining years carrying a poignant reminder of his visit to New York: a scar over his heart in the shape of a cross.

Castro Comes to Harlem
272 West 125th Street

Say what you want about Fidel Castro's politics. As a hotel guest, he was the worst. Castro visited New York in the fall of 1960 to speak at the United Nations. Of course, it wasn't easy for the cigar-chomping dictator to find hotel rooms for himself and his 85-member entourage. Nobody was particularly eager to host Communists in those days. A nervous State Department helped out, though, booking rooms for the Cubans at the Hotel Shelburne, 303 Lexington Avenue.

Fidel and his gang turned the hotel upside down, yelling and marching through hushed hallways in their battle fatigues. They ripped telephones out of walls and littered the carpeted floors with cigar butts, empty rum bottles, and how-to books on revolution. Simply put, they demonstrated little respect for private property.

The Shelburne, already hosting the Cubans reluctantly, demanded that Castro pay $10,000 for property damage. Fidel huffed and puffed and led his troops into the streets, declaring he would sleep in Central Park if no other hotel would take him in. It wasn't necessary. The Hotel Theresa at 125th Street and Seventh Avenue was happy to offer accommodations.

For the next week, Castro's contingent turned the Theresa (now an office building) into party central with plenty of singing, drinking, and heavy breathing. Outside the hotel, crowds cheered wildly for Fidel. Even Soviet leader Nikita Khruschev stopped by for a visit. Years later, in 1990, Nelson Mandela, the leader of the South African anti-apartheid movement, chose the same corner for a huge rally celebrating his release from prison.

Castro ended his visit with a big speech at the UN, charging (accurately, as it turned out) that the United States had been staging a covert war against Cuba and was planning to invade. He went on to give the Theresa four stars while putting in a bad word about the management at the Shelburne.

7

The 1943 Harlem Riot
272 West 126th Street

On a Sunday night in 1943, Mayor Fiorello La Guardia went on the radio and told the people of Harlem to "go to bed."

At the time, the community was in the middle of one of the wildest outbreaks of violence and pillage in the city's history. It started with a single bullet and ended with six people dead and hundreds injured.

The August 1st riot began when a white cop, James Collins, shot a black army private, Robert Bandy, in the shoulder during a confrontation in the lobby of the now-closed Hotel Braddock, 272 West 126th Street. The wound was serious but not fatal.

Nevertheless, a rumor raced through Harlem that night that a white policeman had killed a black soldier. Thousands of blacks streamed into the streets, flipping over cars, setting small fires, and smashing white-owned stores.

Mayor La Guardia stayed awake all night as 2,500 cops dispersed the throngs with bullets, billy clubs, and handcuffs. He banned liquor sales and set a 10:30 P.M. curfew, but the violence went on until morning.

8

Mr. Untouchable
112 West 145th Street

In the 1970s, Leroy "Nicky" Barnes spent Christmas days on Harlem street corners passing out turkeys to poor people. At the same time, he was selling forty pounds of heroin a month out of the Harlem River Motor Garage, 112 West 145th Street, and pulling down $250,000 a week. Young women were hired to package the smack in the back of the garage. Cars would drive in for what appeared to be repairs. They would leave with as much as $50,000 worth of the white powder.

Barnes was a ruthless businessman. He didn't particularly care for people who betrayed him. One foe, a man who liked to play golf, was found with bullet holes in his head at the 18th hole of the Moshulu golf course in the Bronx.

Still, Barnes was a hero to many Harlemites, who treated him, as one cop sneered at the time, "like the goddamn Pope." You couldn't help but admire his flash: he drove Mercedeses and Maseratis, owned three hundred suits, sixty full-length leather coats, and apartments in three cities. Barnes was the original Superfly, a real-life version of Leroy Brown, the baddest dude in the whole damn town.

Barnes beat criminal raps thirteen times, enough for the *New York Times* to dub him "Mr. Untouchable." The government finally got its case together in 1978 and convicted Barnes at age 45 of running "the largest, most profitable, and most venal drug ring in New York City." He was sentenced to life in jail.

From prison, Barnes renounced his drug-dealing days and proclaimed his whole life had been "shallow." He became a close confidant of federal mob investigators, helping them convict forty-four murderers and drug dealers from 1980 to 1990.

Even the Harlem River Motor Garage went straight. It's now a supermarket. The turkeys aren't free anymore, but there are some pretty good specials during the holidays.

9

David Dinkins: Crime Victim
148th Street and St. Nicholas Avenue

Almost all New Yorkers have a crime story. They wear it like a badge of honor or a battle scar. Pity the politician who can't say he has been mugged at least once in his life. He doesn't have a chance of getting elected in the crime capital.

David Dinkins likes to tell the story about the night in the early 1950s when he was robbed while managing a liquor store at 148th Street and St. Nicholas Avenue. It has been nearly forty years since the incident and the sixtysomething mayor is a little fuzzy on the details—like when the holdup occurred.

But Dinkins can remember one thing very clearly—what it felt like to stare down the barrel of a pistol. "In my fear, the gun looked about the size of a cannon," Dinkins has recalled. "I handed him every dollar."

As mayor, Dinkins doesn't have to worry much about being held up. He spends many a night on the town, parading through galas in a black tux and white scarf. Someone once called him the Mayor of the United States. He has the protection to prove it: at least three detectives and a host of uniformed officers guard him around the clock.

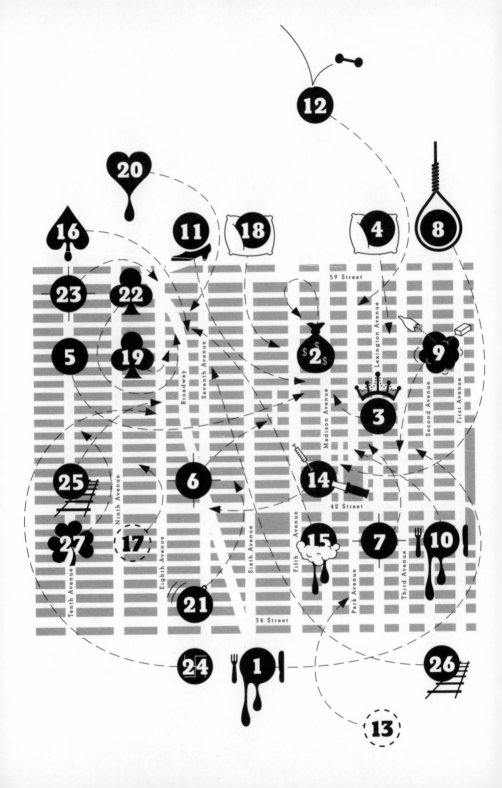

5

Midtown
Mayhem

(East River
to the
Hudson River,
59th to 34th
Streets)

THE REGISTER OF MIDTOWN NOTORATI reads like a guest list for a posh dinner party. It's our very own Last Supper, a bullet-riddled feast for New Yorkers who never leave home without first calling their lawyers. The dishes are varied: delicious mob hits, sizzling rip-offs, hot political executions, and spicy scandals.

Imagine the spread: a long dining table, crisp white linen, shining silver—all stolen, of course. Here's a tuxedoed Donald Trump seated between Ivana and Marla, Nelson Rockefeller with Megan Marshack. At the head of the table, serving the salad, is the hostess Leona—or is it Imelda? Those jewels all look alike.

Watch mob boss Paul "Big Paul" Castellano ask fellow gunslinger Albert Anastasia to pass the salt. The gangsters complain of severe headaches, but we know that the problem—bullets on the brain—is a bit more serious than that. A little more of that wine, says the ever bloodthirsty Legs Diamond. No problem, answers the Happy Hooker, always eager to oblige.

They're all here, the men and women who left their fingerprints in Midtown: mobster Joe Colombo, infamous gambler Arnold Rothstein, actor Gig Young, who earned a place at the table not by winning an Oscar, but by killing himself and his wife all in one day.

Yes, that's Nathan Hale still mouthing off about the Revolution. Even New York's most famous missing man, Judge Crater, managed to make it after more

than fifty years. Who could blame him? The meal is catered by the
Westies, lords of that bastion of fine criminal cuisine, Hell's Kitchen.
Bon appetit.

The Mideast

Dead Meat
246 East 46th Street

They don't talk about it much, but restaurant owners in New York City
know there's one way to guarantee success.

Pray for a mob hit.

Before the winter of 1985, Sparks Steak House was popular among
businessmen looking for a prime rib and a refreshing martini. Now, Sparks
is known everywhere, from Ohio to Oregon, from New Jersey to New
Hampshire. Even in the smallest villages of the Soviet Union, husbands
and wives have been overheard mentioning "Sparkovich" when planning
visits to New York.

The reason: the murder of mob boss Paul Castellano. Or perhaps we
should credit John Gotti, who is responsible for sending a hit squad to
assassinate Castellano and his driver Thomas Bilotti outside Sparks, 246
East 46th Street, on December 16, 1985.

The rush-hour kill was mob dinner theater at its best: the gunmen
wore wooly hats, spoke into walkie-talkies, and fired semiautomatics.
Castellano and Bilotti were shot six times each as the pair climbed out
of a black Town Car. Castellano's cigar slipped from his fingers and
he collapsed on the sidewalk in front of a sign that said, NO STANDING.

Most mobsters, not to mention Sparks' owners, weren't exactly weeping over Castellano's forced retirement at 70. Big Paul, it was agreed,
was a big bore. He lived in a mansion he called the "White House" on
Staten Island. The $3.5 million home featured two impressive columns
out front and two Dobermans roaming the grounds. Paul liked to putter

around in velvet slippers and a blue bathrobe, occasionally take a dip in his Olympic-size pool, play bocce in the backyard, or make the moves on his petite Colombian maid.

Unlike most criminals, Castellano actually bragged about his legitimate business investments, including the distribution of Perdue chickens. It was only fair, some reasoned, that a Godfather who boasted about poultry should get knocked off in front of a steak house.

Gotti, on the other hand, had character—and not only because he claimed he was a plumber and was said to fear flying. Here was a gangster yuppies could love. He wore floral print ties and $2,000 double-breasted silk suits, drank fine wine, and hung out at Regine's and other trendy Manhattan nightclubs. A "mob star," one biographer called him. After the Castellano murder, Andy Warhol created a stenciled rendering—his last—of Gotti that *Time* magazine put on its cover under the headline THE NEW GODFATHER. New Yorkers knew better. They called him the "Dapper Don."

The name stuck. In 1992, Gotti went to jail, convicted of ordering the killing of Castellano and ten others. Even if he gets out, we're confident that Gotti—like Big Paul—will also face an early retirement. The mob may not obey the law, but it does have a deep abiding respect for poetic justice.

2

Trump: The Carnival
Trump Tower, 725 Fifth Avenue

Think of Donald Trump's life as an overpriced carnival. Trump Tower, with pink marble and an eighty-foot waterfall, is the Fun House. The "21" Club is the concession stand. Check out the Donald & Ivana Bumper Cars. Or the Marla Maples Roller Coaster.

Donald, of course, is the main attraction, the ringmaster, his stage name "The Man Who Has Everything" or "The Amazin' Trump." He's a thrill-o-minute—juggling ex-wife Ivana, girlfriend Marla, casinos, hotels, a 50-room triplex . . . and a raging fear of going bald.

We marveled in the late 1970s when he had the gumption to knock down the very tasteful, very elegant Bonwit Teller to make room for his 68-story glass Fun House at 56th and Fifth. We gasped when he destroyed Bonwit's fifty-year-old Art Deco friezes—while preservationists, editorial boards, and good government groups screamed for his scalp.

Donald the Magnificent has done more than replace elegant old landmarks with monstrous glass skyscrapers. He also found time to pose for *Playboy,* buy a football team, and create a board game with himself as the theme. He fixed Wollman Rink in Central Park when the city couldn't, then bought the Plaza Hotel, his very own airline, a huge yacht named the *Trump Princess,* and mansions in two states. He even found the time to worry about nuclear war, volunteering at one point to negotiate arms deals with the Soviets.

Nothing was beyond the Great Trump's powers, or so he said. He wrote a best-selling book, *The Art of the Deal,* in which he included such riveting details as how he hates parties, thinks lunch is a waste of time, and, yes, even interrupts work at the office to take calls from his nine-year-old son.

Of course, "The Man Who Has Everything" can't *do* everything. He couldn't make Ivana understand his lust for Marla. Donald met Marla in the same place he married Ivana, the Marble Collegiate Church on Fifth Avenue at 29th Street, and he kept a suite for her at the St. Moritz Hotel at 50 Central Park South, a few blocks from Trump Tower.

The Marla scandal and the Donald-Ivana split was the topic of international intrigue and the beginning of a down period for the Trump Carnival. As 1991 turned into 1992, Donald was having cash-flow troubles and had started selling off casinos, hotels, even his yacht. He still had Marla and the Fifth Avenue Fun House, but that was about all.

Leona
Helmsley Palace Hotel, 455 Madison Avenue

Never mind that Leona Helmsley didn't pay taxes or that her servants claimed she liked being hand-fed baby shrimps between laps in her swimming pool. We're fascinated by Leona for another reason: facial flexibility.

It's not everyone who can splash on a little lipstick, flash a smile, and manage to look like a cross between Liberace and the Joker.

Such talent, we're sure, takes many hours of hard work, as does managing the quite imperial, 961-room Helmsley Palace Hotel at 455 Madison Avenue. So it's doubly impressive that Leona, self-annointed Queen, also found time to be a criminal.

In 1989, she was convicted of tax evasion in a trial that featured a former maid testifying that the Queen once said, "I don't pay taxes. The little people pay taxes." The case was a landmark in judicial circles after Leona's lawyer, Gerald Feffer, introduced what quickly became known as the "tough bitch defense," in which he noted that being a bitch may not win one friends, but it's still quite legal—in New York, anyway.

Beyond anything, Leona's trial proved that the Helmsley Palace—with its crystal chandeliers, circular stairways, and gold-framed portraits of obscure British royalty—is certainly imperial, but no one should ever work there, certainly not while Leona is boss.

Just ask the help. Pity the kitchen workers who once served the Queen damp lettuce, or the maids who failed to dust the windows or fluff the pillows. "If she should stumble on a speck of dirt in a hotel room or, God forbid, a roach in a hotel room, all hell breaks loose," her lawyer said.

Outside the Palace's iron gates, the public knew little of Leona's penchant for pettiness. They did know about the "Just Wild About Harry" birthday parties she threw for her husband, the doddering King of their $5 billion real estate empire. And they also knew the hotel ads, which spotlighted a glimmering Leona and the caption: "The only Palace in the world where the Queen stands guard."

The scandal that brought down Leona was first reported by the *New York Post,* which discovered that she was billing Helmsley enterprises millions of dollars for personal expenses, everything from a pool enclosure for their $11 million Connecticut estate, to a $45,681 clock in the shape of the Helmsley Building, to her silk lingerie. Together, the $5 billion couple saved themselves a meager $1.2 million in federal income taxes.

Harry, at 80, was judged too senile to testify, although there were pretrial reports that he was happily vacationing in Florida. The judge in 1990 fined Leona $7 million, plus $2 million in restitution, and then sentenced her to four years in prison.

Still, nothing could keep Leona off the airwaves. "I can't believe people are so cruel," the Queen told a television interviewer. Tears streamed down her cheeks. She knew she'd have trouble getting used to her new lodging—a Kentucky prison.

The Happy Hooker
155 East 55th Street

Xaviera Hollander, perhaps the happiest hooker of them all, was no hands-off brothel proprietor. Xaviera not only balanced the books, she was more than willing to jump in bed for cash herself. Communicating flesh to flesh was never a problem for the Dutch-born Xaviera, who liked to say that sex was her favorite hobby—until she realized it could also be quite lucrative.

In 1971, Xaviera ran her sex shop out of a penthouse apartment at 155 East 55th Street. The love nest boasted several amenities, including a swimming pool on the terrace, circular mirrors over the beds, and a photography exhibit featuring hundreds of shots of blonde, green-eyed Xaviera in the nude.

The cops raided the brothel on July 23, 1971, arresting Xaviera, six co-workers, and four clients, including a prominent and very embarrassed businessman from Elyria, Ohio. Xaviera said she was shocked—simply shocked—that anyone would dare suggest that sex was being sold in her home. She claimed she was an interior decorator and was insulted when the police rolled their eyes and asked why it was that she had six tele-phones in her apartment, each one with a different number.

The cops, it turned out, had known about Xaviera's business for months. Her name had emerged during the Knapp investigation into police corruption. Hollander, investigators learned, had paid out $1,100 a month in bribes for police protection.

Getting busted ruined Xaviera's business, and the government's de-cision to deport her in 1972 didn't help either. But there was a silver lining. A major publisher paid $100,000 to Xaviera to write *The Happy Hooker,* a moving tale in which she recounts her journey from Holland, where she won the 1966 Outstanding Secretary of the Year award, to East Side madame. We recommend the passage in which Xaviera describes a particularly steamy afternoon she once spent with a German shepherd. The book sold more than a million copies.

Today, Xaviera is a kind of madame emeritus, no longer in the prostitution business, but writing a column about life between the sheets for a porn magazine.

5

Murder at St. Pat's
Fifth Avenue Between 50th and 51st Streets

The sign at the entrance to St. Patrick's Cathedral reads: WELCOME. PLEASE HELP MAINTAIN THE PRAYERFUL ATMOSPHERE IN A HOUSE OF GOD. On September 21, 1988, Jorge Delgado walked into the cathedral and it was clear he hadn't come for prayer. For one thing, he was naked, except for a pair of red and white gym socks. In his hand, he clutched a bouquet of red carnations.

Jorge was six foot five inches tall and weighed 250 pounds. It was impossible for the few parishioners in the church at the time not to notice him, especially when he stalked toward a man and a woman kneeling in prayer and hit them in the face with his fist. A cop tried to intervene, but Jorge smashed him on the head with a wrought-iron prayer stand.

As screams echoed through the cathedral, Delgado walked to the main altar, picked up another prayer stand, and attacked John Winters, a 77-year-old church usher. Jorge hit Winters on the head seven times until he fell down dead. Moments later, a second cop arrived and shot Delgado in the chest as he raised the prayer stand to strike again. Delgado was dead by the time an ambulance arrived.

The following day, the police reported that Delgado had been arrested eleven times and hospitalized seven times for mental illness. Priests at the cathedral said he had been ejected on several occasions for disrupting masses. It also turned out that on the morning of the attack, Delgado had visited the cathedral and was blessed by John Cardinal O'Connor, the Roman Catholic Archbishop of New York.

6

Date with Death
50 Rockefeller Plaza

Dennis Sweeney may have been insane, but at least he knew it was rude to kill without first making an appointment. Unfortunately for Allard Lowenstein, Dennis was on time.

Lowenstein was a prominent political activist and had been a congressman in the 1960s, leading campus demonstrations for civil rights and an end to the Vietnam War. Allard, a pal of Bobby Kennedy, was proud to say he ranked seventh on Richard Nixon's "enemies list" and was well known for leading the "Dump Johnson" movement in 1968.

One of those who helped Allard was Sweeney. They met at Stanford University, where Allard taught political science and Sweeney was a student.

By 1980, no one seemed to be protesting anything anymore. Allard spent more time on his law practice. Sweeney, on the other hand, was experiencing emotional problems. Some wondered if he was losing his mind, particularly after he told friends that the CIA had put mind-controlling electrodes in his teeth, which prompted him to rip the bridgework from his mouth.

For reasons no one can figure, Sweeney was also tormented by what he thought were the sounds of Allard's voice in his head. He telephoned Lowenstein in March of 1980 and asked to see him. They'd long ago had a falling-out, but Allard was never one to turn someone away because of a disagreement over politics or strategy. On March 14th at 4 P.M., Sweeney entered the reception area on the ninth floor of 50 Rockefeller Plaza. Allard greeted him with a handshake and led him to his office.

"You're sick, Dennis, you need a psychiatrist," Allard said after a few minutes. Sweeney answered by pulling out a Spanish-made pistol and fired seven times, striking Lowenstein in the chest, stomach, and torso. As Allard lay dying, Sweeney left the room, put his weapon in a secretary's in-basket, and took a seat until security guards swept in and cuffed him.

Paramedics raced Lowenstein to nearby St. Clare's Hospital, but he died seven hours later. Old friends rushed to Allard's side. They broke into tears, as well as protest songs, including "We Shall Overcome." Months later, a judge ruled Sweeney insane and sent him to a psychiatric hospital.

7

Assassinated: Meir Kahane
Marriott East Side Hotel, 511 Lexington Avenue

Militant Rabbi Meir Kahane despised the stereotype of the Jew as a bookworm too scared to use his fists. The founder of the Jewish Defense League, a Brooklyn boy, urged Jews to battle oppression with guns and bombs. "Never again!" was his fiery, fist-pumping call-to-arms.

Little surprise, then, that Kahane, at the age of 58, ended up with a bullet in his head. On November 5, 1990, he was shot to death by a Muslim while giving a speech to devotees inside the Morgan Room at the Marriott East Side Hotel. The alleged gunman, El Sayyid Nosair, an air conditioner repairman employed by the city, fled from the hotel, but was captured outside during a wild shoot-out with a US Postal Service police officer who happened to be passing by. Shot twice, Nosair was arraigned in a hospital bed at Bellevue and later acquitted by a jury that nonetheless convicted him of possessing the gun that police said was used in the killing. A judge hit Nosair with the maximum sentence, up to twenty-two years in prison, saying the jury's decision contradicted "the overwhelming weight of evidence and was devoid of common sense." Some called Kahane's death New York's first political assassination since Malcolm X was murdered in 1964.

Kahane was ordained as a rabbi as a young man, but he wasn't wholly satisfied with the synagogue life. He went by an alias, Michael King, and wrote a book that supported the Vietnam War. As Michael King, Kahane hung out in East Side singles bars and apparently had affairs with non-Jewish women, including a model who jumped off the Queensborough Bridge in 1966 because she was despondent over their relationship.

Kahane was a controversial figure no matter what circle he traveled in. During the 1970s, he moved to Israel and served in the Knesset, only to get thrown out of the country because many found his taste for confrontation dangerous and offensive. Among Kahane's favorite ways to spend a day was marching into Arab villages and provoking riots by calling the residents "dogs."

8

Nathan Hale
44th Street and Vanderbilt Avenue

Nathan Hale, hanged for spying on the British during the Revolutionary War, is most famous for his last words, uttered just before the Brits slipped a noose around his neck: "I only regret that I have but one life to give for my country."

Great quote. It got him a statue outside City Hall. Trouble was, he never said it, or at least that's what many historians claim. No one asked, but we suspect Nathan's last word was something more like, "Ouch!"

British soldiers caught the blond, blue-eyed wonder-rebel snooping around Brooklyn on September 21, 1776. They charged that he was spying on their military installations. Nathan, with pen and paper in hand, claimed he was a schoolteacher. The Brits smiled, stuck a bayonet in his face, and placed him under arrest. The following day British commanders, who prided themselves on being civilized, executed Hale, 24, possibly at a site where the United Nations now stands, or at 63rd Street and Third Avenue.

Besides the City Hall statue, there is also a fresco, located at Hale House on East 51st Street, that depicts his trial and death, as well as a plaque at the Yale Club at 44th Street and Vanderbilt Avenue. (Hale went to Yale.)

Draft Riots
Third Avenue and 46th Street

For three long days in the summer of 1863, New York hosted its very own Civil War, a citizens' revolt that started on East 46th Street and nearly leveled the city. Before it was over, nearly a hundred thousand people were rampaging through the streets, destroying buildings, looting stores, and setting most of Manhattan on fire.

Some observers blamed the hot weather for the revolt; others, the uneducated lower classes. Actually, it was President Lincoln who provoked the violence by instituting a Civil War draft that allowed rich people to buy their way out of military service for $300.

Irish laborers, already getting dirt wages for dangerous work, were incensed. The only people they hated more than rich bosses were freed slaves arriving from the South, who competed for their jobs. On the morning of July 13th, several thousand workers, along with members of the city's most lethal street gangs, stormed draft headquarters at Third Avenue and 46th Street.

The rioters destroyed the draft lottery wheel and torched the building. They swarmed streets and underground tunnels, swinging knives, pickaxes, and crowbars, killing as they went. The city's 800-man police force was overwhelmed. Three officers were slain and countless others were injured, including the chief, who was chased and stomped unconscious by a mother whose son was headed for war. The rioters looted stores, hotels, and warehouses. They burned down mansions, a ferry terminal—even the Colored Orphan Asylum on 43rd Street west of Fifth Avenue, where 250 children barely escaped out the back door.

Mayor George Opdyke fled from his ornate home and went into hiding, where he wired for troops. By the time the militia rode in and quieted the mayhem, as many as 1,500 to 2,000 may have died, according to some histories.

The draft, suspended during the riots, was soon restored without incident. Bankers, merchants, and lawyers crept back into town. The

gangs returned to the fringes of society. Blacks and Irishmen returned
to their joyless places at the bottom of the economic ladder. "This is a
nice town to call itself a center of civilization," sniffed the diarist George
Templeton Strong.

10

The Boss of Bosses
230 Park Avenue

In 1931, Mafia chieftain Salvatore Maranzano appointed himself Boss of
Bosses. To celebrate the self-promotion, four men impersonating police
officers burst into his Midtown office, stabbed him in the throat, and shot
him four times in the heart.

So much for fancy titles.

Maranzano's death climaxed what was known as the Castellammarese
War, a bloody battle known more to mobologists than to students of
military history. The war pitted Maranzano's gang—whose roots were
in Castellammare del Gulfo, Italy—against soldiers loyal to a man who
also called himself boss, Joe Masseria. In two short years, sixty gangsters ended up in the city's morgue, including Masseria, who was shot
during a poker game in a restaurant on Coney Island (see Brooklyn
tour).

No one was happier about Masseria's death than Maranzano, who
proclaimed that the Castellammarese War was over. He invited five
hundred gangsters to a meeting hall in the Bronx where, surrounded by
crucifixes and paintings of Jesus, he proclaimed that organized crime
would now be called "Cosa Nostra" (Our Thing).

Maranzano spelled out the hierarchy by which the mob still operates
today—a structure he envisioned after reading about Caesar. At the
bottom of the pyramid would be soldiers; at the top, bosses. Soldiers
couldn't talk to bosses unless they went through the guys in the middle,
the captains, or capos. Of course, he, Salvatore Maranzano, would rule
everyone as *Capo di Tutti Capi*—the Boss of All Bosses.

Let's just say that not everyone was pleased with this arrangement,
especially the very temperamental Lucky Luciano, who was quickly mov-

ing up the mob ladder and would soon become a major boss himself. Nor was Lucky happy to learn that he was on Maranzano's hit list, which also contained the names of such underworld titans as Al Capone, Vito Genovese, and Frank Costello.

On September 10, 1931, Maranzano invited Luciano and Genovese for a "meeting"—that's what he called it—at his Midtown office, suites 925 and 926 at 230 Park Avenue at 46th Street. Luciano feared a setup. He dispatched four men dressed as cops to visit Maranzano a few hours before his own appointment. It looked like a raid until the fake cops took out knives and guns and Maranzano was dead.

As the gunmen left the building, they passed Vinnie Coll, otherwise known as "Mad Dog," a psychopathic yet proficient assassin from the Bronx. Maranzano had hired Coll to kill Luciano and Genovese that day. But hearing that Maranzano had been deposed, Vinnie turned around. He was no fool. He knew he had the afternoon off.

11

Imelda: The Tour
Olympic Tower, 631 Fifth Avenue

The Philippines was her home; Manhattan was her shoe store. Imelda Marcos, a.k.a. "Size 7N," owned three thousand pairs of fancy footwear, many of them purchased right here in Midtown.

Welcome, then, to Imelda's Very Expensive Shoe Tour.

Start at Gucci's, 685 Madison Avenue, which delivered five pairs— or $1,000 worth of leather—to Imelda's door each week. Also try Walter Steiger, 739 Madison; Charles Jourdan, 769 Madison (the gold lamé pumps go for $1,500 a shot); and Susan Bennis/Warren Edwards, on West 57th Street, where you can pick up an alligator pump for a mere $2,450. The lizard backless slippers aren't bad, either. They're around $850.

For jewelry, antiques, and other supplies, Imelda preferred Fred Leighton on Madison, where she could spend $5,000 to diamond-brighten her earlobes. Imelda was quite popular at Van Cleef & Arpels on Fifth. No wonder. In one afternoon, she once plunked down $43,000 for silverware, $234,000 for antique jewelry, and $100,000 for a diamond-and-ruby necklace. At another shop, she even dropped $6,000 for a few dozen boxes of chocolate.

The shoes, the jewelry, the sweets—that was the least of it. Imelda and her loving despot husband, Ferdinand, were also wallet-happy when it came to buying apartments and skyscrapers.

Which brings us to the second part of our Imelda odyssey, the Real Estate Tour.

Let's start small (relatively) with the Olympic Tower, 51st Street off Fifth, where Imelda and Ferdinand owned a $2.4 million condo—owned it secretly, that is, in the name of Imelda's secretary, Vilma Bautista.

True, it wasn't like home, the Malacañang Palace in Manila, where Imelda's closet was large enough for two thousand gowns, five hundred bras, and all her pumps, including a set of blinking disco shoes. But how could she complain? There were six bedrooms, five bathrooms, gold faucets, Persian rugs, and delicious views of St. Patrick's Cathedral, the Empire State Building, and Central Park.

Even better, they could stay at the Philippine UN consulate, a seven-story town house at 15 East 66th Street, which they stocked with $100 million in regal frills. Imelda liked to tidy herself in front of a George III mirror, while her seamstresses slept in the basement, in bug-infested cubicles and a cramped room that locked from the outside.

If it was music she wanted, there were three Steinway pianos and a pillow-strewn disco room. The art ranged from Van Gogh to Monet to two oversized oil portraits of Imelda, entitled *The Triumph of Purity* and *The Triumph of Beauty*. If she just wanted to rest, she could stretch out on a $3,000 lace bedspread and $9,000 canopy bed bearing the crest of Czar Nicholas II.

Ferdinand Marcos had a thing for skyscrapers, including a 70-story building at 40 Wall Street; the Herald Center shopping mall on Sixth Avenue and 34th Street; a 26-story office building with an ornate lobby at 200 Madison Avenue; and, of course, the world-famous Crown Building at 750 Fifth Avenue.

Where's the crime, you ask? None was proved, but prosecutors charged that Ferdinand and Imelda paid for the goodies with $200 million they stole from American investors and the Philippine national treasury.

Ferdinand, of course, was very conveniently dead by the time the matter went to trial at Manhattan Federal Court in 1990.

Imelda didn't dare wear her $1,200 Gucci alligator high-heels in front of a jury. Instead, she wore basic black shoes. They matched her black dress, dark sunglasses, and the black rosary beads she was rolling between her fingers.

Perhaps the attire reflected her somber mood. Her husband was dead, after all, and she was a former First Lady in exile from her homeland. Or maybe Imelda merely wanted the jurors to think she was just like them—and not the "pig" all the newspapers made her out to be (OINK! squealed the headlines).

The jurors weren't fooled about her lifestyle, but they couldn't bring themselves to blame her for what was mostly her husband's corruption. Imelda was acquitted on her 61st birthday. She dashed out of court and straight to St. Patrick's Cathedral. With a gaggle of photographers snapping away, she knelt in prayer and smiled publicly for the first time in a long while. "Thank you! Thank you!" Imelda said. "God bless America."

12

Goodbye
465 Park Avenue

These were the last words of Alvin Rodecker, as recorded by his wife on the occasion of his 60th birthday, June 23, 1960:

"Holy cow! We're really celebrating!"

In the next instant, a ten-pound dumbbell dropped from the sky and struck Alvin Rodecker on the head. He died the next day.

The dumbbell fell eight stories from an apartment window at the Ritz Tower Hotel at 465 Park Avenue. The apartment, you should know, belonged to actress Arlene Francis.

It was an accident, of course. Arlene wasn't home at the time. The weight had been wrapped in a towel and used to prop open a window screen. A maid knocked it off the ledge.

No charges were filed, but Francis eventually agreed to pay Mrs. Rodecker a $175,000 legal settlement for her incalculable grief.

The Midwest

13

Thanks for the Memoirs: The Disappearance of Joe Bonanno
36 Park Avenue

Gangsters are not traditionally known for penning their memoirs. Al Capone, for example, never got around to writing, say, *The Capone Papers, Living with Syphilis*, or *My Life of Brutally Killing Hundreds and Hundreds of Men.*

Joe Bonanno, on the other hand, wasn't so modest. In 1983, he wrote *A Man of Honor*, a 406-page tome recounting his life in what he called the "Tradition." The Mafia? No such thing, wrote Joe. Just a bunch of guys who care about family.

Included in the book is the story of how Bonanno was kidnapped by his relative on an October night in 1964. It happened quite conveniently just hours before Joe was to testify before a grand jury about the mob— or, as he would put it, the "family."

Bonanno, 59 at the time, and his attorney, William Maloney, were returning to Maloney's apartment at 36 Park Avenue. Suddenly, two men came up from behind on the street and grabbed Bonanno by the arms. "C'mon, Joe," one of the men said, "my boss wants to see you." Maloney tried to intervene, but when the other thug took out a gun he remembered he was a lawyer—not a fighter—and ran inside to call the cops.

Bonanno was thrown into a car and not seen again for nineteen months. He claims he was driven hundreds of miles to the upstate home of Stefano Magaddino, who happened to be Bonanno's cousin. The kidnapping was apparently the mob's way of telling Joe to retire. At the time, Bonanno was making noises about killing the heads of New York's other crime families, including the ever-powerful Carlo Gambino.

Bonanno resurfaced one morning in 1966, walking into a federal courtroom in lower Manhattan and introducing himself to a judge. He was wearing a gray silk suit and a dark tie. The cops examined the labels for clues to where he had been, but Joe, clever as a fox, was wearing the same clothing he wore the night he disappeared.

Soon after, Bonanno, along with his beloved Doberman pinscher, Greasy, retired to Tuscon, Arizona, where he still lives.

14

Times Square
42nd Street

No single crime ever made Times Square famous. A million and one murders, stabbings, and robberies were enough to do the trick. Times Square, Main Street in the City of the Notorious. Quaint, isn't it?

Gathered here on any night are drug dealers and murderers, rapists and thieves, hustlers, pimps, and boy prostitutes. Leave anyone out? Oh yes, the arsonists, pedophiles, junkies, and perverts—they're very sensitive to a slight.

In one recent year, seven crimes a day were reported on 42nd Street between Seventh and Eighth avenues, known as "The Deuce," the neon heart of Times Square. An electronic headline zipper high above 42nd Street announces the latest catastrophe: COP SHOT, EAST SIDE WOMAN SLAIN, or FIVE DEAD IN BROOKLYN.

But what makes Times Square really special are the opportunities. It's helpful if you're interested in pharmaceuticals—as in crack, smack, cocaine, and speed.

Did someone say Uzis? Got 'em. A license to drive? Got it. A license to practice dentistry in the State of New York? Got that, too.

We haven't even mentioned sex. Where else can you talk to a "real live nude girl" through a hole in a dark booth; or peruse quality literature in a truly "adult" bookstore; or pay for a night of romance in a hotel where you're bound to lose your limbs and wallet if not your life.

And the movies—who can forget that finely woven tale of cannibalism, *Make Them Die Slowly?* Yes, it played Times Square along with *Debbie*

Does Dallas, Deep Throat, and *Escape from New York,* to name but a few.

Of course, Times Square has been Sin Central for most of the century. But the sinning was a tad less shocking before 1950. Those were the days of "girlie" shows, bawdy musicals, and dirty dime novels. On any given night, Babe Ruth, J. Edgar Hoover, and Jack Benny could be spotted grabbing a bite at Sardi's, Lindy's, or the Stork Club.

Those were also the days before the Port Authority Bus Terminal was built. A charming addition that was. Dante's Terminal, it became. Not only is it filthy and dangerous, but you can't even call for help. It's the only bus terminal in the world where the pay phones are padlocked at certain hours so drug dealers can't use them for business.

Never been to Times Square? Better get there fast. There's a plan kicking around to clean it up. That means turning it into the kind of Main Street found in most other cities and towns. You know, nice office buildings and clean streets. Politicians imagine a bright future and promise no more porn, no more sex shops, no more psychotic slashers, kidnappers, and drug abusers hanging out in Times Square.

Lots of luck.

Barber Shop Special
Park Sheraton Hotel, 870 Seventh Avenue

The barber-shop murder of mob boss Albert Anastasia in 1957 ranks among organized crime's greatest hits. Performance judges should note that the killers struck and escaped in broad daylight on one of the busiest streets in Western Civilization.

Consider also that Anastasia was no pussycat. If anyone ever commissions a Mount Rushmore for mobsters, they would have to include the fistlike mug of the man known as the Lord High Executioner. Albert Anastasia didn't just kill because he was told to. He killed because he liked to. Some people collect stamps. Albert collected corpses.

Anastasia was a chief executive officer of Murder Incorporated, the death squad that carried out murders for the mob—some say as many as four hundred—in the 1930s. This was no pull-the-trigger, splatter-the-walls operation, although they did plenty of that. Albert and the boys also liked to hack people to death with ice picks, set them on fire, even throw them in the East River with slot machines tied to their ankles.

Very good at his craft, that Albert, and very successful. He lived like a top exec in a 20-room mansion across the Hudson River in Fort Lee, New Jersey. No doubt the residents of Bluff Road were intrigued by their neighbors, particularly when the Anastasias surrounded their home with a ten-foot-high fence topped with barbed wire.

For thirty years, dozens of mob-busters dreamed of sending Albert to the electric chair. Never happened. Not many witnesses were interested in testifying against him. Those who were interested ended up in the morgue just when they were supposed to be on their way to court. Imagine that.

The only chair Anastasia ended up in was the No. 4 barber chair at the Park Sheraton Hotel, at 56th Street and Seventh Avenue (now the Omni Park Central). By 1957, the mob had grown tired of Albert's murderous ways, and that could mean only one thing: goodbye, Albert.

Anastasia visited the Park Sheraton on October 25, 1957, for a clip and a shave. Two gunmen, both wearing business suits and sunglasses, sauntered in and fired ten times. Five of the bullets hit Albert in the back. He fell out of the chair and flopped on the linoleum floor. There were eleven witnesses—customers and barbers—but none could describe the gunmen to the police. "I've never seen so many people go blind at once," one investigator grumbled.

Albert never saw anything either. He had a steaming hot towel wrapped around his face. Anastasia was buried in a simple, $900 maroon coffin with rosary beads entwined in his fat fingers. No one outside his immediate family attended his funeral, not even the top mob bosses who had, so many times in the past, requested his murderous services.

More interest was shown in Anastasia's death chair, which was eventually auctioned off for $7,000. His Bluff Road mansion was purchased for $75,000 in the late 1950s by the comedian Buddy Hackett.

16

Dead Man's Poker
Park Central Hotel, 870 Seventh Avenue

Albert Anastasia wasn't the only gangster to check out at a hotel at 870 Seventh Avenue. In 1928, gambler Arnold Rothstein, legendary for fixing the 1919 World Series, was shot at the same address after welshing on a poker debt.

Rothstein wasn't a big-name villain like Anastasia or Al Capone, but he was a major influence on the underworld's younger members. Think of Arnold Rothstein as the dean of Crime High, a kind of mob finishing school for major bad boys like Lucky Luciano, Meyer Lansky, Frank Costello, and Legs Diamond.

In Bribery 101, Rothstein taught the value of paying off cops and politicians. In Protocol 101, he preached that upstanding gangsters mingle with mayors and judges and steer clear of the spotlight, flashy suits, and colorful ties. Arnold dressed in the pinstripes of a Wall Street banker and earned power nicknames any CEO would envy: The Brain, The Fixer, Mr. Big. Some simply knew him as the J. P. Morgan of the Underworld.

Rothstein demonstrated an aptitude for crime at an early age. His father, an Orthodox Jew, caught Arnold at the age of three trying to stab his brother. "I hate Harry," Arnold screamed as his father grabbed the knife from his hand.

Of course, bad things have a way of catching up with bad people, and Arnold was no exception. He got his after a marathon three-day poker game in which he lost $320,000 and refused to pay. Six weeks later, on November 4, 1928, the man Arnold lost to supposedly invited him to room 349 at the Park Central Hotel (it was later named the Park Sheraton). Shortly after 10 P.M., Rothstein was seen stumbling out onto the street, a bullet wound in his stomach.

Arnold lingered in a coma for two days and died on Election Day. If he had survived, he apparently would have collected $570,000 for correctly betting that Herbert Hoover would become president and Franklin

D. Roosevelt would be elected governor of New York. Arnold's alleged assassin, meanwhile, was arrested but then cleared.

Judge Crater
332 West 45th Street

The public knew little of State Supreme Court Judge Joseph Force Crater prior to August 1930. He had an apartment on Fifth Avenue, a wife, and a few mistresses. At 41 years old, he liked to part his hair dead-center and wear spats, choke collars, and Panama hats. Nothing special. Just another ordinary Joe.

Life for the Craters changed on August 6, 1930, the day the judge disappeared. This made Crater very famous. Now everyone wanted to know about him. That's the way it works in New York: sometimes you have to vanish to get any attention.

No one could accuse the police of not trying to solve the Crater mystery. Case no. 13595 was closed in 1979, more than a half-century after the judge was last seen outside the former Billy Haas' Steakhouse at 332 West 45th Street.

Crater had gone alone to the restaurant, popular in its day among politicians, judges, lawyers, and gangsters. He bumped into two friends, including an attractive showgirl, with whom he ate dinner. At 9:15 P.M., Crater told his friends he was late for a show, *Dancing Partner,* at the Belasco Theater. The judge said goodnight, hopped into a cab, and drove off into infamy.

Several explanations for Crater's disappearance have cropped up over the years. Some claimed that Legs Diamond was dispatched by the mob to murder Crater, who was apparently the target of a police investigation into judicial corruption. Others suspected that Crater, whose nickname was "Good Time Joe," was killed for having an affair with a gangster's girlfriend.

Of course, the theories were never proven, and generations of cops were left with nothing to do but follow up on calls from tipsters who had spotted Crater in different locations around the world. At different times, the judge was reportedly seen prospecting for gold in the California desert, herding sheep somewhere in the Northwest, and running a bingo racket in Africa.

Rocky Horror Show
13 West 54th Street

Think living in this town is risky?

Try dying here.

Better yet, try being Nelson Rockefeller and dying here—late at night in the company of an attractive blonde less than half his age.

Gosh, Rocky left us with a lot of unanswered questions.

What *was* he doing with Megan Marshack that January 26th night in 1979 when he had a fatal heart attack? Of course, Rocky didn't live to answer the questions and Megan wasn't talking.

Instead, the Rockefellers presented an official spokesman, one of those communications experts trained to dance around tough questions. Hugh Morrow's initial explanation was that Rocky died in his office at 30 Rockefeller Plaza and was with a security aide and his chauffeur. Morrow gave the time of death as 10:15 P.M.

But the next day, Morrow changed his tune. Rocky, it turned out, actually died not at the office but in his splendid old townhouse at 13 West 54th Street. The heart attack, Morrow said, actually occurred at 11:15 P.M., an hour later than first reported. Morrow also added that Rocky was in the company of Marshack, his 25-year-old assistant, with whom he was working on an art book project.

The revised account only prompted more questions, not the least of them concerning Megan's fashion sense: Why was she dressed in a black evening gown for what was supposedly an evening of work? Secondly, if Rocky was stricken at 11:15 P.M., why did Marshack place a frantic call an hour earlier to Rocky's neighbor? Paramedics arrived at 11:16 P.M., moments after being summoned, but were too late to save Rocky.

The questions lingered like cheap perfume—the kind Rocky wouldn't have been caught dead buying for his wife, or any other woman for that matter. Morrow maintained a steady hand: he claimed Marshack had called for help as soon as Rocky was stricken. The initial reports about time and place, he said, were incorrect only because she was in a state of shock. Period. End of discussion.

Rocky's wife, Happy, declined an autopsy and had her husband's body cremated the next day. Marshack was soon let go from her $60,000-a-year job. Rockefeller remembered her in his will, saying she didn't have to pay back a $45,000 real estate loan from the family. To this day, she has refused to talk publicly about her last night with Rocky.

19

Studio 54
254 West 54th Street

From the moment it opened it 1977, Studio 54 was a strobe-lit, cocaine sandbox for the rich and shameless. Here was a nocturnal playpen for Truman Capote and Halston, Jack Nicholson and Cher, a home away from home for Andy Warhol and Bianca Jagger, Elton John and Farrah Fawcett. Even the First Mother, Lillian Carter, couldn't resist. She danced one night to Donna Summer disco tunes with pretty, muscled boys in satin boxer shorts.

Did someone say cocaine? It was everywhere. You knew it was so: a huge spoon lowered from the ceiling and dumped artificial snow on the dance floor. And why not? The Vietnam War was over. The demonstrations were done. It was time to party. It was time to talk about *moi.*

Outside the club each night, hundred of young men and women waited behind red velvet ropes, hoping, praying that owner Steve Rubell would deem them worthy to get in. "Steve," they would beg, "Steve. Over here."

Rubell, five foot five and always surrounded by beefy bodyguards, was arrogant and well connected. Roy Cohn, the mob-connected and unabashed Commie-hunter of the 1950s, was his attorney. Rubell raked in $600,000 a week, storing the cash in garbage bags in Studio's rafters.

Of course, he didn't bother telling that to the tax man, reporting instead an income of only $55,675 his first year. The IRS returned the favor in 1978 by charging him with illegally hiding $2.5 million.

Rubell spent thirteen months in prison for tax evasion with partner Ian Schraeger as the 1970s ended. After jail, he sold Studio and made millions in the hotel business. He died at 45 in July 1990 of what his publicist said were complications from hepatitis and septic shock.

The standing-room-only service at Riverside Memorial Chapel on Amsterdam Avenue didn't have a guest list, but there was a coterie of bodyguards at the door. Most of the old glittering crowd didn't make it, but Calvin Klein and Bianca Jagger were there, both dressed in stylish black and hiding their tears behind designer sunglasses.

Gig Young Becomes a Star
205 West 57th Street

They met in 1978 on the set of a trashy thriller called *The Game of Death*. Oscar winner Gig Young had already married and divorced four wives, including "Bewitched" star Elizabeth Montgomery. But Gig, 61, handsome and graying at the temples, was willing to take another chance. Who could blame him? Kim Schmidt, 31, an actress, was beautiful, blonde, and half his age.

Gig and Kim were married in September 1978 at City Hall in New York. They lived in Young's apartment at the luxurious Osborne, 205 West 57th Street. Friends said Gig adored his new bride, although there were some who wondered why no one had been invited to the ceremony.

Just three weeks later, Gig gave his most memorable performance. Not that his acting career wasn't illustrious—he had starred with Clark Gable in *Teacher's Pet* and won the Oscar starring with Jane Fonda in *They Shoot Horses, Don't They?*

Sometime during the day of October 19, 1978, Young shot his new bride in the head. Then he turned the gun on himself. Someone found the bodies hours later fully clothed and sprawled out on their blood-soaked, king-sized bed. In Gig's hand was the .38-caliber revolver.

No satisfactory explanation has ever been given for the murder-suicide. Gig's fans were left with one mysterious detail. On a desk in the bedroom where the bodies were found, a diary was opened to September 27th. The entry said: "We got married today."

21

Only the Loathsome
145–151 West 44th Street

Future generations looking back on the economic boom of the 1980s will learn about a loathsome creature who roamed New York City's landscape, searching, itching, salivating to turn anything that didn't move into a condominium. In those days, real estate developers were the Pirates of Finance, known for tearing down elegant old buildings and erecting glass towers in which no one but the very rich could afford to live.

No one fit the bill of dastardly developer better than Harry Macklowe. In early January of 1985, Macklowe bought four vacant tenements on West 44th Street. He hoped to knock the buildings down and replace them with a hotel, preferably with his own name on the awning.

Only one obstacle: two of the buildings were boarded-up Single Room Occupancy hotels serving poor and elderly residents. The city was instituting a moratorium on demolishing SRO hotels. City Hall drafted the law after critics charged that Mayor Koch had turned the city over to developers at the expense of the lower and middle classes.

On January 7th, with only two days to go before the moratorium would take effect, Macklowe did what many Pirates of Finance do when blocked by the government. He broke the law. In the dark of night, Macklowe ordered a wrecking crew to demolish the buildings, even though he didn't have a demolition permit, protective scaffolding, or assurances that the water and electricity had been turned off.

But Harry did have Eddie Garofalo, a protegé of John Gotti, directing the destruction. Eddie, who was murdered in a mystery shooting five years later, took care of the job while the city slept. The next morning, city officials and New Yorkers were outraged. Harry apologized and paid a $2 million fine. Big deal. Today, the 43-story Hotel Macklowe towers over the spot.

22

Murder at the Hotsy Totsy
1721 Broadway

The rubber-legged men carried out of the old Hotsy Totsy Club on Broadway weren't always drunk. Sometimes they were just plain dead. Not surprising, since the Hotsy Totsy's owner was Legs Diamond, who, in the 1920s, was highly regarded in the field of homicide.

Legs, it seems, could also be a pleasant host as long as patrons kept their eyes shut while inside the club. Otherwise, they were liable to end up in court testifying against gangsters, if not the bottom of the East River.

Case in point: one night in 1929, Legs and gangster pal Charlie Entratta got into a drunken argument with two men. Suddenly, guns were drawn and bullets were flying. In seconds, the two men, one of them nicknamed Red, were lying on the floor of the club in a puddle of blood.

For the next eight months, the cops searched everywhere for Legs, but all the witnesses to the double murder—including the bartender, three customers, a cashier, and the hat-check girl—either disappeared or died very unnaturally. The following March, ten months after the shootings, Legs walked into a police precinct in Midtown and said, "You guys looking for me?"

It was a fine time to surrender since no one was left to testify against him. The Hotsy Totsy murders were never solved, leading one newspaper to write: "The solution is locked up in the graves of dead men and in the minds of a few men still alive who are anxious to keep on living until their time comes to die from natural causes."

Legs, known for surviving dozens of bullet wounds, finally died in his sleep a year later in an Albany hotel room. The police found him in his pajamas, with three bullet holes in his head.

23

Goodbye, Colombo
Columbus Circle

The feds knew him as a bigtime Mafia boss, but Joe Colombo said it just wasn't so. The talk about his gambling and loan-sharking empire, his hijacking business—it was all a lie. Instead, he described himself as a simple guy from South Brooklyn, a real estate salesman, living on $20,000 a year.

"Call me Joe," he'd say, offering a licorice stick. He was short, balding, muscular. He even dressed like a salesman—checked jackets, wide ties, and gray fedoras.

"Mafia? What's the Mafia?" Joe would ask. "There's no Mafia. Am I the head of a family? Yes. My wife and four sons and a daughter. That's my family."

Colombo claimed to hate that word, *Mafia*. He felt it was offensive to law-abiding Italian-Americans—like himself. In 1971, he formed the Italian-American Civil Rights League and was able to convince the makers of *The Godfather* to cut references to "Mafia" and "Cosa Nostra" from their script.

Joe took his campaign further, sponsoring Italian Unity Day, an anti-discrimination rally in Columbus Circle. Thousands showed up that June 28, 1971, holding red, white, and green banners. Many waved to Joe. "Hi ya!" he shouted back.

Apparently, not everyone was happy about Joe's organizing efforts. Jerome Johnson, 24, wearing press credentials and a camera around his neck, walked through a ring of a thousand cops and shot Colombo in the head, neck, and face. The mob chief crashed to the ground, less than a thousand feet north of the statue of Christopher Columbus. Pandemonium broke out. Johnson himself was shot dead, apparently by a Colombo bodyguard.

Joe was rushed to the hospital, paralyzed for life, able to move only a thumb and finger. Investigators believe Crazy Joe Gallo, Colombo's arch rival in South Brooklyn, arranged the hit. Of course, Crazy Joe himself didn't last too much longer (see Little Italy tour).

Others say mob boss Carlo Gambino, fed up with Joe's need for publicity, hired the killer. In the shadow of Colombo's paralysis, his underground empire crumbled. He died of a stroke nearly seven years after the shooting, on May 22, 1978. He was 55.

24

A Nazi Rally at Madison Square Garden
Eighth Avenue and 49th Street

In 1939, Adolf Hitler's fans in New York held a huge rally for their favorite führer at the old Madison Square Garden, at Eighth Avenue and 49th Street. Some 28,000 people bought tickets to the February 20th event. Eighteen thousand attended.

The Garden didn't exactly turn into Nazi Germany, but the rally's organizers did hang anti-Semitic banners from the balconies. Thousands dressed up in Nazi uniforms and wore gold tiepins in the shape of swastikas. The speakers attacked Jews and President Roosevelt while praising Hitler, Aryans, and, for some reason, George Washington.

Outside the Garden, fifty thousand counter-protesters jostled with the police, waving "Smash Hitler" signs and denouncing anti-Semitism. The Socialist Workers Party warned of concentration camps one day springing up in America.

Fiorello La Guardia's name was attacked inside the Garden. Outside, he took heat as well, for not stopping the rally. The mayor, who'd been the first major politician to denounce Hitler, said he'd never sink to the level of the Nazis by supressing free speech.

25

The Flutist
IND Subway Station, Eighth Avenue and 50th Street

On a June morning in 1979, Renee Katz stood on a subway platform waiting to take a train to high school. Graduation was a week away and then she would be off to college, possibly a music conservatory in New England. Renee, a doe-eyed 17-year-old from Queens, dreamed of playing the flute professionally.

All she had to do was survive another morning rush hour underground in the New York City subway system. She didn't make it. Renee Katz was the victim that morning of a crime that nearly broke the city's heart. For no apparent reason, a man wearing orange pants pushed her off the platform at 50th Street and Eighth Avenue and into the path of an arriving E train.

At first, the hundreds of commuters packed on the platform didn't seem to know what had happened. And then, after the subway screeched to a halt, everyone could hear Renee screaming. She was lying in the tracks, lucky to be alive, her right hand severed, her dreams of playing the flute finished.

Renee was taken to a nearby hospital where a team of laser microsurgeons worked feverishly for sixteen hours to reattach her hand. The doctors rescued Renee's hand but couldn't do anything about her dexterity, which was essential, of course, for playing the flute. Renee had lost movement and feeling in her slender fingers.

She was deluged with thousands of get-well cards from New Yorkers. Violinist Isaac Stern sent flowers. A businessman anonymously donated $3,000 for the doctors' bills. Her classmates and principal, from the High School of Music and Art, conducted a special graduation ceremony at her hospital bed.

Renee never made it to music college, but she found a new career. Inspired by the professionals who nursed her to health, she became an occupational therapist. She married her high school sweetheart, a constant companion during her ordeal.

The cops never found the man who pushed Renee onto the tracks. At one point, they charged a 26-year-old man with the crime, but a jury acquitted him after several witnesses couldn't place him at the scene. Not very surprising, since it happened during rush hour.

Death of a Utah Tourist
IND Subway Station, Seventh Avenue and 53rd Street

He came to New York from Provo, Utah, for the US Open tennis tournament. Brian Watkins, 22, was an ardent tennis fan with short hair, big ears, and an enthusiastic grin. He may have lived in a community that called itself Happy Valley, but he loved New York. He knew all about its pleasures and pitfalls. He and his family looked forward to their annual sporting pilgrimage.

In the summer of 1990, Brian was killed on a Midtown subway platform while defending his mother from a gang of muggers, who set upon the Watkinses as they waited for a train to take them downtown to a restaurant in Greenwich Village. The family's tragedy became a symbol of raging violence in a city embroiled in a particularly murderous summer, during which more than two dozen children, teenaged and younger, were wounded or killed by gunfire. Brian's death turned the city's troubles into a national topic of conversation. *Time* magazine ran a cover story with the headline THE ROTTING OF THE BIG APPLE.

Brian died, in part, because the family did something most tourists— not to mention New Yorkers—wouldn't dare to risk: they tried to fight back. The family had decided to take the subway from their hotel, the New York Hilton, to a restaurant in Greenwich Village. They were waiting for a D train at 53rd Street and Seventh Avenue when eight teenagers surrounded them.

The pack, which called itself F.T.S., or Fuck This Shit, had an initiation rite that required new members to mug someone. It so happened that on the night they attacked the Watkinses, the gang was trying to raise money to get into Roseland, the dance hall at 239 West 52nd Street.

One of the youths demanded money from Brian's father, then sliced open his back pocket with a box cutter. A second grabbed Mr. Watkins' money clip holding $200. Another gang member kicked Brian's mother in the chest. That was more than Brian could take. He lunged at the thugs, one of whom stabbed him in the chest with a four-inch, silver handled butterfly knife.

Police had little trouble rounding up the gang. "Where's the party?" a key witness had asked the teens as they streamed out of the station. "Roseland," one replied. When the cops arrived, the youths, with nicknames like "Rocstar" and "Skor," were eating mescaline and dancing to Madonna. The ringleader concealed a knife in his shoe. The alleged killer, Yull Morales, 19, was soon indicted for murder along with the seven other gang members. By 1992, seven of the eight, including Yull, were convicted of murder and robbery, a sentence carrying a term of twenty-five years to life in jail. The eighth and last defendant was facing a separate trial as well. The judge called the teens "predatory beasts."

As a result of the killing, Mayor Dinkins, who was forced at one point that summer to deny that New York was turning into Dodge City, started a program that was supposed to flood the streets with 2,500 new cops. Seven months after he died, the city opened the Brian Watkins Tennis Center for youths, on the East River near the Williamsburg Bridge. An anonymous donor made the $1.7 million facility possible.

27

The Westies
Hell's Kitchen

Nostalgia night with the Westies, a gang of murderers and loan sharks who once ruled Hell's Kitchen, wouldn't exactly be a tender affair. These were not tender men. They were gangsters without expense accounts, men who cared more for leather jackets and stale beer than for silk suits and fancy wines. They drank recklessly, killed for no reason, and then delighted in dumping bodies in the East River.

A trip down memory lane with the Westies would have to include a stop at the now-defunct Leprechaun Bar, 608 Ninth Avenue, where gang member Mickey Featherstone, who would eventually destroy the Westies by testifying against them in court, shot a drunken man in 1970 for demanding that he buy him a drink. Mickey's partner Jimmy Coonan, another well-mannered gent, once killed a man for calling his brother a "sissy."

Who can forget the morning Mickey, Jimmy, and Eddie "The Butcher" Cumminsky were sitting around the now-closed Sunbrite Bar, 736 Tenth Avenue, passing around a milk carton containing the genitals of one of their victims? Or how about the time they shot a guy named Rick and then cut him into six pieces all because he didn't pay back a $1,250 loan?

Hell's Kitchen always had a reputation for turning out first-rate rogues. The Westies inherited the lawless tradition laid down by early-twentieth-century Irish gangs like the Parlor Mob, the Gorillas, the Gophers, the Whyos, and the Dead Rabbits. Gangster Owney Madden, who owned the Cotton Club in the 1930s, was a Hell's Kitchen graduate, as was Vinnie "Mad Dog" Coll, hitman-extraordinare in the 1920s and 1930s.

Hell's Kitchen has been renamed Clinton by real estate speculators, but its reputation lives on as a neighborhood where bodies tend to disappear. In search of the remains of long-missing thugs, in 1979 the cops dug up the grounds behind the Skyline Motor Inn at 50th Street and Tenth Avenue. They came up with some bones, but they belonged to dogs, not enemies of the Westies.

The Westies were put out of business in 1987 when Mickey Featherstone was arrested for murder and started singing about the gang's dark past. Jimmy Coonan, the gang's leader, went to jail for life, as did plenty of others. Mickey is a member of the Federal Witness Protection Program, living somewhere in America. He has a new name, but plenty of Westies memories to keep him staring at the ceiling late at night.

6

Below the Belt

Murray Hill, Gramercy Park, and Chelsea

(34th to 14th Streets, River to River)

HOW COMFORTING TO THINK OF BIG BAD New York City as a collection of small neighborhoods. Just below midtown, for example, are Murray Hill and Gramercy Park on the East Side, Chelsea on the West.

Imagine them as urban sanctuaries, pockets of brownstone warmth within the skyscraper-cold metropolis, their mission to offer a peaceful break between the madness of midtown and the pandemonium of the Village.

How charming. How quaint.

How optimistic.

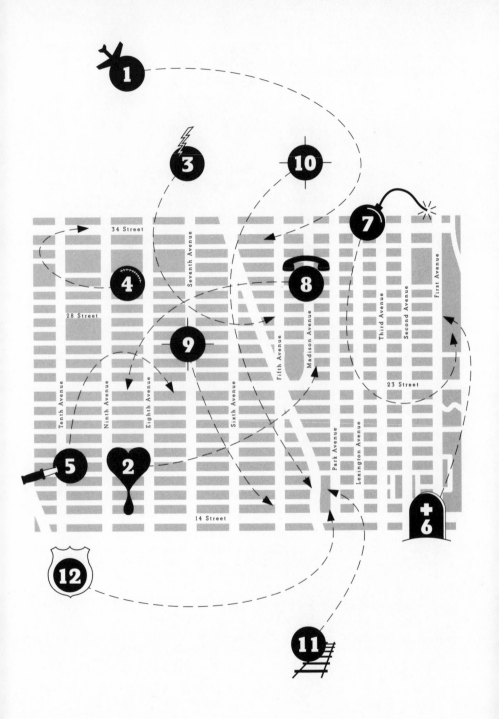

1

Plane Crash at the Empire State
Building
350 Fifth Avenue

Don't miss the Empire State Building, unless, of course, you're traveling in an airplane. Unfortunately, US Army pilot William Smith Jr. couldn't resist. In 1945, he crashed a B-25 bomber smack into the skyscraper's 79th floor.

The newspapers of the day, ever sensitive to tragedy, declared the disaster SPECTACULAR!, even though Smith, a copilot, one passenger, and eleven people inside the building were killed. No doubt the papers were referring to the plane's last moments in the air, when it swooned, slalomed, and finally punched a hole in the northwest face of the Empire State—all at two hundred miles per hour.

The 102-story monolith swayed like a tree in a storm as fiery bits of building and aircraft rained down on rooftops, back lots, and pedestrians on the street. Miles away, Queens residents thought the sudden flash in the sky was lightening. Others, closer to the scene, wondered if a kamikaze pilot had attacked Manhattan.

The plane's engine, dislodged on impact, landed on the building's 78th floor and hurtled down a long hallway until it broke through the sky-scraper's southwest wall and fell atop an apartment house a block away. Eleven Catholic war relief workers in room 7915 on the 79th floor were incinerated in a flash. Emergency workers discovered them burned in their seats, one with a notebook in his lap, another holding a pencil in hand. A third victim, the papers reported, was found carrying a postcard of the Empire State Building in his jacket pocket. Among the twenty-six survivors was Betty Lou Oliver, a stenographer, who fell eighty floors in an elevator car after its cables snapped.

Smith had been flying to the New York area from Bedford Field, near Boston, running up practice miles for a war assignment in the Pacific. Army investigators suspected he lost his way in the blinding fog. It is also possible his rudder failed. Fortunately, the crash occurred on a

Saturday before 10 A.M. Only fifteen hundred people were inside the
Empire State at the time, far less than the normal weekday crowds of
fifteen thousand.

The accident left no lasting scars, mostly because the management
spent $1 million to make the Empire State as good as new. Room 7915
still exists and its tenants, employees of an importer of industrial cables,
know exactly where the plane hit. If they're not too busy, they'll show
you the spot.

2

Edifice Complex: The Rise and Fall of Stanford White
51 Madison Avenue

We could list forever the achievements of the great nineteenth-century
architect Stanford White, whose legendary works include the memorial
arch at Washington Square Park and the former Tiffany mansion, a mas-
terpiece of Romanesque Revival.

But why bother when we can talk about his sex life instead. Especially
since it relates to another of our favorite subjects: his bloody death atop
one of his most masterful and majestic creations, the old Madison Square
Garden at 51 Madison Avenue.

White, delightfully dapper with his red handlebar mustache, was well
known for spending as much time mingling between the sheets as he did
sitting alone in front of the drawing board. Surely, his plump wife was
not pleased, but Stanford—or "Stannie," as she called him—had warned
her to lose weight or his attention would wander. "Fat is fatal," Stannie
once told Mrs. White.

The architect had many love nests around town, but his favorite was
his art studio at 22 West 24th Street, which he surrounded with mirrors
above and around a canopied bed. Hanging from the ceiling was a red
velvet swing, on which beautiful blondes and brunettes swayed in the
nude to Stanford's endless delight.

White's love at the time was 16-year-old Evelyn Nesbit, a model and
chorus girl whose angelic face brightened countless advertisements and
calendars. Nesbit had moved to New York from Pittsburgh with her

mother. They were poor and lonely in the big city, but Mama Nesbit was no fool. She dangled Evelyn before rich and powerful men and, soon enough, Stanford White came calling with invitations to dinner, theater tickets, and jewels.

For a while their relationship was platonic—at least until Stanford decided it was time for Evelyn to take a ride on his swing. One night he brought her back to his studio and poured her several bottles of champagne. She passed out and awoke hours later, naked, hung over, and unable to remember how she got that way. She also noticed she was lying in Stanford's bed and—surprise, surprise—he was stretched out next to her.

Evelyn remained friends with Stanford while dating other men, including the actor John Barrymore and a deranged but not bad-looking young man, also from Pittsburgh, Harry Kendall Thaw.

Thaw had a history of beating women, but he was also a millionaire and, therefore, quite an eligible bachelor. In 1905, Thaw asked Evelyn to marry him. She agreed, but before they could celebrate, Harry insisted that Evelyn recount the night she slept with Stanford. Evelyn obliged. One telling, though, wasn't enough. Thaw, always the romantic, demanded that she tell him the story over and over again until he had worked himself into a jealous, frothing rage.

The following year, on June 25, 1906, the Thaws attended a performance of *Mam'zelle Champagne* at the elegant rooftop theater of Madison Square Garden. Seated a few feet from Harry and Evelyn was Stanford White, who had designed the building, including its garden, starlit roof, and replica of the statue of Diana in the Nude. (The building was torn down in 1925 and replaced with the New York Life Insurance building.)

Bored with the performance, Evelyn announced she wanted to leave. Thaw, in a straw hat and heavy overcoat, agreed. But he seemed troubled. His lips twitched and his eyes narrowed. He stood and walked stiffly to White's table, where the architect was vigorously applauding the showgirls. As a singer crooned, "I could love a million girls," Thaw removed a gun from his coat and fired three shots into the back of Stanford's head. "I'm glad I killed him," Harry said as the architect thudded to the floor, dead at 52. "He ruined my wife."

The district attorney tried to ruin Thaw, but Harry's lawyer was able to argue that his client suffered from "dementia Americana," a mental disease, he said, that afflicts husbands trying to protect and defend their wives' honor. White was portrayed as a nefarious philanderer, with no regard for morality in general and young girls in particular.

"That bastard's death saved hundreds of innocent girls," Thaw said. Harry was sent to an insane asylum, where he stayed until 1915, only to return for another six years of incarceration after brutally horsewhipping a teenage boy.

By this time, Thaw had divorced Evelyn. She starred in a silent film about the scandalous White murder, but her career nose-dived into a traveling cabaret and teahouse act. Her audiences were predominantly male, which was only natural, since her name was synonymous with sin.

3

Giving Up Is Hard To Do: Louis Lepke Surrenders
28th Street and Fifth Avenue

Crime may not be the best way to get to heaven, but nothing beats it for becoming well known in post offices. In the 1930s, Louis Lepke's mug shot hung in mail rooms everywhere after FBI boss J. Edgar Hoover branded him "the most dangerous criminal in the United States."

Lepke had the resumé to deserve it. Not only was he said to have ordered the execution of seventy men but he also earned millions every year forcing garment manufacturers to pay him for protection—protection, we might add, from his own gang of murderous goons.

The police and FBI in 1937 were fed up with Lepke. The cops charged him with a litany of crimes, everything from selling narcotics to extortion to murder. In one slaying, a clothing merchant was shot seventeen times after he threatened to tell the world of Lepke's terror tactics.

But Louis didn't hang around long enough to be handcuffed. He disappeared for two years. Law enforcement officials posted a $25,000 reward for his capture "Dead or Alive" and poster-sized pictures of his impish mug were plastered in candy stores and on front pages and street corners across the country.

The police, showing off their great powers of description, noted in the poster that Lepke's eyes were "piercing and shifting" and that his ears were "prominent and close to head." Under the heading "Peculiarities," the cops noted that Lepke liked to "frequent baseball games."

The police search was nationwide, but Lepke stayed in hiding in Brooklyn, growing a mustache, gaining weight, and sleeping in different apartments while bodyguards stood outside. Lepke became an embarrassment to the authorities because they couldn't capture him—that is, until the government put up the reward money.

His life now worth a considerable pile of cash, Lepke became convinced he was safer behind bars. His own cronies, including one known as "Moe Dimples," provided additional bait by making him believe the feds were willing to negotiate a relatively light sentence and would send him to prison for five years, tops.

Lepke decided to surrender, but he insisted that gossip columnist Walter Winchell be there to greet him. That way, Lepke reasoned, the feds wouldn't shoot him on sight.

On August 24, 1939, an anonymous caller told Winchell and Hoover to go to 28th Street and Fifth Avenue. A little man wearing sunglasses walked out of the shadows. It was Lepke. Winchell had a huge scoop, but it was wiped off the front page by the news that Hitler had invaded Poland.

Lepke, of course, didn't get out of prison after five years. On March 5, 1944, at 11:16 P.M., he was executed at Sing Sing in upstate New York. A reporter at the time noted that the fearless Lepke's "lower lip quivered," but that he was otherwise expressionless as he was strapped into the electric chair.

Fame & Misfortune: A Model Is Slashed
455 West 34th Street

Each year, thousands of young women from around the world land in New York hoping to become stage stars, dancers, writers, or fashion models. Marla Hanson came looking for fame in the mid-1980s. She got the fame, sure, but at a terrible price: a razor slashing that left an eight-inch curlycue scar across her picture-perfect face.

Hanson, honey-haired and petite, moved to New York in search of a modeling career. She was just beginning to get work when she crossed paths with a native, Steve Roth, who was a television makeup artist. Roth talked big, but he didn't have much to talk about. He got his job through connections, namely his father, who was senior makeup artist at one of the networks. When Roth was feeling really big, he liked to harass people, sometimes sexually, with his fat mouth. When Marla was around, Roth became lewd and suggestive.

Marla didn't like Steve much, but she put up with him because he might be able to find her modeling work, and because he was looking for someone to rent his two-bedroom co-op apartment. Marla and another model snapped up the pad at 455 West 34th Street that spring, in 1986. As Hanson would later put it, "There's no reason not to be nice to someone who can help you."

True perhaps, but it can also be dangerous, especially if you're a beautiful woman trying to make it in New York City. No sooner did Marla move in than Roth, with his own key, began letting himself in, uninvited. He asked her to dinner and, when that failed, badgered her about her personal life. He liked to call her a lot of names, all of them less than flattering.

Fed up with Roth, Marla moved out within a month. When she asked him to return her $850 security deposit, he stalled. After several weeks, Roth convinced her to meet him at Shutters Bar, which is located on the ground floor of the apartment building.

Roth downed a hard drink; Hanson sipped a soda. She was exhausted from a late-evening shoot. He asked if he could hand her the deposit money outside. Putting his arm around her shoulder, he guided her around the corner onto Dyer Avenue, a grimy, desolate street off 34th Street between Ninth and Tenth avenues that leads directly to the Lincoln Tunnel. "If I was a photographer," Steve grumbled, "you would go out with me."

Just then, two of Roth's pals appeared from nowhere, sprinting toward Hanson and slashing her face with double-edge razor blades. She fell to the sidewalk, screaming as they fled into the darkness. When the police arrived at Shutters, Roth claimed he didn't know the attackers, but one of them later implicated him in the crime. That night, however, Roth accompanied Marla to the hospital, even slipping an arm around her waist as she bled.

As Marla recuperated from surgery the next day, she was deluged with cards and flowers from strangers who had read about the attack in the papers. It was all over the news for weeks, even months. As time went on, though, some people blamed the victim. Picking up on a tired theme, a lawyer for one of the slashers called Hanson "a woman who preyed on every man in this city."

The jurors didn't see it that way, and Roth and his fellow losers were sent away for five to fifteen years.

Don't worry about Marla. After her face was smoothed by plastic surgeons, an elderly New York philanthropist promised her $20,000 a year for life, no strings attached. Marla, today a celebrity regularly mentioned in gossip columns, now lobbies for victims' rights.

Sid and Nancy
The Chelsea Hotel, 222 West 23rd Street

The entrance to the Chelsea Hotel is decorated with plaques celebrating the famous writers who once lived within the Chelsea's red-bricked walls. Arthur Miller wrote *After the Fall* here, and William Burroughs wrote *Naked Lunch*. The Chelsea was also home to Mark Twain, Thomas Wolfe, and Dylan Thomas, at least until he drank himself to death.

But the hotel's management is more bashful when it comes to Chelsea alumni Sid Vicious and Nancy Spungen, punk rock's very own Adam and Eve.

Maybe it's because Sid and Nancy wore their hair spiked and stuck safety pins through their noses.

Or maybe it's because the couple was staying at the hotel when they planned a double-suicide. Sid conveniently backed out at the last minute, but only after sticking most of a seven-inch hunting knife into Nancy's stomach.

Whatever the reason, the management at the Chelsea, those men in suspenders standing behind the front desk, frown at the mere mention of Sid and Nancy. They don't like to admit that the couple stayed at the Chelsea and that the hotel even got rid of their death nest, room 100.

Sid, of course, played bass for the Sex Pistols, one of England's more dubious contributions to mankind in the 1970s. The band, led by Johnny Rotten, was known for such charming antics as spitting at their fans, calling Queen Elizabeth dirty names, and vomiting onstage. The Sex Pistols broke up in 1978 and Sid and Nancy moved to New York. On October 11, 1978, Nancy was found beneath a bathroom sink at the Chelsea, stabbed to death in her negligee.

A judge ordered Sid to a drug rehab clinic, but freed him after he posted bail. Vicious walked out of Manhattan Criminal Court wearing an "I Love New York" T-shirt. Standing by his mother, he told reporters, "I want a slice of pizza."

That night, Sid shot heroin at another girlfriend's apartment at 63 Bank Street. He overdosed and died in his sleep.

Cuckoo's Nest
485 First Avenue

New York may drive you crazy, but think twice before checking into Bellevue Hospital. Bellevue boasts a world-famous nuthouse and a refrigerated morgue where most of the city's 2,000-odd murder victims end up before heading for the cemetery, crematorium, or a potter's field.

Those in charge at the hospital are very sensitive about Bellevue's reputation, reminding anyone who'll listen that it has many fine doctors, that it's the country's oldest medical center, and that it has been the site of many historic advances, including the first use of the hypodermic needle in 1856.

Still, there are tragic reminders that Bellevue is no General Hospital. In 1989, for example, a homeless man wearing a lab coat and a stethoscope raped, robbed, and murdered a promising young doctor on the hospital's fourth floor. The killing of Kathryn Hinnant, then 33 years old and five months pregnant, was horrifying enough. Even worse, it occurred in a public hospital patrolled by a squad of security guards.

Hinnant had been missing for nearly twelve hours before her husband, led by a Bellevue supervisor, thought to look for her in her lab. Pushing the door open, they made out the outline of her body, sprawled in darkness beneath the piercing beam of a still flickering slide projector she had been using when she was attacked.

Later that day, the police arrested Steven Smith, a 23-year-old drifter, at a men's shelter on Ward's Island in the East River. The cops found Smith after several homeless men at the shelter told them he was seen carrying Kathyrn's credit cards, as well as her fur coat with her initials sewn inside.

Smith, the police discovered, had been living on Bellevue's 22nd floor in a storage area where no one could find him. Raised by a poor, troubled family in Brooklyn, Smith suffered from mental illness and had once swallowed a bottle of detergent after his girlfriend rejected him.

To some, Smith symbolized the failure of the city's mental health system. He was hiding out in Bellevue, an institution that is supposed to care for the disturbed. Why didn't doctors spot him as potentially dangerous and place him under the state's care?

Others indicted the police. Only nine days before slaying Dr. Hinnant, Smith had been arrested for stealing hypodermic needles from a physician's office. After being charged with petty larceny, the police let him go.

At the three-week trial, Smith testified that he was not a "normal man" and that he strangled her because "she had on a red dress. Her hair looked nice. She looked like a real lady."

On his last day in the courtroom, Smith folded his arms and laid his head down to sleep. He had already been judged sane. Someone woke him up to hear the judge's sentence: fifty years in prison.

7

Bombs Away with "No Hands" Morales
Bellevue Hospital Prison

Some journalists called him Willie "No Hands" Morales. Others preferred "No Chin." The choices were plenty after the Puerto Rican terrorist lost his fingers and part of his face when a bomb he was constructing blew up in his Queens apartment.

Willie liked to build bombs and plant them anywhere capitalism was sold. As a result, he was sentenced to ninety-nine years in jail. Before being led off to a prison ward in Bellevue Hospital for his first day behind bars, Willie cried, "They're not going to hold me forever. No judge is going to hold me forever."

Sure enough, a month later, on July 29, 1979, Willie cut a hole in a window screen in the hospital prison and, after tying elastic bandages together into a makeshift rope, managed to lower himself forty feet to freedom without anyone seeing.

The police launched a massive manhunt for Willie, but he eluded them for four years, during which time he was linked to a number of bomb scares, death threats, and explosions. Willie was credited, for example, with the 1982 New Year's Eve bombings of several government buildings in Lower Manhattan and Brooklyn. Three police officers were maimed in an explosion at Police Plaza at the base of the Brooklyn Bridge.

Mexican police caught up with Willie in a small town in Mexico in May of 1983, after a shoot-out in which one officer was killed. The US government demanded that Willie be returned to New York, but the Mexicans decided to keep him.

President Reagan was peeved when he learned that Morales was allowed to leave a Mexican jail for good behavior after serving just four and a half years. In protest, Reagan ordered his ambassador to Mexico to return home.

Morales now lives in Cuba.

8

Dial-a-Murder
314 West 23rd Street

Even when it comes to murder, gangsters are known to show manners, which might explain why the big bosses of the 1920s and 1930s were offended by one of their own, the nefarious triggerman with the pencil-thin mustache, Vincent "Mad Dog" Coll.

Vinnie, an eager beaver when it came to homicide, was quite the role model for up-and-coming sociopaths from his home turf in the Bronx. By the time he was 22, Vinnie had murdered an estimated thirty-five men.

The crime kings didn't mind as long as the victims were bookies, bootleggers, and other forms of hoodlum life. But bumping off kids was a no-no. That was where the bosses, child-care advocates all, drew the line. Vinnie, of course, didn't know nothing about lines—or drawing, or kids, for that matter.

On a sweltering night in 1931, outside a social club in East Harlem, Coll and his gang ambushed members of Dutch Schultz's mob. Vinnie was trying to take over Dutch's bootlegging empire, which was a risky proposition because Dutch had a mean temper and many gangsters at his disposal.

Machine guns exploded, hot lead ricocheted everywhere, but none of Dutch's boys went down. Instead, Vinnie wounded four children, including a baby in a baby carriage. A fifth child, a five-year-old named Mikey, was shot in the heart.

In those days, the shooting of kids was still unusual in New York City. The newspapers branded the incident THE MASSACRE OF THE INNOCENTS and Coll a "mad dog baby killer." Edward Mulrooney, the police commissioner at the time, discarded police protocol. "Draw first," he ordered his men, "and give it to him."

Coll savored the attention. He grew his dastardly mustache and hired a savvy lawyer, who convinced a jury that no one could prove Vinnie had squeezed the trigger.

Smug as ever, Coll walked out of court. The mob, still anxious to retire him, put up $50,000 for anyone who could deliver his corpse. At one point, Dutch Schultz walked into a Bronx police precinct and promised to buy a new home in the suburbs for the cop who could bring him Coll's head.

Dutch was spared the expense. On February 9, 1932, Coll telephoned gangster Owney Madden from a phone booth at the London Chemist Drugstore, 314 West 23rd Street. Vinnie didn't tell Owney where he was, but Madden was able to trace the call while he was on the line. Within minutes, a team of assassins arrived at the drugstore and disconnected Coll's call by shooting him fifteen times in the face and chest.

The drugstore closed long ago and a Chinese restaurant is now located on the site. Among its offerings are Hacked Chicken and Sliced Beef, but nowhere on the menu is there anything called Mad Dog Coll.

9

The Anarchist
Fifth Avenue and 15th Street

Everyone in the New York of the 1930s seemed to know the charming pro-labor agitator Carlo Tresca—at least everyone who hung around Union Square, that beehive of change-the-world, rally-the-masses ideologues. Tresca, who edited an Anarchist Italian journal, fought for the little guy against the famous "isms" of the day—Stalinism, Fascism, and Capitalism.

Naturally, Tresca inspired many detractors, including Italian dictator Benito Mussolini, who didn't appreciate Carlo criticizing his murderous regime. On July 11, 1943, Tresca was shot to death on the southwest corner of Fifth Avenue and 15th Street after leaving his nearby office and walking across the street to a tavern with a colleague. A gunman cloaked by the shadows of a wartime dimming of lights shot Tresca in the face and the back. Carlo's pipe fell out of his mouth and his round glasses slipped off his nose as his head hit the curbstone. The working-class hero, 68, was no more.

His murder was never officially solved, but detectives were sure the killer was Carmine Galante, a young thug who would eventually become a Mafia boss. Some suspected that Mussolini, reaching out to his friends in Vito Genovese's crime family in New York, had ordered Tresca silenced. Another theory had it that a rival New York editor, Generoso Pope, to please his friend Il Duce, had ordered Tresca killed.

Galante claimed he had nothing to do with the shooting and that he was at a showing of a new movie, *Casablanca,* on the night Tresca died. Of course, Carmine was unable to recount the film's plot to the cops, nor explain why a black 1939 Ford with his license plate number—IC9272—was seen speeding away from the spot where Tresca hit the ground.

Some suspect Tresca was murdered by a parent who was enraged that Carlo had made advances on his daughter. That would not be unlike Tresca. With his black cape, blue eyes, and rolling *r*'s, he had a habit of ogling, and attracting, a pretty ankle. He was once jailed for molesting a neighbor's daughter, described in court papers only as being "under 16." Tresca also dated famous strike organizer Elizabeth Gurley Flynn until roughly the time her 23-year-old younger sister gave birth to Carlo's son.

Six thousand mourners and a procession of a hundred cars showed up at Tresca's funeral, everyone from former lovers to famous writers to anonymous assembly line workers. For years to come, people annually placed flowers on the spot where he died.

10

Popped Artist
33 Union Square West

Valerie Solanas envisioned a better world, but, unfortunately for Andy Warhol, it didn't include men. Solanas founded the Society for Cutting Up Men, or SCUM, dedicated to the creation of a "swinging, groovy, out-of-sight female world."

"The male," Valerie wrote in SCUM's single-spaced, 21-page manifesto, "is a leech, an emotional parasite, and therefore isn't ethically entitled to live or prosper."

Warhol, of course, surrounded himself with strange, creative characters. Not just the famous dropped by—the likes of Truman Capote, Jane Fonda, and John Lennon—but also hipsters dancing on culture's cutting edge and no-names who spray-painted their genitals or dyed their hair pink or draped themselves in the American flag.

Solanas, of course, fit right in. In fact, Warhol invited her to play the part of a tough lesbian in one of his early underground films, *I, Man*.

"Those disgusting pigs, men," Valerie improvised on camera. Funny stuff. Really. Later, she wrote a movie, which she stylishly titled *Up Your Ass*.

In 1968, Solanas set aside her film ambitions and focused on her true passion—murdering all men, including one who was known to enjoy dressing up like a woman, Andy Warhol. Andy, said Valerie, was getting in the way of her film career. "He's too controlling," she said.

On June 5, 1968, Valerie went to 33 Union Square West, where the Factory, Warhol's headquarters, was located on the fifth floor. Valerie, her eyes darkened by mascara, her lips a lipstick red, waited patiently while Andy talked on the phone. When he hung up, she pulled a gun from her trenchcoat and shot him four times in the chest.

"I can't breathe," Warhol said, hitting the floor. At the hospital, doctors declared Andy clinically dead, but he managed to survive. The ugly surgical scars were, of course, permanent.

Solanas was long gone by the time the police arrived, but she turned herself in later that night. Released on bail, she phoned Warhol at the Factory on Christmas Day in 1968 and threatened to repeat the shooting if he didn't convince Johnny Carson to invite her on "The Tonight Show." Warhol hung up and promptly ordered his staff to install a double door and a buzzer entry system.

Several months later, Solanas was ruled incompetent to stand trial but later pleaded guilty to first-degree assault, for which she spent two years in state prison. Months after her release in 1971, she was arrested for sending letters to mogul Howard Hughes. In one letter, she wrote: "I have a license to kill."

It was the beginning of many short prison stays for Valerie. Recently, when one of Warhol's friends tracked her down by phone to a supervised housing complex in northern California, she had all but forgotten about her animosity toward Andy Warhol. She was still trying to push her anti-male manifesto, though.

HAPPINESS IS A WARM CELL:
George Metesky, a.k.a "The Mad
Bomber," behind bars after sixteen
years of planting time bombs
around New York. He was captured
in 1957. (*Daily News*, used with
permission.)

GREAT MOMENTS FROM THE NEWSPAPER
WAR: A *Daily News* photographer
strapped a hidden camera to his ankle
to snap a shot of convicted husband-
killer Ruth Snyder as she died in the
electric chair in 1928. The result was
the paper's most famous front page.
(*Daily News*, used with permission.)

GREAT MOMENTS FROM THE DRUG
WAR: Disguised as thugs, Rudy
Giuliani and Al D'Amato traveled
to Upper Manhattan in 1986 to
score crack from drug dealers.
Rudy and the Fonz hoped to highlight the city's drug scourge. Even
critics had to concede the two pols
were convincing as criminals.
(AP/Wide World Photos)

TOURIST DISTRACTION: An airplane struck the Empire State Building in 1945. Thousands of New Yorkers showed up to inspect the damage. (AP/Wide World Photos; *Daily News*, used with permission.)

RUNNING ON EMPTY: Frankie Yale after Capone's gang shot him down on 44th Avenue in Brooklyn in 1928. (*Daily News*, used with permission.)

NICE CUFF *(above)*: The Dapper Don, John Gotti, being escorted by the feds from the Ravenite Social Club on Mulberry Street in 1990 after he was arrested for the murder of Paul Castellano. (Reprinted with permission of the *New York Post*.)

YOU BET YOUR LIFE *(left)*: Arnold Rothstein is said to have fixed the World Series in 1919. Nine years later, a gunman fixed Arnold after he welshed on a $320,000 poker debt. (*Daily News*, used with permission.)

CLIP JOB: Mobster Albert Anastasia before and after his last haircut at the Park Sheraton Hotel on Seventh Avenue in 1957. All eleven witnesses came down with amnesia when the cops came around. (AP/Wide World Photos)

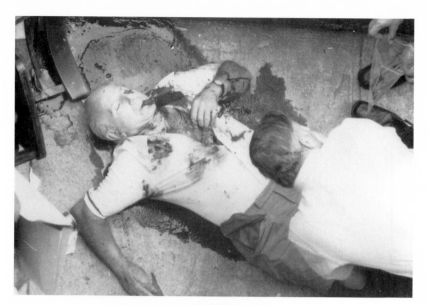

SOMETIMES A CIGAR IS JUST A CIGAR: Sometimes a gangster is just plain dead. Carmine Galante, lunching at a Brooklyn restaurant in 1979, survived the main course but didn't make it to dessert. "We give special attention to outgoing orders," read the sign over the eatery's entrance. (Reprinted with permission of the *New York Post*; *Daily News*, used with permission.)

MOMMY WEIRDEST: Alice Crimmins of Queens was drop-dead gorgeous, with two adorable children. Soon the kids were dead and Alice was charged with their murder. (AP/Wide World Photos)

PUNK ROCKED: Sid Vicious of the Sex Pistols checks out of the Chelsea Hotel in 1978 leaving his wife in their room upstairs, where she lay dead from a stab wound. (Reprinted with permission of the *New York Post*.)

FRIED: Umberto's
Clam House in Little
Italy owes its success
as much to its fried
shrimp (fabulous) as
to the famous 1972 hit
on Crazy Joe Gallo
(rubbed out on his
birthday). (Reprinted
with permission of the
New York Post.)

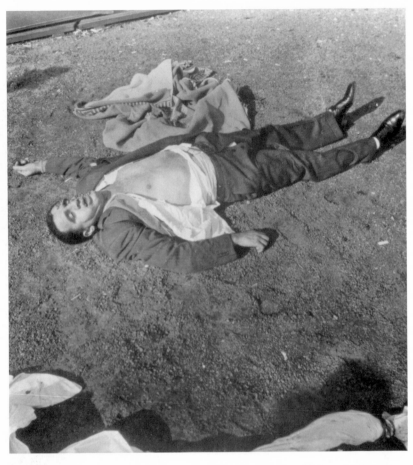

AFTER THE FALL: Not even a 24-hour-a-day police guard could keep mob canary
Abe "Kid Twist" Reles from falling six floors out a window at Coney Island's
Half Moon Hotel in 1941. The Kid was dead before he could say "tweet-tweet."
(New York City Municipal Archives)

Blood on the Tracks, 1991
Union Square Station East

Robert Ray, his blood laced with alcohol after a day and night of drinking Scotch and beer, sat in the dark of Union Square Park as the faint wail of sirens grew louder, as police cars, ambulances, and fire trucks, their flashing lights swirling on dozens of surrounding buildings, converged on the chaos wrought by the city's worst subway crash in sixty-three years.

Ray saw the paramedics and the cops rush down into the Union Square subway station, a steaming, smoky hole on this August 28th night in 1991. The carnage from the 12:10 A.M. disaster was unreal: five dead, more than 250 injured. Here was a subway twisted and mangled, turned into an accordion, stripped like a sardine can. One witness said it felt as though a plane had crashed underground.

From the park, Ray could see the paramedics carrying bodies laid out on stretchers to the street. He could see Mayor David Dinkins stand before a battery of television cameras and announce that a southbound Lexington Avenue subway train had crashed two hundred feet north of the Union Square station and that it was a miracle more people weren't killed. The mayor said the police were looking for the train's missing motorman, identified as Robert Ray.

Several hours later, Ray, 38 years old, arrived at his apartment in the Bronx where several transit police officers were waiting for him. Soon, he admitted to the officers that he had been drinking for hours before work (although later his lawyer would claim Ray got drunk after the crash); that he was having problems with his girlfriend; that the train had crashed at a speed upwards of fifty miles per hour as he was nodding off at the controls.

A blood test was administered and Ray was found to have twice the amount of alcohol in his system that is allowed by law. Less than twelve hours after the crash, he was charged with five counts of manslaughter.

It was the city's worst subway crash since 1928, when sixteen people died and one hundred were injured when a train derailed and crashed at

Times Square. In 1918, ninety-seven people were killed and two hundred were injured in a subway wreck in Brooklyn (see "Off the Beaten Track" in the Brooklyn chapter).

City officials could have been satisfied with Ray's speedy arrest, except that there were disturbing facts beyond his drinking which no one could ignore. For one, he showed up late for work. Ray had a record of absences and tardiness, and he had once been reprimanded for running a red signal.

In addition, several subway employees and police officers on board could have tried to stop the train before it crashed. Each saw Ray overshoot at least two stops and speed recklessly on his southbound course. At one point, the conductor asked over the loudspeaker, "Hey, what's going on?" No response came from the front of the train. When the conductor asked again, Ray said, "Ah, don't worry, I'm all right."

Among those who heard and were no doubt comforted by those words were a security guard, a medical technician, a hotel housekeeper, a nursing aid, and a janitor—the men and women who would die on the Woodlawn Express.

12

Michael Stewart
Union Square Park, 14th Street

On a late September night in 1984, eleven police officers arrested Michael Stewart for writing graffiti on a subway wall. It should have been a simple collar, but less than an hour later the cops delivered Michael to the emergency room in a coma. His face and body were battered and bruised. Eighteen days later, he died.

Stewart's death was a tragedy teetering on a travesty. The city's medical examiner declared that Michael died of a heart attack, even though he had obviously been beaten up. Stewart's friends, family, and others were outraged by the diagnosis, charging that the cops, all of them white, had killed Michael Stewart simply because he was black.

So began one of the most racially charged and divisive cases in New York City history. At issue was the city's reputation as a place where blacks and whites could coexist, along with the reputations of the police department, the district attorney, and the medical examiner, who was initially accused of mishandling evidence to protect the cops.

Stewart, 25, with cornrow braids and a toothsome smile, was gentle, even passive, around his friends. He spent many nights hanging out with artists and musicians in the East Village. On the night he ended up in a coma, September 15th, he had been dancing and drinking beer at his favorite hangout, the Pyramid Club. It was around 2:30 A.M. when he began the trip back to Clinton Heights, a middle-class Brooklyn neighborhood where he lived in a brownstone with his mother and father, a retired transit worker.

While waiting for the L train in the IND station beneath First Avenue and 14th Street, Stewart took out a black Magic Marker and scribbled RAS in foot-high letters on a tunnel wall. If these letters had any significance, no one knows. To the police, they signified a crime in progress. At 2:50 A.M, a pack of transit officers surrounded Stewart and arrested him.

The cops drove Stewart to a makeshift police station at the northern end of Union Square Park, directly outside the Parsons School of Design dormitory at 31 Union Square West. Here, they began beating him. Twenty-seven students said they witnessed parts of the attack from their rooms. One, Rebecca Reiss, said she heard Stewart yelling, "What did I do, what did I do?" And then: "Oh, God, please help me, someone help me."

The cops later insisted Stewart had flown into a drunken frenzy and the eleven officers subdued him with "justifiable force." The explanation seemed preposterous since Michael was alone and armed with nothing more than a felt-tipped marker.

Manhattan District Attorney Robert Morgenthau, relying on the accounts of the Parsons students, indicted six of the cops, three of them for criminally negligent homicide, assault, and perjury. The other three faced lesser charges.

Morgenthau ran into snags in gathering evidence. One of his problems was the medical examiner, Dr. Elliot Gross. The day after the autopsy, Gross had removed Michael's eyes, which might have provided evidence of a choke-hold. Gross said he was merely following routine procedure.

A month later, with questions everywhere, Gross changed his autopsy finding. Instead of a heart attack, Gross said Stewart actually died of a

spinal-cord injury. During the trial that followed, Gross offered yet another version: three different traumas—a fall on a pavement, alcohol, or
blunt force—could have caused Stewart's death. In other words, Gross
claimed, he really didn't know why Stewart died. Still, all charges of
misconduct against the medical examiner were dismissed.

After twenty-two heated weeks in court, marked by emotional outbursts in the courtroom and protests outside, a jury acquitted all of
the cops. They pointed to several factors in reaching the verdict,
including the possibility that the officers acted in self-defense. It seems
that a blood test taken just after Stewart arrived at Bellevue found he
had been drinking. Also, none of the student witnesses could pin a
specific kick or punch on a specific cop, since they were watching from
a distance.

The case ended where it began, with a creative young life snuffed
out and bitterness all around. A transit police spokesman declared,
"We didn't kill Michael Stewart—we did nothing wrong." The Transit
Authority didn't bother disciplining any of the cops involved in Stewart's
death but did revamp their arrest procedures to eliminate the hog-
tying of suspects.

It was hardly a satisfying resolution for the Stewarts, who sued the
city for $40 million, only to receive $1.7 million, much of which paid off
legal fees. "We have witnessed the last act of a farce," the Stewarts'
family lawyer said after the settlement was announced.

7

Pillage in the Village

RESIDENTS OF GREENWICH VILLAGE AND the East Village think they're living in the city's only true bohemia, neighborhoods of cafes and dingy bars and cramped $1,000-a-month, bathtub-in-the-kitchen apartments.

If only writers, revolutionaries, and, yes, even stockbrokers, could afford the rents.

It's all so romantic, Greenwich Village and its narrow winding streets, the tree-shaded townhouses, the little shops selling pink Art Deco teacups.

You almost forget about the stray bullets.

For a reminder, trek east to Alphabet City, Avenues A through D, where life is a little cruder, where people don't need a good reason to kill. Just a gun. Or a knife. Or a drink.

The crime here is more artful than anything as simple as one mobster shooting another, or one gang fighting another (although there is plenty of that). Let's face it, murder is sometimes the only reasonable way to end an argument on human rights, not to mention real estate or double-parking.

Whatever the case, it's often difficult to distinguish the criminals from the victims down here, since everyone seems to prefer dressing in black.

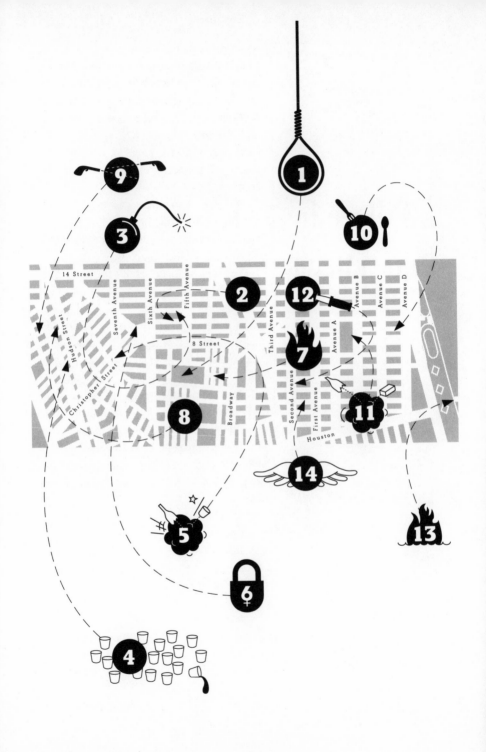

Greenwich Village

Where the Skeletons Are
Washington Square Park

Washington Square Park is not only home to the flying Frisbee and the cigar-sized marijuana joint, but buried beneath the ground are the skeletons of some ten thousand New Yorkers.

Feel better now? We knew you would.

Washington Square was where the city discarded the victims of the yellow fever epidemics that swept through New York between 1797 and 1819. The scourge was so bad that the city's gravedigger was given free rent at a shack on Thompson Street, on the south side of the square.

The hangman, on the other hand, paid his own rent. But he, too, was a busy municipal worker. New York ran a gallows in the center of the square until about 1819, executing everyone from petty thieves to axe murderers. After that, the city leaders decided that capital punishment was better meted out in more secluded areas. It seemed more civilized that way and better for the city's image.

Joel Steinberg
14 West 10th Street

Joel Steinberg's landlord started getting the calls less than a month after Steinberg was arrested for murdering his six-year-old daughter, Lisa: Was the Steinberg apartment available? How much was the rent? Did it have southern exposure?

Tasteless questions, perhaps, but not in a city where real estate is known to bring out the worst in people. Steinberg's building was well known long before he and Hedda Nussbaum moved in. Mark Twain lived in the five-story walkup in 1900, as the plaque at the entrance reminds visitors.

Years later, another tenant, a psychic, wrote a book claiming the building was haunted by evil spirits and that she could see Twain's ghost floating in the stairwell. A number of tenants of the building, the writer claimed, had died under mysterious circumstances.

The book aroused the interest of journalist Lewis Grossberger, who visited the building in 1974. Grossberger interviewed a number of tenants about the book, including a man living in apartment 3W. The man, an attorney named Joel Steinberg, scoffed at the ghost stories.

Thirteen years later, on November 2, 1987, two police officers knocked on Steinberg's apartment door. It was 6:35 A.M., and just two minutes earlier Hedda, a writer and editor of children's books, had dialed 911. "My daughter seems to have stopped breathing," she told the operator.

Standing in the couple's living room, the officers could see the makings of an atrocity. Walls were smeared with dirt and blood. The carpet was soaked with urine and chairs were overturned. A stash of cocaine was found in a desk drawer, and unused VCRs, TVs, car radios, and tape decks were piled everywhere.

The officers could see that Lisa's 16-month-old adopted brother, Mitchell, was tied to a chair by a four-foot length of rope. Steinberg emerged from a bedroom carrying Lisa, her body naked and bruised. She wasn't breathing, but she still had a slight pulse. As more officers began arriving, the cops raced Lisa to St. Vincent's Hospital on West 12th Street and Seventh Avenue. Hedda, who had bruises on her face and body, told the police that Lisa had fallen while roller skating.

In the emergency room, Steinberg, his dark eyes fidgeting behind aviator glasses, explained to doctors that Lisa had only vomited and that she would be fine. Then, as his daughter struggled for her life, he left the hospital and went home.

Hundreds of strangers attended Lisa's funeral, many of them weeping and carrying flowers. Steinberg, with his sneering scowl, turned into one of the city's—indeed, the nation's—most detested villains. Ed Koch, the mayor at the time, called Steinberg a "monster" and recommended he be "dipped" in boiling oil.

Steinberg is now serving an eight-to-twenty-five-year sentence in state prison for first-degree manslaughter, while Hedda lives outside the city. Their adopted son, Mitchell, now lives with his biological mother outside the city. The Steinbergs' one-bedroom apartment was eventually rented, but only after Joel gave up the lease in exchange for not having to pay the landlord $25,000 in back rent. The apartment was quickly grabbed at twice Steinberg's $550-a-month lease. Before moving in, the new tenants made sure the landlord had completely renovated the apartment.

Blown Up
18 West 11th Street

Sure, go ahead and leave your sweet, loving daughter home alone while you take off for a Caribbean vacation. It's the hip thing to do, especially in 1970 when being hip is so important.

Only one warning: be sure your sweet, loving daughter isn't passionately committed to the violent overthrow of the United States government.

Poor James Wilkerson. He should have asked more questions.

In March of 1970, he left his daughter Cathlyn, then 25 years old, in his Village town house while he flew south for rest and relaxation. Mr. Wilkerson knew Cathlyn was a radical and that she had even once clobbered a Chicago cop over the head with a billy club.

But explosives? Who was to know?

Mr. Wilkerson, Dustin Hoffman, and the rest of the world, to name just a few.

At just before noon on March 6th, Cathlyn and a bunch of radical pals accidentally blew up her father's handsome, brick-faced home at 18 West 11th Street while building bombs in the basement. The blast rattled store windows several blocks away and scorched walls of the two adjoining brownstones.

Living in one of those brownstones was Hoffman, at the time a young actor who had recently starred in a film called *The Graduate.* Moments after the explosion, Dustin was seen scampering from his building, a Tiffany lamp under his arm.

Cathlyn Wilkerson and her friends, all members of a militant antiwar faction known as the Weathermen, were preparing to attack universities, corporations, police stations, and other government buildings. But they didn't plan on thirty sticks of dynamite accidentally exploding. Three of Cathlyn's confederates died in the blast.

At first, the police suspected that a gas leak was to blame for the explosion, but they became suspicious of foul play after they couldn't track down Cathlyn and another woman, Kathy Boudin. The women had apparently raced from the apartment naked and, after borrowing some clothing from a neighbor, vanished.

Wilkerson turned herself in ten years later and was sentenced to eleven months in prison for negligent homicide in connection with the explosion. Boudin wasn't captured until 1981, when she participated in a Brinks armored truck holdup in which two cops and a security officer were killed. She was sentenced to a prison term of twenty years to life.

Cathlyn's father eventually sold his rubbled lot and the new owners built a modern, space-age home, provoking howls of esthetic protests all along the block. But the neighbors grew more accepting over time, especially after the newcomers stashed a Teddy bear in their front window. Some took it as a welcome sign that the kids inside were too young to play with dynamite.

Last Call for Dylan Thomas
The White Horse Tavern, 567 Hudson Street

If drinking booze were an Olympic event, Dylan Thomas, the red-haired writer and poet, would have won the Gold. Dylan's arena was the White Horse Tavern, where he spent his last night on earth, November 9, 1953.

Dylan was a regular at the White Horse, his favorite table in the corner near the bar. Maybe it was the low-lit, cozy atmosphere that drew him here. Maybe it was the conversation, sometimes about such relaxing topics as death and dying. Most probably it was the drink, specifically the bottles of whiskey glowing behind the long wooden bar.

On Dylan's last night, he showed remarkable showmanship with the bottle. First there was one shot of whiskey. Then two, four, and then eight and ten shots.

Dylan was beginning to turn red from head to toe.

Eleven shots made him slur, 13 made him stagger, 15 made him fall, and 17—yes, 17 shots of whiskey—made him collapse on the sidewalk outside the bar and die.

Dylan knew what he had accomplished. Great artists always do.

Before his last breath, he reportedly mumbled: "Seventeen whiskeys. A record, I think."

Stonewall Riot
53 Christopher Street

Gay rights as a national movement was born on a summer night in 1969 after police officers and homosexuals battled outside the Stonewall Inn, a bar at 53 Christopher Street frequented then and now by gays. A tablet outside the bar commemorates the rioting, which continued sporadically over a two-day period.

The cops claimed they raided the bar, allegedly owned at the time by mobsters, because it was serving alcohol without a liquor license. But those inside the Stonewall, with its blackened windows and $1 admission charge, thought they were being picked on because of their sexual preference. Bottles were thrown at the police. So were pennies, trash cans, and parking meters.

Thirteen protesters were arrested in the June 27th melee, and four people, including a cop, were injured. The Stonewall Riot, as it came to be known, is credited with inspiring the formation of gay rights groups nationwide. It was the first time that gays collectively engaged in civil disobedience.

Few outside the gay and liberal communities had much sympathy. The day after the riot, the headline on the front page of the New York *Daily News* read: HOMO NEST RAIDED, QUEEN BEES ARE STINGING MAD. The story began this way: "She sat there with her legs crossed, the lashes of her mascara-coated eyes beating like the wings of a hummingbird. She was angry. She was so upset she hadn't bothered to shave. A day-old stubble was beginning to push through the pancake makeup. She was a he. A queen of Christopher Street."

Thanks in part to gay activism, such blatantly homophobic prose has gone into the closet. At least, it doesn't appear much in newsprint anymore.

Babes Behind Bars
10 Greenwich Avenue

The Women's House of Detention on Greenwich Avenue was never home to Ma Barker or Bonnie Parker of Bonnie and Clyde fame. But the jail held some pretty tough ladies, all the same.

The House, a rust-colored high-rise on a charming block lined with coffee houses and gourmet markets, served soggy spaghetti, watery coffee, and worm-infested prunes, among other delicacies. The cots were made of iron, the tables of metal. The washbowls were filthy, mice seemed to scamper everywhere, and there was one unenclosed toilet for every two-inmate cell.

It was bad enough to make a tough lady cry.

"Dehumanizing degradation," said the accused Communist Elizabeth Gurley Flynn after a stay at the House in 1951.

"The Barbizon it ain't," said Bea Garfield, a notorious East Side madame after spending ninety days in the same clink in the late 1950s.

Andy Warhol's man-hating nemesis, Valerie Solanas, was among those locked up in the House in 1968. Ethel Rosenberg was imprisoned there in the early 1950s.

Antiwar protester and Bennington College student Andrea Dworkin was sent to the House for a weekend that same year. Afterward, she complained of a "barbaric" internal exam by one of the female staff doctors.

Reddish-haired beauty Alice Crimmins also stayed at the jail after killing her three-year-old daughter in 1968. She was the last famous femme fatale to hold her own in the House.

The jail was razed in 1968 and the inmates were ferried to a new prison complex on Riker's Island. Today, the Jefferson Market garden occupies the spot where the House once cast its shadow.

Triangle Shirtwaist Factory Fire
29 Washington Place

New York City suffered its worst industrial disaster in 1911 when the Triangle Shirtwaist Company near Washington Square Park caught fire. One hundred and forty-six workers, most of them young Italian and Jewish girls from the Lower East Side, were killed.

The blaze was apparently ignited after someone on the eighth floor accidentally set fire to a pile of scrap cloth. Many of the five hundred workers were getting ready to leave when the alarm rang. The bells caused the long rows of sewing machines to automatically shut down. In minutes, thick gray smoke and flames billowed across the top three floors of the ten-story building.

The girls scrambled. Several rushed to emergency exits, but the doors had been locked by the owners, who were nervous that employees would steal from the company and leave before work was over. Workers crowded onto the factory's rickety fire escape, which collapsed under the weight. Inside, two elevator operators made countless trips up and down but couldn't save everyone.

Dozens died jumping from the ledges, some while holding hands, others with their clothes and hair aflame. Their bodies, clad in ankle-length cotton dresses and blouses buttoned to the neck, piled on the sidewalk below. The fire took only a half-hour to exact its toll, and within days, a hundred thousand New Yorkers were weeping and praying over the mass grave for the victims dug at Mt. Zion Cemetery in Maspeth, Queens.

The tragedy galvanized the national labor movement, spawning an array of legislated safety reforms in factories, including mandatory fire drills, fire escapes, and limits on working hours for children.

Such laws, had they been on the books before the fire, would have been enough to send the factory's owners to jail for manslaughter. Instead, Isaac Harris and Max Blanck were acquitted. The owners paid a mere $75 to each of the twenty-three families of the victims who filed lawsuits. The Asch Building, as it was called, didn't even burn down. Harris and Blanck had made sure their investment was fireproof.

Today, New York University holds classes in the building at 29 Washington Place, now known as the Brown Building. Outside, at Washington Place and Greene Street, is a tablet dedicated to the victims of the fire from the International Ladies Garment Workers Union. "Out of their martyrdom," it reads, "came new concepts of social responsibility and labor legislation that have helped make American working conditions the finest in the world."

8

Pay Phone Shooting
Jane and Greenwich Streets

The telephone lines in John and Vicki Reisenbach's Jane Street apartment building were out of order on a sultry July night in 1990. John, a 33-year-old advertising executive, needed to call a colleague. It was 11 P.M., not too late, it would seem, to walk out into the cobblestoned, Old World charm of Greenwich Village.

John was gone for more than a half-hour when Vicki Reisenbach, upstairs with the couple's three dogs, became concerned. Vicki went outside to look for her husband. Nearing the pay phone at the corner of Jane and Greenwich, she saw the receiver dangling by its cord. Then she saw a swirl of flashing red and yellow lights. Twenty feet from the phone booth, police officers and paramedics were huddled over a man lying in the street.

The man, Vicki noticed, was wearing a familiar button-down shirt and penny loafers. "Is that my husband?" she asked.

John Reisenbach had three bullet wounds in his chest. Nothing had been stolen from his pockets, which only made his murder more senseless and disturbing. No matter how many times it happens, New Yorkers are never able to comprehend a murder of an innocent in a relatively safe neighborhood. But it's a story as old as the city itself.

Of course, the Village isn't all brownstones, soft lights, and flower boxes. The western end of the neighborhood, over by the meat-packing district along the West Side Highway, has a seamy side, particularly at night, when transvestites, drug dealers, and drifters take over the street. In 1990, a vestpocket called Abingdon Square Park had turned into a settlement camp for homeless men and women, many of them alcoholics and crack addicts. They slept on benches under a statue of a pistol-toting World War I soldier.

It was here where detectives thought they found the answer to Reisenbach's slaying. Based on a tip from a transvestite who called herself Porsche, the cops arrested William Emerson, a disheveled Vietnam veteran who was living in the park. Eight months later, though, District Attorney Robert Morgenthau conceded that key pieces of evidence were missing and that there were contradictions between accounts offered by several eyewitnesses. The case was dropped and Emerson was cleared of the charges. No one else has since been charged with Reisenbach's murder.

On the first anniversary of Reisenbach's death, neighbors draped the phone booth with purple and black streamers, a Xerox copy of a photo of John, and an offer of a reward for information that would help catch his killer.

Dueling Forefathers: Alexander Hamilton and Aaron Burr
Shoot It Out
80 Jane Street

He was a widely respected political theorist, the founder of a newspaper, and a former secretary of the treasury. Alexander Hamilton was a smart guy, no question. But he wasn't always so bright.

Hamilton's first mistake was agreeing to a gun duel in 1804 with Aaron Burr, the country's vice-president. His second was not firing his gun in the hope that Burr would do the same.

Not a wise choice, since Burr despised Hamilton for blocking his dreams of becoming governor of New York, or even president.

Standing across from Manhattan on the banks of Weehawken, New Jersey, Burr pulled the trigger. The mortar hit Hamilton in the belly. He fell on his face, doomed to die as his son had in a duel only the year before.

As the sun rose over New York City that July 11, 1804, Hamilton's friends rowed him across the Hudson River to Manhattan and an old friend's house at 80 Jane Street, parts of which still stand today. He lay moaning for hours and died the next afternoon at the age of 47. He was buried in the cemetery outside Trinity Church on lower Broadway.

Killing Hamilton didn't do much for Burr's career. He became a political outlaw in New York and a black sheep in Washington, especially after he was convicted of Hamilton's murder. The court's ruling was later reversed.

About the only place that hailed Burr as a hero was the corrupt Tammany Hall, whose leaders were more than happy to see the reform-minded Hamilton bite the dust.

East Village

10

The Monster of Tompkins Square
700 East Ninth Street

He carried a rooster under one arm and a copy of *Mein Kampf* under the other. He had long blond hair, a beard, and, depending on his mood, he called himself "Jesus Christ" or the "God of Marijuana."

Daniel Rakowitz was just another psychopath hanging around Tompkins Square Park—except, of course, that he chopped up his girlfriend and claimed he fed her remains to homeless people.

It was an act that made Dan special, even in New York City.

Still, Rakowitz did have his reasons, which he willingly revealed in a sweet Texas drawl. He mutilated the body of Monika Beerle, a 26-year-old dancer from Sweden, after she threw him out of her apartment at 700 East Ninth Street. As far as Dan was concerned, that just wasn't right, especially given how difficult it is to find an apartment in New York.

In September 1989, a month after Beerle died, the police charged Rakowitz, then 30 years old, with murder. Dan confessed everything to the cops, even inviting them to preserve his statement on videotape. Camera rolling, he explained how a satanic cult friend killed Monika and how he carved up her body and dropped her head in a pot of boiling water. He even led officers to the Port Authority Bus Terminal, where he had concealed her skull and bones in a bucket of kitty litter.

Rakowitz maintained that he turned Monika's body parts into a soup he served to people living in Tompkins Square Park—a claim the police refused to believe. The headlines' writers needed no convincing, christening Rakowitz "The Butcher" and "The Monster of Tompkins Square."

Once he got into court, Rakowitz forgot his confession and claimed he was as innocent as he was sane. No one, not even his lawyer, believed him, especially after Dan said God sent him to Earth to preach the virtues of smoking pot.

The highlight of his six-week trial came when Rakowitz pulled a tantrum in court, accusing the guards of stealing his copy of *Mein Kampf*. Perhaps it was such outbursts that prompted the jury to find him not guilty by reason of insanity. The judge mandated an indefinite stay at an upstate mental hospital.

Led away for the last time, Rakowitz thanked the jury for a fair trial. "I hope someday we can smoke a joint together," he said, smiling and waving goodbye.

What a Riot
Tompkins Square Park

A park is a place for children and dogs and baseballs and bicycles. In most cities, that is. In the East Village, the park is a place for anarchists and drug addicts and unemployed stockbrokers.

And that's on a nice day.

Tompkins Square Park has also served as a war ground for bloody battles between the police department and those who don't much respect authority—especially when it is carrying guns and nightsticks and trying to evict homeless people.

On a hot August night in 1988, a dozen cops on horseback rode into Tompkins Square to shut it down for the night. It was 1 A.M. and the neighbors had been complaining for weeks about the noise coming from the park and the dozens of men and women who had turned it into a settlement camp.

No one wanted to leave, particularly the two hundred gathered to protest the curfew. Suddenly, rocks and bottles were flying, and white teenagers, some of them with ponytails and dreadlocks, were chanting, "Kill the pigs!" Moments later, four hundred additional police officers arrived to join in a four-hour fight that became known as the Battle for Tompkins Square. It was a bloody riot in which at least fifty people were injured.

When the sun rose on glass shards and bloodstains, the police insisted they had done their job. But then Clayton Paterson, a local artist who was never without a video camera, made public a tape showing that many cops had actually behaved brutally that night, whacking people with their nightsticks without provocation. The video also showed that other officers, wishing to remain anonymous, had covered their badge identification numbers with black tape, a clear violation of the department's regulations. Police brass were embarrassed, especially after 121 people filed brutality complaints.

Afterward, rioting in Tompkins Square became a kind of rite of summer—that is, until 1991, when Mayor Dinkins padlocked the park for renovations and posted officers to keep everyone out but dog walkers and basketball players.

It wasn't a crackdown on poor people, the mayor insisted, just a $2 million renovation to make the park a park again. Those who had been accustomed to sleeping there moved their worldly possessions to a rubble-strewn lot nearby, which they promptly dubbed "Dinkinsville."

12

A Writer on the Cutting Edge
79 Second Avenue

Jack Henry Abbott may not be the kind of guy you take home to mother, but he is the only author in literary history to write a best-seller and land on the FBI's most-wanted list—all at the same time.

It's a tough feat to achieve without a little help. In Abbott's case, the help came from Norman Mailer, with whom Abbott had lots in common. Not only did both like to write, but they also shared a fondness for knives. Mailer once stabbed his wife (not fatally); Abbott once stabbed an inmate (fatally).

Mailer met Abbott in the 1970s while writing *The Executioner's Song,* a sympathetic portrait of Gary Gilmore, the death row convict from Utah. At the time, Abbott and Gilmore were prisoners at the same penitentiary. Abbott considered himself an expert on criminal justice issues, having spent twenty-five years behind bars, fifteen of them in solitary confinement. His crimes: a jail break, robbery, and murder, just to name a few.

Abbott wrote Mailer a series of letters about life in prison. Mailer loved Abbott's writing and turned the letters over to *The New York Review of Books,* which published them in 1978.

Editors at Random House were intrigued. They published Abbott's writing in book form. *In the Belly of the Beast,* which features advice on how to murder someone with a single thrust of a knife, hit the stores in 1981 and sold well. Mailer wrote the introduction, which no doubt helped land the book a favorable review in the *New York Times.*

That's not all Mailer did for Abbott. He got him paroled at least three years early and invited him to New York City. In June of 1981, Abbott moved to a halfway house on the Lower East Side. Instantly he was a celebrity, interviewed by *People* magazine and "Good Morning America."

The literati—Mailer, Jerzy Kosinski, and William Styron among them—couldn't get enough of Abbott, inviting him to parties and art openings. Beautiful women, including the daughter of a French count, desired Abbott's company. Maybe it was the tweed jacket–handcuff look, his sandpaper-rough cheeks, the rattlesnake glare, the wire-rimmed glasses.

Abbott wasn't in the city long before he broke the law again. On July 17, 1981, he took two stylish beauties to BiniBon, then a restaurant at 79 Second Avenue. Abbott needed to use the bathroom, but a waiter, Richard Adan, told him the restaurant's toilet was only for employees.

Abbott was irate. He challenged Adan to a fight. They went outside, where Abbott took out a knife and stabbed Adan in the heart, using the technique he had described so vividly in his book. Abbott fled all the way to Louisiana, where the police caught him hiding out in an oilfield.

Abbott, found guilty of first-degree manslaughter, went back to jail for another fifteen years. A judge ruled that all his book royalties are to be turned over to Adan's family.

Mailer could have expressed sympathy for Adan's family, or even apologized for being a poor judge of character. Instead, he defended Abbott and said he regretted that he was convicted. "He will either grow or deteriorate in prison," Mailer said at that time. "If he grows and develops and changes, and I feel he has a chance on the street again, then I will help him."

No Picnic
East Third Street Pier

The *General Slocum* steamer began her ill-fated journey at the East Third Street pier on the sunny morning of June 15, 1902. She carried 1,400 German-Americans, mainly children and mothers from St. Mark's Lutheran Evangelical Church of 328 East Sixth Street (now a synagogue). The excited parishioners were on their way to their annual church picnic.

They never got there. The ship, named for a Civil War hero, caught fire after passing through Hell Gate, a narrow, turbulent channel in the waters off Harlem. The skipper could have beached the vessel and saved the day. Instead, he stepped on the gas and fanned smoke, flames, and pandemonium, sending 1,031 passengers to their deaths.

The tragedy, the most horrific fire in the city's history, sent thousands of German immigrants on the Lower East Side spinning into despair. For days, hearses jammed the streets as families buried their dead.

Within a year, the skipper was sentenced to ten years' hard labor for criminal negligence. A small monument, an eight-foot-tall white shaft showing a boy and girl, was erected in Tompkins Square Park near the corner of East Sixth Street and Avenue A for the kids who died. The time-worn marker reads: "They were Earth's purest children, loving and fair."

14

Hell's Angels
77 East Third Street

Free country, you say? Perhaps, but not in front of 77 East Third Street, otherwise known as the Manhattan branch of the Hell's Angels Motorcycle Club.

Try parking your car in front. Legally, you can. But remember: the Angels didn't create an illegal parking lot for their motorcycles by being sweetie-pies.

The Angels have resided on the block since 1968, serving as a kind of scarecrow—albeit one dressed in leather and painted with demonic-looking tattoos—against junkies and muggers. They've also kept a fair number of yuppies from moving in.

One result is that the block is among the safest in the city, although the Angels have had their problems with the law. On July 4, 1990, two Angels allegedly tossed a handful of M-80 firecrackers into a burning metal trash can. The ensuing explosion killed a 14-year-old boy. The two Angels were charged with manslaughter and assault.

Don't let that stop you from passing by. But we recommend against saying hello. Or pointing. Or parking out front.

8

Paradise Lost

Little Italy, SoHo, the Lower East Side, and Chinatown

Shake hands with a real, live gangster!

It's all possible in the section of the city where murder is as traditional as a plate of fettucine, a bowl of wonton, maybe even a knish.

Mulberry Street, stomping ground for top members of the Gambino and Genovese crime families, is terrific for gangster-gazing. Hang around long enough and you might even get hit with a bullet meant for an up-and-coming don.

It was in Little Italy, SoHo, Chinatown, and the Lower East Side that crime—New York–style, that is—originated more than two hundred years ago. Here is where the immigrants came to settle; here is where the city's first street gangs formed.

In the middle of it all, at the intersection of what is now Bayard and Mulberry, was The Collect, a swamp the town fathers paved over to make way for a slum (a century later, politicians would call such initiatives urban renewal).

So began crime's Eden, a place for young thugs to rape, rob, and pillage—that is, until some of them earned enough to pay other poor slobs to do the dirty work. Ah, the good old days, when SoHo was known as Hell's Hundred Acres, and Mott Street was a shooting gallery for the Chinese tongs.

How heartwarming to think that no matter how dangerous life is today, back then it was just as bad.

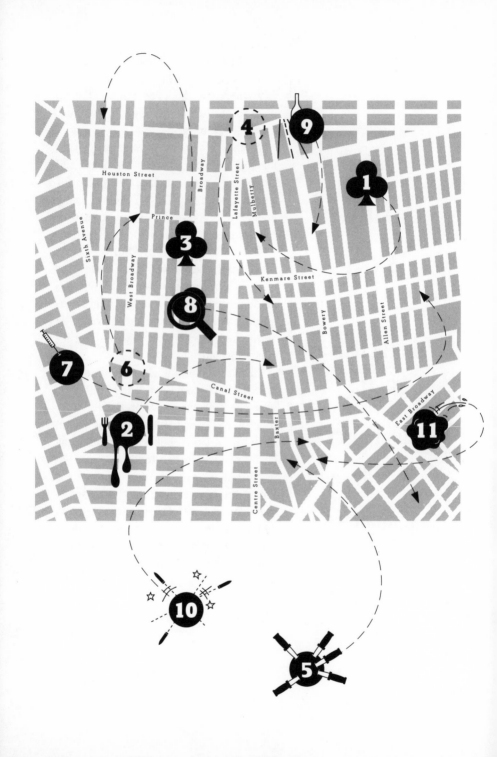

Little Italy

1

Hangin' with the Hoods
Ravenite Social Club, 247 Mulberry Street

When he's not locked behind bars, John Gotti and his merry band of gangsters can be found Tuesday and Wednesday nights on Mulberry Street, hanging out in a brick-faced storefront known as the Ravenite Social Club.

Impress your friends with the information, but don't plan on dropping by unannounced. Nor is it too wise to set up across the street with a lawn chair and video camera. The Dapper Don—"Johnny-boy" to his friends—gets a little jumpy around strangers.

In other words, no autographs.

The Ravenite, with its white-framed windows and screen door, is a kind of a clubhouse, or boardroom, where Johnny and the boys sit around and compare pistols. Outside, the Cadillacs and limos are lined up along the curb. Inside, the club features a few card tables, a color TV, and a refrigerator stocked with soda and beer. If Gotti wants to call an executive session, he can retreat to an empty apartment one flight up.

Sometimes Gotti and his hoods, including brother Pete, stroll south along Mulberry, their diamond pinky rings and chunky gold watches gleaming in the night. Maybe they stop for a bite at Paolucci's or Taormina or Cafe Biondo—no waiting for a table for them. Maybe they circle the block. Or maybe they just stand still, their fat necks twitching in shiny suits.

Mostly they just stay at the Ravenite, which, for those specializing in the study of John Gotti, has been the scene of several quite historic events. It was here, for example, that dozens of gangsters attended a party just days after the 1985 murder of Paul Castellano. Gotti, still relatively unknown, was the fete's center of attention, a fact noted with great interest by detectives watching from across the street. The following day, reporters were proclaiming Gotti the new Godfather.

The Ravenite is also where Gotti, mob sage, has proven he has lots to say about, you know, lotsa things. The police and the FBI, ever eager to understand the criminal mind, secretly installed microphones at the Ravenite just to capture Johnny-boy's musings.

Our favorite was Gotti's great sorrow over the untimely passing of Paul Castellano: "He deserved it."

It was such commentary that inspired federal agents to drop by the Ravenite on December 16, 1990, and arrest Gotti, along with several of his top underlings, charging them with eleven murders and racketeering.

A white silk scarf around his neck, Gotti was led from the Ravenite in handcuffs while a dozen of his soldiers, some wearing sunglasses despite the late hour, stood on the sidewalk cursing the cops under their breath.

Hoodlum on the Half-Shell
129 Mulberry Street

The linguini with pesto, the fried octopus, the clams oregano—these are all excellent reasons to visit the restaurants of Little Italy. But we have a better reason, especially if you like games. We call it "Find the Bullet Hole" and there's no better place to play than Umberto's Clam House, at 129 Mulberry Street.

We'd tell you to look for the actual bullets, but most of those are long gone, having been deposited one night in 1972 in the body of a gangster known as "Crazy" Joe Gallo.

Poor Joey. All he wanted was to get away from his gang and the clubhouse on President Street in Brooklyn, where he kept a lion chained in the basement to intimidate his enemies. But all Joey got were three bullets in the middle of his shrimp, scungilli, and soda—and on his 43rd birthday, no less.

Not a peaceful way to go, but Joey was never much of a pacifist. He's credited, for example, with planning two of mob history's most famous hits—Albert Anastasia in 1957 and Joe Colombo in 1971.

Still, Joey didn't like to think of himself merely as a guy with a gun. He fancied himself an oil painter and an intellectual, talking endlessly of Balzac, Kafka, and even a little Sartre.

In the last years of his life, Joey even tried to turn himself into an upstanding citizen. He wined and dined with big names, including the actor Jerry Ohrbach, with whom he was often seen at Elaine's, a fancy-schmancy writers' hangout on the Upper East Side. Gallo even had plans to tell his life's story to Ohrbach's wife for a book.

All in all, life was good for Joey when his birthday came around on April 7, 1972. Dressed in a dark blue pinstripe suit, he took his bodyguard, his new bride, and his 10-year-old stepdaughter to the Copacabana. From the stage, comedian Don Rickles introduced Joey to the crowd. Not bad for a guy who once spent eight years in prison for extortion.

At 4 A.M., Joey and his party left the Copa and piled into his black Cadillac. They drove downtown to Umberto's, which had opened two weeks before. It was around the corner from police headquarters, a fact of little concern to one of Umberto's silent partners, Matty "The Horse" Ianiello, a well-known mobster who made millions off pornography.

Matty was at the Clam House when Joey and his gang swept through the doors and sat at two butcher-block tables in the back. Joey, of course, was facing the door. At one point, he went to the bathroom in the basement. "You could bury a lot of bodies down there," he said when he returned.

As the Gallo party gabbed and gobbled, a balding middle-aged man wearing a tweed overcoat stepped into the restaurant through the rear entrance. "Motherfucker!" the man shouted, pulling out a pistol and firing more than a dozen shots at Gallo. One bullet struck Joey's left elbow. Another hit his left buttock. The fatal shot blew his back open. Everyone in the restaurant, including his wife and stepdaughter, screamed and flopped on the floor for cover. Gallo staggered outside to Hester Street, where he fell down dead at 5:23 A.M. in front of his car.

When the cops arrived, Joey's sister was bent over his body. "He was a good man; he changed his image!" she cried. "That's why they did this to him." No one was ever arrested for the shooting, but the police believe Gallo was killed by soldiers loyal to Joe Colombo, who were looking for revenge.

To this day, most people only go to Umberto's because of the Gallo shooting, which is fine, only don't expect to see gangsters still sprawled on the floor. The mess was cleaned up long ago. But do check the kitchen door in the rear, about three feet above the floor. Yes, that's it. A bullet hole, timeless proof that Joey Gallo got what he ordered.

3

The Oddfather
225 Sullivan Street

Most gangsters choose something silk, or something double-breasted when surrendering to the police. Not Vincent "The Chin" Gigante, considered by some to be the most powerful gangster in the free world. Vincent showed up for an arrest in pajamas, a blue bathrobe, and slippers.

Gigante has always had a special way of greeting the cops. Once, federal investigators broke into his 225 Sullivan Street apartment to serve him a subpoena. They found The Chin in the shower, naked and holding an umbrella over his head.

His brother Louis, a priest and former city councilman, claims Vincent suffers from "auditory and visual hallucinations and delusions of persecution." In the last twenty years, Louis has tried to convince several judges that Vincent was too crazy to stand trial, including a judge in 1991 when he faced racketeering charges.

The cops who follow The Chin around think otherwise, claiming that he commands an army of two hundred soldiers and earns more than $100 million a year from loan-sharking, extortion, and drug sales. In fact, investigators insist that Gigante's empire is as big—if not bigger—than John Gotti's.

Vincent began his gangster life as mob boss Vito Genovese's chauffeur, an entry-level position in the mob. He hit the front pages for the first time in 1957 when he was accused of trying to shoot Frank Costello (see

Upper West Side tour). The charges were dropped after Costello claimed that he couldn't identify Gigante or anyone else as the shooter.

Now in his late sixties, Gigante seems to like things in pairs—at least when it comes to women and their names. His wife Olympia lives in a house in Bergen County, New Jersey, but he prefers to sleep most nights with mistress Olympia in her place on the Upper East Side of Manhattan. Vincent spends his days at 225 Sullivan Street, a humble tenement between Bleecker and Third streets. The initials "Y. G." are scribbled over one of the mailboxes (for Gigante's mother, Yolanda) in the entranceway, but we don't recommend ringing the doorbell.

In the afternoon, The Chin, in his bathrobe, slippers, and cap, likes to walk across the street to the Triangle Civic Improvement Association at 208 Sullivan Street. The windows are blackened and the door is often padlocked, but, according to investigators, this is where Gigante and his close associates play pinochle.

The feds claim The Chin talks business late at night, strolling the side streets of SoHo and Little Italy, whispering to confederates or to himself. Sometimes, particularly when he feels that he is being watched by the police, he starts muttering to himself in the middle of the street. Once, after he spotted undercover cops, Gigante, dressed in his bathrobe, fell to his knees on the sidewalk in front of a church and began to pray.

Where Have You Gone, Joe the Baker?
385 Broome Street

Caffe Roma's cannoli are a treat and don't miss the cheesecake and cappuccino. Definitely compliment the chef, but don't bother thanking the owner, at least not the one who helped open the joint. He's been missing since 1977.

Eli "Joe the Baker" Zeccardi was a man of much weight and many talents. Not only was he an underboss for mob kingpin Vito Genovese, but he also found time to own one of our favorite dessert stops, at 385 Broome Street.

That is, until April 27, 1977, when Eli, 67 years old, told his wife he was on his way to the cafe. It was common for him to spend his days there meeting with men who operated his multimillion-dollar loan-sharking business.

We're not sure if Mrs. Zeccardi is still waiting up for Eli, but the police have given up the search. On several occasions in the months after he disappeared, investigators thought they had found his torso floating in the waters off Brooklyn or the Bronx. But the body parts turned out to belong to other long-lost wise guys.

5

A Murder a Day: Five Points
Intersection of Bayard, Park, Worth, Mulberry,
and Baxter Streets

It is called Columbus Park these days, the concrete plaza behind the Manhattan Criminal Court buildings, where kids play basketball and stickball and senior citizens spend afternoons sitting on park benches. More than one hundred years ago, though, this patch was known as Five Points, a world-famous slum raging with despair, disease, and the city's earliest street gangs—the Dead Rabbits, the Roach Guards, and Plug Uglies, to name just a few.

Conditions were so bad that Jacob Riis, the crusading journalist, called Five Points a "human pigsty" populated by "thieves, murderers, pickpockets, beggars, harlots, and degenerates of every type." Charles Dickens, in the 1840s, wrote that Five Points is home to "all that is loathsome, drooping, and decayed." Dickens toured the slum—accompanied by cops, of course.

Five Points, a paved-over swamp, was located at the intersection of what was then known as Orange, Cross, Anthony, Little Water, and Mulberry streets. Now they're called Baxter, Bayard, Park, Worth, and Mulberry streets. The nineteenth century brought thousands of immigrants, many of them Irish, who crowded into the area's airless, soot-filled tenements. In one year, 1852, census takers visiting Five Points found that 155 children, all younger than five, had died, many of them from cholera.

Landlords named their buildings "Gates to Hell" and "Brick Bat Mansion," but none were more squalid than the Old Brewery on Pearl Street, on the site of what is to be a new federal courthouse behind One Police Plaza. The writer Herbert Asbury, in his 1927 classic, *The Gangs of New York,* wrote that the Old Brewery resembled a "giant toad with dirty, leprous warts."

It was here that police estimated one murder was committed every night for fifteen years—a lot for one address, even by modern standards of crime. Not surprising, then, that tenants named a hallway "Murderer's Alley" and a room the "Den of Thieves." A thousand families lived in the five-story building, where in the basement a five-year-old girl was once robbed and stabbed to death after showing off a penny. The Brewery was knocked down in 1852 and workmen clearing the site carried out bags of human bones.

Sometimes, the gang warfare at Five Points got a tad out of hand. In 1857, for example, the city called in the state militia to quell a fight between the Dead Rabbits and the Bowery Boys, but not before ten people had died and dozens of others had been injured.

In the 1880s, the police found in the pocket of one gangster, Piker Ryan, a member of the Whyos, a list of services he was willing to render, along with the charges. A punch cost $2, while two black eyes cost $4. Piker would chew someone's ear for $15, or shoot them in the leg for $25. He charged $100 for "doing the big job."

Piker Ryan wasn't much to fear, especially at the turn of the century when Five Points gangs included members like Al Capone and Lucky Luciano. Their experience on the city's streets was so inspirational that the two men were among the founders of organized crime, a venture that would make them world famous and their operations about as big as US Steel.

SoHo

6

Missing
Prince and Wooster Streets

He left for school early one spring morning in 1979, a six-year-old boy, blond, blue-eyed, and carrying a bag with figures of elephants stitched on the outside. It was the first time Etan Patz ever walked on the streets of New York City without a grown-up.

Julie Patz, Etan's mother, was anxious watching her son leave, but she knew he was only walking two blocks west from their apartment on Prince Street to the corner of Prince and West Broadway, where he would catch a bus for school.

More than ten years later, Mrs. Patz and her husband, Stanley, are still waiting for their son's return. As far as the police know, Etan reached the corner of Prince and Wooster streets on May 25, 1979, and was never seen again.

The police department assigned five hundred officers to the case. On foot and in helicopters, they searched rooftops and back alleys and checked out thousands of tips. They even consulted psychics, one of whom assured them that Etan was safe because God was looking out for the Patzes.

The cops scattered 300,000 posters of Etan throughout the city, all of them stamped "MISSING." Etan's smiling face seemed to hang on street corners everywhere, a touchstone for every parent's worst fear for their children.

The days of waiting for Etan to come home turned into weeks, months, and then years. The posters eventually came down. Police officers were reassigned. All that was left was National Missing Children's Day, marked every May 25th, the day Etan disappeared.

As Etan's 18th birthday came and went, investigators kept the case open. In 1990, the police targeted a man who pleaded guilty to molesting an eight-year-old boy in Pennsylvania. The man said he had abducted Etan, but the cops could never prove his claim.

There have been some particularly cruel moments for the Patzes, who never seemed to give up hope. In the months after Etan disappeared, Julie Patz poured out her heart to a friend, who turned around and wrote a novel entitled *Still Missing*, about a little boy who is kidnapped. Hollywood bought the rights to the book for $450,000, which didn't bother the Patzes nearly as much as that in this fictionalized version, the little boy comes home.

Lower East Side and Chinatown

7

Buying Heroin with Jane Fonda's Kid
139 Essex Street

Acting seems to run in the Fonda family, even when there's no audience or movie camera. Jane's daughter Vanessa, for example, put on a most dramatic performance for the police in 1989 when she and her boyfriend Thomas Feegal were busted for buying heroin outside 139 Essex Street.

Trouble was, the cops didn't buy the act.

Who could blame them? Vanessa, then a student at Brown University, claimed they were purchasing the smack for "research purposes."

Or how about this line, delivered with feeling after she saw the cops slap handcuffs on her beau: "You can't just take him!" Vanessa yelled. "You've got to take me, too!"

The cops, of course, didn't mind and hauled the two off to the local precinct. Feegal, carrying a hypodermic needle when he was busted, was charged with possession and sale of narcotics. Vanessa was arrested for obstruction of justice and disorderly conduct.

She was eventually sentenced to three days of community service. Her then-divorced parents, Jane and French film director Roger Vadim, didn't attend the hearing in Manhattan Criminal Court. But they issued a jointly written statement about the bust. "Vanessa," they said, "is a good daughter."

8

The Rosenbergs
Apartment GE11, Knickerbocker Village, 10 Monroe Street

The FBI came for Ethel Rosenberg in the summer of 1950. She was alone with her two young sons in Knickerbocker Village, a middle-income housing development a mile from the teeming tenements where she grew up.

Julius Rosenberg, already arrested for allegedly giving atom bomb secrets to the Soviets, had prayed his wife would remain free, but FBI boss J. Edgar Hoover had other plans.

Hoover was curious about this child of Jewish immigrants, who once sang on street corners for the American Communist Party. So curious, in fact, that he sent nine G-men to her modest apartment to rifle through her underwear and coat closets for evidence of "un-American activities."

They didn't find anything, but one G-man got tough with Michael Rosenberg, Ethel's son, not yet eight years old, who was listening to the Lone Ranger on the radio.

"Turn it off," the G-man growled.

"No," Michael said.

"Yes," the G-man said, switching the volume off.

So much for a cold war standoff. The feds weren't going to let anyone stand in their way, least of all a little kid.

They had started investigating the Rosenbergs after Ethel's younger brother, David Greenglass, a mechanic at the Los Alamos atomic bomb factory, told them that Julius was the head of a Soviet espionage ring.

Actually, David was the one who was accused of being a spy, but he was trying to save his own hide—and his wife's. That's when he ratted on sister Ethel.

Three years after the feds knocked on Ethel's door, and just after President Eisenhower refused to intervene, the couple was sent to the electric chair at Sing Sing. Julius required the standard three volts, Ethel needed five.

9

The Boulevard of Bad Manners
The Bowery

The nation's most famous skid row began in the 1700s as a bucolic country lane, De Bouwerie, which led from the southern tip of Manhattan to outlying farms, including Peter Stuyvesant's, at what is now Astor Place.

But the farms died and the cows headed upstate. New York was becoming a center of immigration and De Bouwerie was paved in 1837 to accommodate the traffic. Poor and working-class immigrants started jamming into tenements. Felons and hobos and drunkards weren't far behind.

Oh, how they loved the Bowery, with its endless rows of saloons, pawn shops, brothels, tattoo parlors, drug dens, and flophouses. Proprietors gave catchy names to their haunts—the Hell Hole, Cripples' Home, or McGurk's Suicide Hall at 295 Bowery, a building that still stands.

Where else but at the old Bowery Theater on Canal Street could you hurl pennies and chicken bones at actors earnestly performing Shakespearean sonnets. Where else but on the Bowery could you pay to watch boxing matches and dogs eating rats. The champion dog, a fox terrier named Jack, managed to digest one hundred rats in eleven minutes. The whole neighborhood was proud.

This was democracy as the founding fathers never imagined, a boulevard without churches, but with its own gang, the Bowery Boys (who were eventually immortalized on film), and an eight-foot-tall goon named Mose, who carried a butcher's knife and a beer keg on his belt, and who liked to hoist horse buggies in the air just to scare the passengers.

Such was life on the Bowery for more than a century, until the late 1970s, when people with money began moving in. Today, the boulevard is cleaner and quieter, the big theaters demolished to gravel lots, the flophouses replaced by sterile rehab centers and a men's homeless shelter, the old warehouses converted to lofts by artists and bankers. Many welcomed the changes, but others, longing for the days when the Bowery had character, mourned the passing of the neighborhood.

Wonton Destruction
Chinatown

Admire Chinatown's pagodas. Walk Pell Street, Bayard, and Mulberry. Eat the spare ribs, the steamed dumplings, the prawns sautéed in garlic sauce.

Maybe even catch a famous Chinatown pastime—a bloody gang war in the middle of Mott Street. Watch the bullets fly. See the bodies fall. It's all very exhilarating—except, of course, when you've been shot in the back.

Chinatown has a rich tradition of violent warfare between its gangs, or tongs, as they are known. Ruling Chinatown in the early 1900s was Mock Duck, the leader of the Hip Sing tong, who giggled like a hyena, had terrible eyesight, and liked to shoot into crowds with both eyes closed.

Mock Duck's chief rival was Tom Lee, the white-bearded leader of the On Leong tong, whose 13 Pell Street headquarters was the site of the city's first opium den (these days, the building is controlled by the Hip Sing tong). Lee ran many gambling parlors and ordered his foes murdered, but the city's political leaders could still count on him to get out Chinatown's six votes on Election Day. For this service the pols chose to overlook his felonious ways, dubbing him the Mayor of Chinatown and making him a deputy sheriff.

Lee ruled the neighborhood until 1900, when Mock Duck took over the Hip Sing and the two tongs battled for control of Chinatown's gambling parlors. Gang war exploded in the streets. By 1909, fifty people had been murdered on Doyers Street, also known as the "Bloody Angle." (Irving Berlin performed at the time at a nightclub at 6 Doyers Street.) Mock Duck himself was shot many times, including once in the belt buckle, but he always managed to survive.

It was not a good idea to mess with Mock Duck, who carried two pistols, a hatchet, and wore a chain-mail shirt. A battle over a young woman named Sweet Flower ended when Mock Duck's soldiers broke into 17 Mott Street in the middle of the night, stabbed her in the heart, and cut off her fingers.

Mock Duck was no less gentle when a local comedian, Ah Hoon, lampooned him in his act. Ah Hoon, a member of the On Leong tong, made fun of Mock Duck's marriage, the way he held a gun, his high-pitched giggle. The act was a big hit with everyone—everyone, that is, except Mock Duck.

In November of 1909, Mock Duck proclaimed that Ah Hoon would die by the end of the year. By December 30th, Ah Hoon was still alive and performed his act at the Old Chinese Theater. Afterward, the police took him to his apartment in what is now 10 Chatham Square. They waited outside his door while he slept through the night.

Moments before midnight, a man seated in a chair made out of rope was lowered from the tenement's roof and suspended in front of Ah Hoon's bedroom window. While Ah Hoon dreamed of new jokes about Mock Duck, the man pulled out a pistol and shot the comedian in the heart.

Today, more than eighty years later, Hip Sing and On Leong still thrive, but they've been joined by lawless street gangs with names like Born to Kill, the Ghost Shadows, and the Flying Dragons.

The neighborhood is no safer, especially since the gangs are poor shots. More often than Chinatown's restaurateurs like to admit, a tourist or two gets caught in the crossfire. In the new Chinatown, it's always safer to eat and run.

11

A Battle for the Ages: Mayor Koch Fights Off a Watercress
13 Mott Street

Of all the battles Ed Koch fought in his twelve years as mayor, none was so dramatic—or so life-threatening—as his epic bout with a watercress.

Or was that a piece of pork?

We'll leave the debate to the historians, but it is universally accepted that on July 26, 1981, the mayor dined at the Sun Lok Kee restaurant on Mott Street with his pal and political ally, David Margolis, the president of Colt Industries.

It was not unusual for Koch to eat Chinese. Rarely a day passed when he wasn't swallowing an egg roll or a dumpling. Indeed, many Chinese restaurants in the city boasted a picture—often out-of-focus—of the smiling mayor surrounded by an admiring kitchen staff.

But things didn't go so swimmingly when Koch dined with Margolis at Sun Lok Kee. Suddenly the mayor began to choke. He couldn't breath. For the only time in his life, perhaps, Ed Koch couldn't talk.

He did have a lip-reader, though. Koch, 58 at the time, turned to Margolis and mouthed the words "I am choking." Then he stood up and put his hands over his head. Margolis jumped into action, performing the trusty save-the-mayor Heimlich maneuver.

The piece of food flew out of Koch's mouth and the mayor was once again able to breathe. He was also able to eat, he noticed, and quickly returned to his meal.

No doubt many people felt sorry for the mayor. Koch blamed the mess on an errant piece of watercress. But this was an election year and Koch's enemies spread rumors that the mayor had actually choked on a piece of pork.

Koch was keeping it quiet, the rumormongers said, to protect his support among Orthodox Jews, whose dietary laws forbid the eating of pig meat. As for the Chinese, they didn't seem to care, as long as the mayor didn't start eating hamburgers for lunch.

9

Down and Dirty

From City Hall to Wall Street

LOWER MANHATTAN, FROM CITY HALL to Wall Street, is among the safest areas of the city, but only at night after all the stockbrokers and city bureaucrats have gone home.

Such is life in Suit Country, where the financier makes a mint (bail money, perhaps) before being sent off to prison, where the mayor makes promises ("More better weather!") before fleeing the city in shame.

Modern corruption, both political and financial, was born in Suit Country.

Boss Tweed, New Yorker? Case dismissed.

The area includes the city's most elegant spires, City Hall, the Municipal Building, and the New York Stock Exchange among them, all spectacular settings for negotiating shady deals. For those experiencing post-greed depression, or remorse, several esteemed houses of worship are nearby, including the nineteenth-century Trinity Church on Broadway.

Foley Square, a few blocks north of City Hall, is home to the federal, state, and city court buildings and serves as a kind of judicial entertainment center for trial buffs and pedestrians passing by. All that's missing is a marquee announcing the trial du jour and ushers showing folks to their seats.

They're so entertaining—Leona, Imelda, the Dapper Don, parading up and down the court steps, smiling and waving

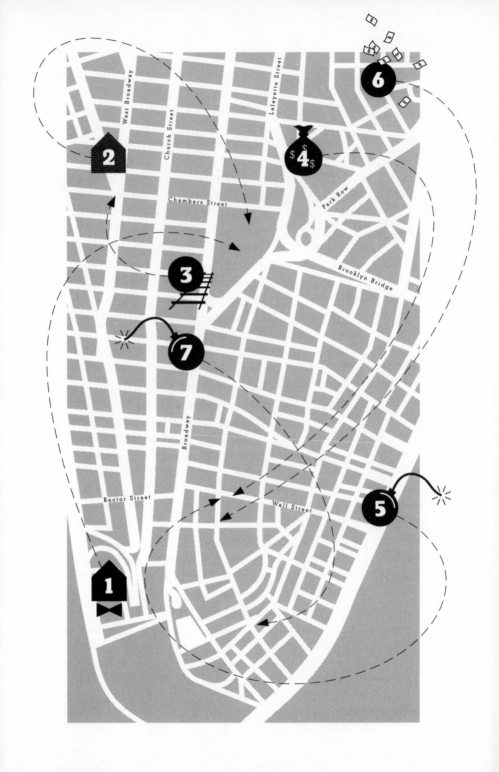

for the cameras as the cops keeping watch soak the city's taxpayers for overtime.

Par for the course in Suit Country.

Hizzoner Dishonor
City Hall

It may look like a wedding cake bathed in light, with its elegant portico, handsome arched doorways, and marbled interior, but City Hall has often seemed more like a fancy playpen for white-collar criminals. The nineteenth-century landmark features a park and a nice view of the Brooklyn Bridge. All in all, a perfect setting for a romantic stroll, a picnic, a bribe.

No mayor has ever actually been hauled from the building in handcuffs, but two, Jimmy Walker and William O'Dwyer, fled to foreign countries amid charges they were taking payoffs and consorting with gangsters. During the 1980s, Mayor Ed Koch preached the virtues of honesty, even as many of his political cronies were being escorted to jail.

Walker, the city's chief executive from 1925 to 1932, was more charming than honest, but that didn't stop New Yorkers from electing him twice. "Gentleman Jim" or "Beau James," as he was known, was Fun City's perfect host for the Roaring Twenties. "I'd rather be a lamppost in New York than mayor of Chicago," he once said. Walker was the nocturnal mayor, tall and thin, and debonair in white custom-made suits— a mayor who loved gambling, whiskey, and beautiful women (even if they didn't vote for him).

Indeed, Walker's philandering was so well known that once, while riding in a parade with Queen Marie of Romania, an ironworker yelled out, "Hey, Jimmy! Have you made her yet?" The police commissioner at the time, Grover Whalen, recalled the scene in his autobiography, *Mr. New York,* a 300-page book in which he details his own accomplishments but fails to mention that he was widely suspected to have been on mobster Lucky Luciano's payroll.

Walker also had many gangster friends, but it was his years in show business that made him particularly well suited for New York City politics. In 1908, Jimmy wrote the song "Will You Love Me in December as You Love Me in May," a hit that earned him $10,000 over thirty years.

As mayor, Walker never showed up at City Hall before noon and only then to play craps with pals and reporters in his basement office (which came with a shower and bedroom and has been used by mayors since). No one complained about Jimmy's work habits until he hiked his mayoral salary from $25,000 to $40,000. "That's cheap," Walker countered. "Think what it would cost if I worked full-time."

At night, Jimmy would kiss Mrs. Walker goodbye and trot about town with his mistress, the leggy showgirl Betty Compton. Once they went to a gambling parlor on Long Island and got caught in a police raid. While Betty was rounded up by the cops, Jimmy slipped into an apron and claimed he was a waiter. Some said they'd never seen Mayor Walker think so quickly on his feet.

Jimmy had a tougher time escaping the law when a state panel found in 1932 that he had taken $1 million in payoffs from contractors seeking business with the city. It was also discovered that he had close ties to gambler Arnold Rothstein, in whose personal papers were found the names of some of Jimmy's top aides.

By late summer of 1932, the wagons were circling. On September 1st, after pressure was applied by Governor Franklin D. Roosevelt, Walker resigned from office. He sailed for Europe and didn't return for eight years.

If New Yorkers were appalled by revelations of corruption within the marbled walls of City Hall, it didn't stop them from electing William O'Dwyer in 1945, just thirteen years after Walker's unhappy exit.

O'Dwyer's integrity had long been the subject of speculation, making him a perfect candidate for mayor. Only three years before his election, he had visited the home of mobster Frank Costello to ask for his help with the campaign.

O'Dwyer, it seemed, was especially fond of gangsters. In 1940, after becoming Brooklyn's district attorney, he claimed he was too busy to investigate racketeering charges against another top thug, Albert Anastasia. Anastasia's pal, it turned out, was on O'Dywer's staff.

The following year, a murder case against Anastasia collapsed after a mob turncoat, Abe "Kid Twist" Reles, fell out of a hotel window while under 24-hour police guard (see Brooklyn tour). Instead of punishing the cop charged with guarding Reles, O'Dywer eventually promoted him to deputy police commissioner.

O'Dwyer was reelected mayor in 1949. As far as the public knew he was keeping his nose clean, but in early 1950 he was privately begging President Truman to appoint him ambassador to Mexico. It wasn't that O'Dwyer had any special talent for diplomacy. On the contrary, he was trying to flee town before Brooklyn bookie Harry Gross testified that he had bribed top police brass, as well as contributed $20,000 to O'Dwyer's mayoral campaign. Truman spared O'Dwyer endless embarrassment and sent him packing two weeks before Gross was arrested.

Following O'Dwyer's mayoralty, City Hall was relatively safe from corruption until 1986, the beginning of Ed Koch's last term. The mayor was a kind of emcee for dozens of scandals, big and small, as his political bedfellows, who cheered his inaugural ceremony on the steps of City Hall, were being charged with robbing millions of taxpayer dollars.

Every day, it seemed, another commissioner or party boss was resigning with his head bowed and a trenchcoat draped over his wrists to hide the handcuffs (a ploy invented, of course, by a public relations man). No matter how bad the news, Koch still traveled the city bellowing "How'm I doin'?"

In 1989, the voters responded by throwing him out of office and electing David Dinkins, whose love of dapper suits and black-tie parties have elicited comparisons to Jimmy Walker. No talk of missing public money, though.

Tweed Courthouse
52 Chambers Street

The Tweed Courthouse behind City Hall may be a monument to nineteenth-century corruption, but that's no reason, as some insist, to knock it down. On the contrary, we say keep it. Turn it into a museum. Open a gift shop. Sell memberships. Call it the Museum of Municipal Impropriety. MOMI for short.

It's perfect for a building unofficially named for the man who ripped off more than $50 million from New York City taxpayers. William Marcy Tweed, the father of municipal corruption, the original Boss of Bosses, didn't need a shotgun to get his way. He had the votes instead.

In 1861, Tweed ordered this Palladian-style courthouse built at a proposed cost of $250,000. So what if the final tab was $13 million? Tweed and his henchmen were more than happy to pocket the difference. So what if a plasterer was paid $133,187 for two days' work and a carpenter got $360,751 for barely lifting a finger? They deserved it. They were the boss's close friends.

Yes, MOMI should feature wax statues resembling Tweed and the rest of the Tammany Hall Democratic political club, which, for a generation, turned the city's treasury into their personal piggy bank. We see a spot for Sam Swartwout, maybe even a whole room—yes, the "Swartwout Room"—for the man who stole $1.2 million from the taxpayers. Or the mustachioed George Washington Plunkitt, who spoke of the "grand opportunities all around," his expression for taking bribes from any and all Wall Street tycoons.

Perhaps there could be an entire wing for Hugh Grant, who juggled many interests, including whiskey, gambling, and the law, which he simultaneously practiced and flouted as only a Tammany man could. As the city's sheriff, Grant earned $42,497 by selling property taken from widows who couldn't pay their taxes. A grand jury called him "slovenly and wholly indecent." The Tammany regime later called him mayor, in 1888.

MOMI would also feature the "Croker Staircase," dedicated to Richard Croker, a street gangster who stole his way to political boss. Croker owned a $500,000 horse farm, a Florida winter home, and a country estate in England—all paid for with bribes he graciously accepted from businessmen, cops bucking for promotions, and prostitutes looking to buy their way out of trumped-up charges.

We see a statue for Tammany police lieutenant Charlie Becker. One of the most corrupt men ever to wear a shield, the broad-shouldered Becker was the perfect pick to head Special Squad No. 1, the police department's anti-graft unit. It allowed him to extort cash from every pimp, crimp, and creep in exchange for letting them stay clear of the law. Becker went to the electric chair in 1915 for ordering the murder of a gambling parlor owner who refused to pay him off.

They were a shameless bunch, the Tammany men, but no one was more criminal than Boss Tweed, who once proclaimed bribery to be the only sensible way to govern New York City. MOMI's gift shop would feature Boss coins commemorating the currency he stole, as well as replicas of the walnut-sized diamond pendant he wore around his neck. You won't find cigarettes: Boss believed tobacco was more evil than a payoff.

Tweed was elected to the city's Board of Aldermen in 1851, a body that was nicknamed "The Forty Thieves." Instantly, he proved he belonged by authorizing the purchase of sixty-nine acres on Ward's Island. Tweed alloted $103,000 in payment for the property, even though it was worth $30,000. He pocketed the difference.

Among his proudest moments, Tweed once ordered the city to pay his friend $170,000 for thirty-five chairs—more than $5,000 each—and got his own dog walker a $25-a-week city job as an English interpreter, even though he couldn't read or write in any language.

Boss's reign ended in 1870, after one of his cronies offered a *New York Times* editor $5 million in cash—taxpayer money, of course—not to expose Tammany's corruption. It didn't work. The *Times* wrote that Tweed controlled the city like "Napoleon ruled France, or as the Medicis ruled Florence." Tweed was arrested in 1871 at his 237 Broadway office. Arriving at jail, he was asked his profession by a police officer. "Statesman," Tweed declared, as he was locked behind bars.

A second trial two years later reversed the conviction, but Tweed was later returned to prison for fraud. The courts let him leave custody each day and go home for lunch, and one afternoon in 1874 he vanished, ducking out the back door of his residence at 647 Madison Avenue. Authorities found him eight months later in Spain, hauled him home, and locked him in the squalid Ludlow Street jail. Stripped of his lunch privileges, suffering from gout and heart trouble, the Boss died behind bars in 1878.

3

Subway Vigilante
IRT Subway, Chambers Street Station

Avoiding muggers may be difficult in New York City, but it helps to take precautions. Here's one: don't dress like Bernhard Goetz.

Goetz had a history of attracting trouble even before he shot four teenagers on a subway train in 1984. Perhaps it had something to do with his fashion sense. The oversized aviator glasses, the wash-n-wear white shirt, the pens sticking out of the pocket—Bernie looked like a poster boy for crime victims.

Or as one of his friends said: "He was a fire hydrant looking for a dog."

Actually, many believe Goetz left his apartment on December 22, 1984, hoping that someone would try to mug him. He had recently purchased a silver-handled .38-caliber revolver, which he tucked under his belt. Goetz found his excuse aboard a crowded IRT express train—car no. 7657—as it sped southbound from Fourteenth to Chambers Street.

Troy Canty, 18, and three friends approached Goetz at the front end of the car. They asked him for five dollars. Goetz, annoyed, responded by pulling out his new pistol and shooting each of the four teenagers. As one of the teens, Daryl Cabey, lay on the floor of the car, Goetz leaned over him and shouted, "You don't look so bad—here's another!" and pulled the trigger. Cabey suffered brain damage and paralysis.

Moments later, the train arrived at Chambers Street, and as the doors slid open, Goetz dashed out and disappeared into the platform crowd. Nine days later, he surrendered to police in Concord, New Hampshire. He wasn't remorseful. On the contrary, he told cops he would have continued shooting if he hadn't run out of bullets. He also said he wanted to scratch his victims' eyes out with his apartment keys.

Goetz returned to New York an instant celebrity. Dozens of journalists camped outside his apartment at 55 West 14th Street, soaking up crucial

details, such as the fact that he went to a coffee shop and ordered a
turkey sandwich.

Bernie became the "Subway Vigilante," as one tabloid called him, hero
to legions of gun nuts who raised tens of thousands of dollars for his
defense, saying he had stood up for innocent people desperately trying
to survive in the New York jungle. The four teens, Goetz's defenders
charged, were carrying screwdrivers in their pockets when they were
shot. Clearly, they were up to no good. Weeks after the shooting, one
of the teens, James Ramseur, 18, was charged in a separate crime with
falsely reporting his own kidnapping. Ramseur was also later arrested
on charges of sodomy, rape, and robbery.

On the other side, many New Yorkers labeled Goetz a murderous
racist itching to shoot someone, especially someone black. An assistant
district attorney described Goetz's personality as a "powder keg waiting
to go off."

Certainly, Goetz had a troubled past. His father was tyrannical, ordering his children to write memorandums after they were scolded. "Dear
Mr. Goetz," Bernhard wrote his dad at the age of ten, "I am sorry I
have been a bad boy." The letter was signed, "Your son, Bernhard
Goetz."

Bernhard's father was convicted in 1968 of molesting two 15-year-old
boys in upstate New York. The case was so embarrassing to the family
that Bernhard, 13 at the time, was shipped off to boarding school in
Switzerland to finish high school.

Twelve years later, Goetz moved to New York and started an elec-
tronics company. For two years he lived at 211 Thompson Street before
moving to 14th Street. Bernie hated the drug dealers and the vagrants
who frequented his block. Prosecutors would later claim he once set fire
to homeless people's possessions. But, more important, Goetz's rage
was stoked by a 1981 mugging in which he saw his attacker arrested
and then out on the street again within hours committing another crime.
It was then that Bernie decided to carry a gun.

After a seven-week trial in 1987 for the subway shooting, Goetz was
acquitted of attempted murder but convicted of gun possession. Later,
he was sentenced to six months in prison. After the trial was over, the
subway gunman, dressed as always in his wash-n-wear white shirt, leaned
over to his lawyer and asked, "Can I go home now?"

4

Do the Hustle: Boesky, Milken & Levine
Wall Street

No guns were brandished, no blood was spilled. The criminals wore starched white shirts and bright red power ties. The getaway cars were stretch limos, specially stocked with liquor, platinum blondes, and cellular phones.

Welcome to the Wall Street crime wave.

The world's financial capital was a regular orgy of impropriety in the 1980s. And you thought those financiers were uptight in their pinstripes. Forget about it. They stole everything but the New York Stock Exchange.

Dennis Levine, a middle-class kid from Queens, was earning $1 million a year as an investment banker at Drexel Burnham, whose headquarters were at 60 Broad Street. Dennis had a $500,000 co-op apartment at 1185 Park Avenue, an $80,000 red Ferrari, and a summer house in Southampton. It would have been enough for most people—most people, that is, except Dennis, who just had to have more.

In 1986, he was arrested for ripping off $12.6 million from insider-trading deals. The federal prosecutors who arrested him took his jewelry, cuff links, watch, money, briefcase, and his wallet. It was enough to touch off a Wall Street panic not seen since the stock market crashed in 1929.

Off Levine went to Al Capone's former home, the US penitentiary at Lewisburg, Pennsylvania. He might have stayed for years, except he chose to loosen his lips for a considerably lighter sentence. In exchange for a two-year term, he gave investigators the proof they needed to nab financier Ivan Boesky, whose Wall Street nickname was "Piggy."

The Great Boesky is famous for once telling a graduating business school class that "greed is healthy." He worked 20-hour days at his Fifth Avenue office, rarely slept, and his daily meal was little more than a piece of fruit. Mostly he gulped cups of coffee—or, as he called it, "the vampire's plasma."

Boesky made hundreds of millions a year and once said he liked to imagine his fortune as a stack of silver dollars. "I wonder how tall that would be?" he asked. "It would be like Jacob's ladder, wouldn't it? A Jacob's ladder of silver dollars. Imagine—wouldn't that be an aphrodisiac experience, climbing to the top of such a ladder?"

Boesky not only fell off his ladder, but ended up behind bars, prisoner no. 13987-054. Of course, he cut a sweet deal for himself with prosecutors—a two-year term and $100 million fine in exchange for the goods to get Michael Milken, the Junk Bond King, whose thorny crown happened to be a black curly-haired toupee.

Milken lived and worked in California, but plenty of his riches—including his world-record $550-million-a-year salary—flowed through Wall Street. Actually, Milken lived modestly in a simple home in Los Angeles without butlers or original Monets hanging on the walls. At dinner, the Milkens poured Kraft dressing on their salads.

Milken's love was his work. Almost single-handedly, he created the junk bond buying frenzy that fueled the corporate raiders of the late 1980s. It paid off handsomely, with Milken earning $1.1 billion in salary between 1983 and 1987.

It was during that year that the Securities and Exchange Commission caught on to Milken's shady dealings, the ones involving the buying and selling of stock on the basis of insider, nonpublic information about corporate deals.

At Manhattan Federal Court, Milken sobbed as he was sentenced to ten years in prison and a $200 million fine for fraud and insider trading. But he must have felt better when he walked out of court. Waiting on the steps outside were dozens of his supporters, all of them Milken lookalikes, curly-haired and wearing blue blazers and red ties just like their fallen hero. He was sent to a federal prison camp in Allerton, California, where he earns 40 cents an hour for cleaning toilets.

5

Only the Pinky Survived
23 Broad Street

In the years following the Russian revolution, Americans were quite fearful of Bolsheviks, Communists, and other forces of violent social change. They had good reason: in 1919, a New York City postal clerk discovered sixteen packaged bombs addressed to prominent Americans, including John D. Rockefeller, J. P. Morgan, and US Attorney General A. Mitchell Palmer.

More than a year later, on September 20, 1920, a horse-drawn wagon pulled up to the corner of Broad and Wall streets, just across from Morgan's 23 Broad Street headquarters. The wagon's driver got out and slipped away as the noontime bells tolled at Trinity Church.

Moments later, a bomb on the back of the wagon exploded, shooting iron shrapnel and fire in every direction. Skulls were crushed and skin was torn. Windows shattered and fragments of glass rained down on brokers working the floor of the Stock Exchange. Five blocks away, a pedestrian was hit by a flying pipe.

The death toll reached 38, and 130 others were injured. Police searched for financier Edward Sweet, but all they could find was his pinky, recovered in the middle of the street and still adorned by a diamond ring. No one was ever charged for the bombing, but investigators assumed Anarchists were to blame.

Today, the Morgan building wears the damage inflicted by the bombing. The scars are located just below the second windowsill from the east end of the building.

6

Yippee! Abbie Hoffman Visits the New York Stock Exchange
Exchange Place and Broad Street

When Abbie Hoffman and fifteen of his friends appeared at the New York Stock Exchange on an August afternoon in 1967, the man at the door refused to let them in. Abbie reminded the man that they had phoned in a tour reservation under the name of George Metesky (see the Upper West Side tour). The man shrugged and shook his head. "Why?" Abbie asked. "Because you're hippies and you've come to demonstrate," the man answered.

Abbie smiled. "Hippies? Why, we're Jews and we've come to see the stock market," he offered. With that, the man at the door furrowed his brow. Visions of newspaper headlines zipped across his brain. According to one telling, the man didn't like what he imagined: STOCK MARKET BANS JEWS!

Quickly, the man stepped aside and allowed Abbie and company to proceed to the visitors gallery overlooking the exchange floor. They giggled, talked of revolution, and pointed at the brokers waving at them from below. Hoffman then took out three hundred very crisp dollar bills and tossed them like confetti onto the trading floor. Men in suits, a reporter wrote at the time, scrambled after the money "like worried mice."

Security guards ushered Abbie outside, but not before one demonstrator proclaimed the exercise an "exorcism of evil spirits in the Stock Exchange." Another stuffed a fistful of cash into his own mouth. Not to be outdone, Abbie held up a five-dollar bill and set it on fire.

At the time, Hoffman was living at 333 East Fifth Street and hadn't yet made his mark on most of the country, or "Amerika," as he would call it. A year later, in what would become known as the Chicago Eight trial, Hoffman and seven others were arrested for inciting a riot outside the Democratic Convention in Chicago.

The Stock Exchange field trip has been recounted in many books, but we highly recommend going straight to the source. Jerry Rubin, Abbie's cohort, wrote about the demonstration in his autobiography, *Do It!*, which he dedicates to "dope, color TV, and violent revolution." Just above the copyright, Jerry, now a stockbroker, recommends, "Read this book stoned."

Abbie also tells the story in *Soon To Be a Major Motion Picture.* American capitalism survived, he notes, but the demonstration was still significant. "Not a drop of blood had been spilled, not a bone broken. But on that day, with that gesture, an image war had begun. In the minds of millions of teenagers, the stock market had just crashed."

The brokers of capitalism didn't exactly head for the hills following Abbie's visit, but they did install bulletproof glass windows in the visitors gallery overlooking the trading floor.

7

Getting Bombed at the Fraunces Tavern
54 Pearl Street

The Fraunces Tavern, with its red-brick Federal-style exterior, is a terrific place to get a taste of what New York was like two hundred years ago. In other words, in simpler days when overthrowing a government didn't get you thrown out of a restaurant.

George Washington loved the Fraunces and it was here that he invited his top troops for a goodbye party in 1783 after the end of the Revolutionary War. What a time they had, grown men in knickers, singing, chugging whiskey, and showing off their muskets.

Today, the tavern's owners are proud of their historic past, but they weren't too pleased when the Revolution resurfaced, this time in 1975.

A bomb exploded in the tavern's dining room on January 24th of that year, killing four Wall Street businessmen and injuring fifty-five others. A fire broke out in the kitchen, windows shattered, and plates, forks, and knives ricocheted across the room. When the smoke cleared hours later, almost half the landmark tavern was a smoldering wreck.

The same afternoon, a terrorist group known as F.A.L.N., already linked to dozens of bombings around the country, claimed responsibility for the attack. A note in a phone booth outside, to which they directed cops, called the blast revenge for the US government's opposition to independence for Puerto Rico.

The radicals compared their cause to that of the American freedom fighters of 1776, who used muskets and mortars to send the British crown a message. "You comfortable Yankees cannot escape," the F.A.L.N note read.

No one today, not even George, would know that the Fraunces had ever been bombed. It has been fixed up and looks as good as old.

part two

—

Badlands

THE OUTER BOROUGHS

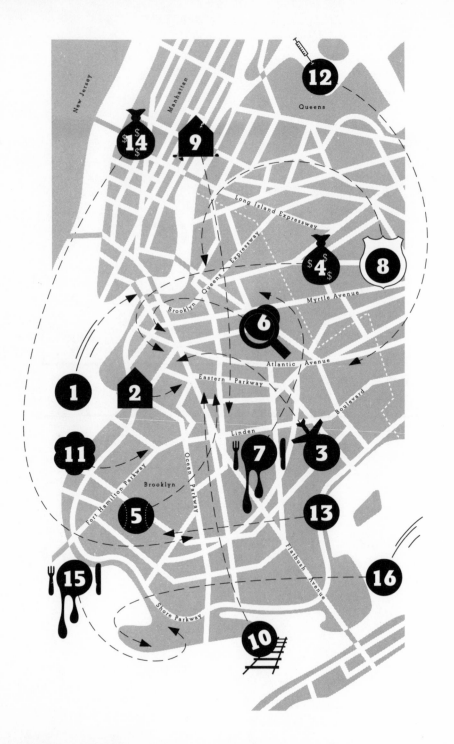

10

A Spree Grows in Brooklyn

BROOKLYN HAS ALWAYS BEEN KNOWN AS the City of Churches. Sort of warms the soul, no? Much better than, say, the City of Gangsters, or the City of Dead Gangsters, or the City of Dead Gangsters Blown Away on Every Corner.

The titans of organized crime—everyone from Al Capone to the boys from Murder Inc.—were born and, yes, educated in Brooklyn. Here is where they went to public school, where they learned to shoot bullets, where they dumped their first corpses before moving on to terrorize the rest of the world. Ah, the memories.

But Brooklyn isn't only about mobsters. As a city, it would be the fourth largest in the United States. "It'd take a guy a lifetime to know Brooklyn t'roo an' t'roo," wrote Thomas Wolfe in *Only the Dead Know Brooklyn*. "An' even den, you wouldn't know it all."

The borough features a dozen neighborhoods, everything from Coney Island to Borough Park to Bedford Stuyvesant, and dozens of ethnic groups, including blacks, Jews, Latinos, Italians, Irish— you name it. Everyone gets along well except, of course, for those rare moments when there's only one seat left on a crowded subway train.

Brooklyn Bridge

Some people look at the Brooklyn Bridge and write a poem, break out the watercolors, maybe pontificate about the miracle of modern architecture.

Not us. We think of all the people who died.

We think of John Roebling, the philosopher and engineer whose idea it was to build the spindly bridge. One afternoon a year before construction began, Roebling stood on the edge of a Brooklyn pier dreaming of when New Yorkers would be able to whisk across the East River without throwing up over the side of a boat.

Perhaps Roebling was distracted by his dream. He didn't notice a ferryboat docking right in front of him. Ouch. The boat crushed his right foot. John rushed home, where a team of doctors cut off his toes. It was painful, sure, but lockjaw and finally death took care of that.

Building the Brooklyn Bridge killed a lot of people, at least twenty by some counts, and injured plenty more. Some slipped off the towers; others were crushed by falling boulders. It was a lot of risk for a salary of $2 a day. Fortunately for those who today enjoy an exquisite backdrop for their daily traffic jam, enough men survived to finish the job.

After John Roebling died, the blueprints of the bridge were turned over to his son, Washington, who was 32 years old. Washington lived to see the bridge's completion, but when it came to medical matters his luck wasn't much better than his father's.

Junior took dozens of trips underwater in pressurized chambers to surpervise work on the bridge's foundation. Life at the river's bottom wasn't all that good for the stomach. Men came up vomiting, their lips blue, their heads pounding. Some just dropped dead. Others, including Washington, damaged their hearing, eyesight, and nerves. Washington spent the last twenty-five years of his life, including most of the time in which the bridge was being built, twitching in a rocking chair.

The bridge opened on May 24, 1883, and seven days later the city hosted a grand ribbon-cutting celebration. Twenty thousand New Yorkers crowded the bridge. The city was feeling mighty proud. No one knows how it happened, but suddenly the herd panicked (some perhaps thought the bridge was about to collapse; others may have been running to avoid a gang of pickpockets). Twelve people died in the stampede and thirty-five were hurt. One witness on the Manhattan shore, the future New York governor Al Smith, said the glorious blue sky was suddenly filled with hats and umbrellas fluttering into the river.

2

Capone
38 Garfield Place, Park Slope

Brooklyn residents don't have George Washington or Thomas Jefferson to boast about as native sons, but who needs ex-presidents—men who wore wigs, no less—when they have America's most famous gangster, Al Capone, instead.

Sure, Al made his name in Chicago in the 1920s, but he developed his considerable appetite for cash, silk pajamas, and bloodshed right here in the county of kings. "I'm no Italian," Al liked to boast. "I was born in Brooklyn."

That wasn't all. Brooklyn was where Al punched out his eighth-grade teacher, smoked his first cigar, and acquired the famous four-inch scar that stretched across his left cheek.

Capone liked to brag that he got the scar while fighting overseas during World War I. Nice story, but we wouldn't base a doctoral dissertation on the testimony of one Alphonse Capone.

The truth is that the scar was the handiwork of Frankie Gallucio, who slashed Capone with a knife at the old Harvard Inn, a Coney Island dance hall, after he said something less than charming about Frankie's sister. Capone held many grudges, but none toward Frankie. After he moved to Chicago, Al hired him as his driver at $100 a week.

A proper Capone tour of Brooklyn includes a stop at 38 Garfield Place, in a neighborhood called Park Slope. Eight-year-old Al and family moved into this two-story brick house in 1907, paying four dollars a month rent. Young Al attended PS 7 with other miniature criminals like Lucky Luciano.

The Irish kids called Al "Macaroni," but never to his face. After school, Al made a few bucks on the side, working as a clerk in a candy store at 305 Fifth Avenue in Brooklyn. He was also the neighborhood pool champion, cueing up nightly at a hall at 20 Garfield Place, a few yards from his home.

As a teenager, Al ran with the James Street gang, a kind of farm team for the Five Pointers, who were wreaking havoc in Lower Manhattan. In 1919, Capone became a suspect in a murder and fled to Chicago. Before leaving, he married a Brooklyn girl, Mae Coughlin, whose family lived in a three-story home, still standing, at 117 Third Place. They were wed at St. Mary Star of the Sea Church on Court Street, where Mae and her family were parishioners. It was a lovely ceremony, even if the best man wore brass knuckles.

In Chicago, Al became famous for ordering the St. Valentine's Day massacre, for feeding three traitors a sumptuous feast before bashing their heads in with a baseball bat, and for finally being sent to prison for income tax evasion in 1931. He was Public Enemy No. 1, but considering that he fed an entire city booze during Prohibition, no one was surprised that when he went to Comiskey Park for a White Sox game, the fans gave him a standing ovation.

There Goes the Neighborhood: Plane Crash in Park Slope
119 Sterling Place

No matter how bad the big city gets, take solace: at least you weren't hit by an airplane. The same can't be said for those who happened to pause at a certain Park Slope stop sign on the snowy morning of December 16, 1960.

One driver, seated behind the wheel of his delivery truck, felt a crunch. He looked out his window and saw that part of an airplane wing had just come to a crashing halt on his roof. The rest of the plane, a United Airlines DC-8, was a few yards away, having turned the Pillar of Fire church at 119 Sterling Place into an ash-filled crater, fifty feet wide and twenty-five feet deep.

New York City's worst airline disaster occurred when the United plane collided with a TWA Super-Constellation over Staten Island, killing 135 people, including six pedestrians and a motorist. The TWA plane crashed onto Miller Field on Staten Island.

One witness said the United jet looked like a "guided missile" as it nose-dived from the sky before flattening the Park Slope church. A housewife compared the sound of the impact to that of a "million dishes breaking at once." Two dozen parked cars and eleven other buildings were cremated in the inferno, along with a bakery, a funeral home, and several apartment houses. Nearby, three elementary schools survived unscathed, as did the children and teachers inside.

Out of the wreckage flew Stevie Baltz, an 11-year-old from Chicago, the only survivor onboard, his clothes in flames. He was thrown from the plane's tail, which was sitting in the middle of the intersection of Sterling Place and Seventh Avenue. Two cops threw their trenchcoats around him and rolled him in the snow to extinguish the fire.

It was Stevie's first trip on an airplane—he was traveling to see his aunt. At Brooklyn Methodist Hospital, he told nurses that he had been so excited he hadn't eaten breakfast. He was supposed to fly two days earlier, but a sore throat had kept him at home. Nine doctors tried to save Stevie, but twenty-six hours after the crash the boy died in his sleep. The 55 cents he had in his pocket was donated by his father to the hospital's poor box.

Where the Money Was: Willie Sutton
340 Dean Street

Willie Sutton lived a long life of crime, but he did have his reasons, not the least of which was that he liked having afternoons off. "Why did I rob banks?" Willie once asked. "Because I enjoyed it. I loved it. I was more alive when I was inside a bank, robbing it, than at any other time in my life."

No wonder there was never a Mrs. Willie Sutton.

Like Al Capone, Willie the Actor learned his crooked ways in Brooklyn, growing up at 183 and then 227 High Street. Home was a fountain of inspiration for Willie's education as a thief. His first crime victim was his grandfather, from whom he stole a quarter when he was ten years old. Willie cried from guilt afterward, but the tears soon dried and two years later, he stole another quarter, this time from his teacher at PS 5, Mrs. Grilli.

Willie eventually graduated to bigger paydays, ripping off twenty banks for $2 million by the end of his life. Still, it was difficult to dislike him. Willie had such style, showing up for bank jobs in a dapper mustache and a street messenger's uniform so as to seem harmless. He deplored violence, never firing a gun and always allowing his captives to use the bathroom. Once, Willie told bank employees not to worry about the stolen cash. "The insurance will cover this," he said, walking out the door.

Besides robbing banks, Willie also had a talent for breaking out of prison. He escaped three times, including once from Sing Sing's vaunted escape-proof cell in 1932. It's an accomplishment he details with charts and considerable pride in his autobiography, *Where the Money Was.*

Sutton's last robbery, at a Manufacturers Hanover Trust branch at 47-11 Queens Boulevard in 1950, was classic Willie. After a month of surveillance, of studying the employees' daily habits (including the fact that the guard unlocked the front door at 8:30 each morning), Willie busted in and lifted $63,000. No one was hurt, of course, although a few of the employees did cry.

Willie hid from the law in a room at 340 Dean Street in Park Slope, where he kept a shot glass on the bureau and books by his bed, including the scintillating tome, *How to Think Ahead in Chess.* The apartment was three blocks from Brooklyn police headquarters.

One afternoon in 1952, nearly two years after the Manufacturers robbery, two officers approached Willie while he tinkered in front of his building with his Chevy. They had a question. "Am I Willie Sutton?" Willie repeated increduously. "Hell no. My name's . . . Gordon—yes, Charles Gordon."

It was a valiant try for freedom, but soon the courts returned Willie to prison. He had been pointed out to police by Arnold Schuster, a 24-year-old Brooklyn resident who saw him on the subway one afternoon and followed him home. Such bravery earned Arnold an early grave and no doubt scared off New Yorkers from assisting criminal investigations in the future. Schuster was shot dead on March 8, 1952, three weeks after fingering Sutton. Mobologists say that Albert Anastasia ordered the shooting after he saw Schuster on television bragging about Willie's capture. "I can't stand squealers!" an angry Albert was supposed to have screamed at his TV.

Sutton's final robbery cost him a life sentence. This time, he did not try to bolt. He grew old and sickly and was finally paroled on Christmas Eve, 1969. As he himself noted ruefully, he had spent nearly half his life in prison, on parole, or on the run. Broke, he was now forced to go on welfare, tapping $78 a month before dying in Florida in 1980. His body was returned home to Brooklyn. Holy Cross Cemetery was one place from which Willie couldn't escape.

5

Home of Dem Bums
Ebbets Field, Bedford Avenue, Flatbush

If Brooklyn ever had a heart, it was the Brooklyn Dodgers, which might explain why many New Yorkers are quite comfortable comparing the team's owner, Walter O'Malley, to a mass murderer.

Nice move, Wally, shutting down Ebbets Field in 1957 and transplanting Brooklyn's heart to Los Angeles. All for a lousy buck.

Thousands stood on Bedford Avenue one afternoon in 1960 and watched a crane tear down the stadium. "Brooklyn died that day," Dodger pitcher Johnny Podres said. O'Malley was universally condemned, and journalists Pete Hamill and Jack Newfield called him the third worst villain of the twentieth century—behind Hitler and Stalin, of course.

The Dodgers were as Brooklyn as a mob shooting. Babe Ruth wore a uniform here, as did Casey Stengel, who once doffed his cap to the fans only to reveal a sparrow nesting on his head. Jackie Robinson broke baseball's color line in Brooklyn, and the Duke of Flatbush, Duke Snyder, hit many a home run into the streets where he and the other Dodgers lived.

None of this evidently meant much to O'Malley, who never seemed to have much affection for the antiquated, cramped charm of Brooklyn (translation: not enough parking space to accommodate the suburban fans). The Dodgers played their last game at Ebbets Field on September 24, 1957, defeating the Pittsburgh Pirates, 2–0. Gladys Goodding, the stadium's organist, played a few sad ballads, including "Am I Blue" and "After You've Gone."

The stadium, built in 1913, was replaced by a 1,327-unit public housing complex bounded by Bedford Avenue, Montgomery Street, McKeever Place, and Sullivan Place, near the Brooklyn Museum. The complex is named the Jackie Robinson Apartments.

6

The Russians Are Coming (In Fact, They're Next Door)
252 Fulton Street, Brooklyn Heights

The FBI was mighty proud when it arrested a Soviet spy living in an apartment building on tranquil Fulton Street in 1957. They were G-men coming to their country's rescue. It's enough to send patriotic shivers down your spine, except in New York, where people only get the shivers if they walk down the street alone.

In other words, most of the city, including the spy's neighbors, were not terribly upset to learn that Rudolf Ivanovich Abel of 252 Fulton Street was gainfully employed by the KGB. Rudolf, his nose long, his lips thin, always claimed he worked in a photographic darkroom. Actually he was a Soviet colonel who spoke fluent English with a fake German accent and traveled under the alias Emil R. Goldfus.

Investigators knocked on his door after another Soviet spy defected and ratted on him. G-men searching his apartment found shortwave radios concealed behind shelves crammed with books by Einstein, his favorite author, and classics in four languages. They also discovered hollowed-out coins, cuff links used to hide microfilm defense data, and a half-eaten cheese sandwich.

Five months later, Abel, then 62 years old, was sentenced to thirty years in a New York state prison for "conspiracy to commit military and atomic espionage." The Soviet press denounced the case as a hoax, or, as they put it, "low-brow crime fiction." The CIA swapped Abel for Gary

Powers, the American U-2 pilot who fell from Communist skies in May 1961 and was taken prisoner. Abel was returned to the Soviet Union the next year. He died in 1971.

Ashes to Ashes
205 Knickerbocker Avenue, Bushwick

Sure, Carmine Galante was a mob boss. Sure, he got rich selling heroin and killing people.

But say this about him: the man had a mighty set of teeth.

No matter how many bullets tore through his chest one afternoon in 1979, Carmine refused to let a lit stogie slip from his bloodstained lips. Even after he died.

It was a Herculean performance in the annals of the mob, where death usually requires gangsters to drop everything. Still, most found Carmine's fate fitting, particularly because he was known in mob circles as "The Cigar."

Galante was a man of many pleasures. He loved opera, jogging, and could quote Descartes, Plato, and Saint Augustine. He enjoyed playing handball, squeezing the tomatoes at Balducci's, and walking the streets of Little Italy, allowing old friends to kiss his hand.

Carmine was someone New Yorkers could be ashamed of from the beginning. Indeed, some swear that when the doctor slapped him on the behind in the maternity ward in 1910, baby Carmine smacked him back. He was off to reform school when he was nine years old, which was fine preparation for jail when he was 17. Later, he went to work for mob chief Vito Genovese and was arrested for shooting a cop. Carmine's biggest assignment, or so police believe, was murdering Carlo Tresca, the Anarchist newspaper editor, in 1943.

Carmine was rewarded for his treachery, rising in the mob hierarchy until he controlled a multimillion-dollar heroin and racketeering empire. Life was good, except that he kept having this urge to wipe out the competition, including the venerable don Carlo Gambino, the mob's patron saint of drug-free crime. Carlo died quite peacefully in 1976, but the mob was fed up with Galante's threats. A meeting of the bosses was called and a decision was reached: it was time to put out the cigar.

On July 13, 1979, Galante ate lunch at Joe & Mary's on Knickerbocker Avenue in Bushwick, now a Chinese take-out restaurant. Carmine's cousin Joe Turano owned the country-style restaurant, which had yellow curtains, flowered tablecloths, and a picture of the Last Supper hanging inside the front door. Out back was a sunny patio with round tables and a vegetable garden.

Galante, wearing a crisp white shirt unbuttoned at the neck, took a table on the patio with three associates, who kept fidgeting and getting up to make phone calls. They toasted Turano's upcoming trip to Italy, munched lettuce and fresh tomatoes, and soaked up the sun.

Shortly before 3 P.M., three men wearing ski masks darted into the restaurant. From a distance of six feet, they fired double-barrel shotguns at Galante's chest. Minutes later, the cops found Carmine on his back, blood dripping from his left eye, the stogie in his mouth, his hand raised to ward off the bullets. Nice try, Carmine. The flies swirled around his head.

New York's Roman Catholic archbishop, Terence Cardinal Cooke, refused Galante's family a funeral mass, noting that church law defines both gangsters and unfaithful husbands as "public sinners." Still, fifty mourners, including lawyer Roy Cohn and lots of elderly women wearing sunglasses, showed up at a service for Carmine at the Provenzano Funeral Home at 43 Second Avenue. Galante was buried in St. John's Cemetery in Queens, apparently without his cigar.

8

Serpico
778 Driggs Avenue

Detective Frank Serpico was a maverick cop. For one thing, he wore a beard and a leather vest and lived in Greenwich Village.

For another, he was honest.

It was an attribute frowned upon by many in the police department in the late 1960s, when patrolmen and detectives were supplementing their incomes with payoffs from drug dealers and pimps. Once, Serpico said, a sergeant handed him an envelope stuffed with $300. Serpico refused the offer and watched as the sarge pocketed the cash.

From 1967 to 1969, Serpico tried to convince the department to investigate corrupt cops, including a Bronx division that was collecting $800 a month from a gambling operation. Nine cops were eventually indicted, but Serpico wasn't satisfied because those sent to jail didn't include any officers of rank.

One top police official, a captain in charge of anticorruption investigations, warned Frank he could end up "face down in the river" if he pursued his crusade. Jay Kriegel, a top aide to then-mayor John Lindsay, also listened to Frank's stories. Kriegel relayed Serpico's charges to Lindsay, who refused to look into them. The mayor understood that challenging the New York City Police Department wasn't the best way to advance his political fortunes.

Serpico became known in station houses across the city as the cop who wouldn't take. Officers feared and loathed him. He could send them to jail. One cop pulled a knife on Serpico in a station house, but Frank countered by knocking the knife away and putting a gun to the cop's head.

It wasn't until just before the *New York Times* spread Serpico's charges across its front page in 1970—the headline read GRAFT PAID TO POLICE HERE SAID TO RUN IN MILLIONS—that Lindsay sprang into action. He created the Knapp Commission, which investigated corruption in the NYPD and led to a massive shake-up and restructuring of the department.

Serpico would testify before the commission, but he nearly died before he got there. On February 3, 1971, Frank and three other detectives staked out a heroin dealer at 778 Driggs Street in Williamsburg. It was decided among the officers that Serpico, who didn't look like a cop in his beard and fatigue jacket, would knock on the dealer's door, apartment 3G. It was just after 10 P.M.

Moments later, he was flat on his back in the hallway, blood gushing out of his cheek. The gun had appeared suddenly, in the darkness of a slightly opened door, the bullet shattering the left side of Frank's face.

Serpico was barely conscious at the hospital, but he could see Mayor

Lindsay standing over his bed. Frank was bitter. Here was the man whose attention he had wanted for months. Lindsay smiled. The mayor said the whole city was proud of Frank's bravery.

In the hospital, Serpico received mail from cops, including one card that had a printed greeting, "Recuperate Quickly"—except "Recuperate" was crossed out and replaced with scribble that said "Die." Another card said: "With sincere sympathy . . . that you didn't get your brains blown out, you rat bastard. Happy Relapse."

Eleven months later, on December 15, 1971, Serpico told his story to the Knapp Commission. He said that the country's greatest police force suffered from cancerous corruption. A retired deputy police commissioner, Joseph Walsh, testified that he knew about Serpico's allegations but hadn't ordered an investigation because the matter "left my mind."

Soon after, Serpico quit the force and left the country, moving to Europe, where he stayed for more than ten years before returning to New York and living on Long Island.

Love Thy Neighbor (Except If It's You-Know-Who)
320 Sterling Street, Crown Heights

New Yorkers may hate rats, cockroaches, and anyone who plays for the Boston Red Sox.

But no one is worse than a lousy landlord.

The folks over at housing court came up with a solution: make the suckers live in what they own.

In 1988, Morris Gross owned 320 Sterling Street, a crumbling tenement with far more code violations than tenants—four hundred points of blight in all, according to the city Buildings Department. Aside from the rodents, the building's residents had to contend with no heat, flooding, and roaches and mice. Lovely.

The tenants took Morris to housing court, known among regulars as "The Zoo," where a judge found him guilty of negligence. No need to send him to prison, though. Instead, the judge sentenced Morris to what he deserved: fifteen days in a third-floor apartment at—where else?—320 Sterling Street.

Two city marshals delivered Morris, then 76, to the building on February 12th. The tenants gave him quite a greeting, cursing him and holding up signs, one of which read, "Welcome, You Reptile."

Morris took care of old number one, though. Before his arrest, he had his third-floor apartment repainted, exterminated, and furnished with a queen-size couch. He also installed a reclining chair. When he rested his feet, he could see his electronic ankle bracelet, there to help court officials keep track of his movements.

Gross's sentence ended after the eighth day when he agreed in writing to spend thousands of dollars on repairs to the rest of the building. He was the first—but not the last—landlord who was humliated by having to live like one of his tenants.

Off the Beaten Track
Empire Boulevard, Flatbush

In the winter of 1918, the men who ran the old Brooklyn Rapid Transit Company were at war with striking employees over wages. The impasse created a host of problems, not the least of which was finding workers to replace motormen who had walked off the job.

Soon enough, the bosses, whose motto was "Safety First," found a solution. They ordered untrained workers to start piloting the abandoned trains. Those who refused would be suspended or fired on the spot.

Eddie Luciano, a 23-year-old dispatcher, had only two hours of motorman training, which, according to the bosses, made him the perfect choice to steer a train. Eddie wasn't in a position to say no. His three-year-old daughter had just died of influenza, leaving him in debt to a hospital and funeral home.

As darkness fell on a chilly November 1st, the stationmaster yelled, "Take her out quick, you're five minutes late." Eddie, tired after ten hours of dispatching work, pulled down the wood controller stick, lurching the train and its 1,000-odd passengers across the Brooklyn Bridge toward Brooklyn on the winding Brighton Beach line.

Luciano quickly realized he couldn't maneuver the train's braking system. The train overshot the end of the first station platform, and the second, by several cars. More than half the passengers got up and left the train.

Eddie lost control as he entered a tunnel leading to the Malbone Street stop in Flatbush. A woman rapped on his door, begging him to slow down. He was traveling 45 miles per hour in a 6-miles-per-hour zone. Suddenly, the train derailed.

Riders screamed as the first car splintered down the center and the second crinkled as easily as tinfoil. Many were hurled like rag dolls against the tunnel's concrete wall, while others were crushed in their seats. Minutes later, two dozen dazed survivors were electrocuted as workers at a BRT power station, unaware of the derailment, reactivated the third rail.

For the rest of the night, rescue workers laid out ninety-seven corpses in rows at the Snyder Avenue police station and in the lobby of Ebbets Field three blocks away. The workers used sheets, suit jackets, and even businessmen's hats to cover the victims' faces. More than two hundred of the wounded were taken in cars and ambulances to Brooklyn hospitals.

Luciano and the management of BRT were charged with manslaughter. Eddie insisted the brakes failed, but his bosses called him incompetent. After six months of legal fireworks, everyone was acquitted. The railroad was forced to install automatic trippers in the tracks, which are designed to slow runaway trains and are still used today. As for the Malbone stop, it was renamed Empire Boulevard to help commuters forget the crash.

11

Frankie Yale
923 44th Street, Borough Park

Oh, how we love a mob funeral! It's almost as good as a mob shooting. The flowers are beautiful, the suits are stylish, and it's always fun to see grown men with guns cry like babies.

New York City's first great mob funeral was in 1928. The honoree was Frankie Yale, an expert in burying bodies not only because he was an accomplished triggerman and bootlegger, but also because he was an undertaker, with a shop at 6604 14th Avenue.

Frankie's $52,000 funeral was more than an occasion for mourning. It was fine entertainment for the whole family, drawing thousands of spectators, who leaned out windows, climped up lampposts, and perched on one another's shoulders for a peak at the silent, slow-motion procession through the streets of Brooklyn.

Frankie was a big man in Brooklyn even before he died, having owned the Yale Cigar Manufacturing Company at 6309 New Utrecht Avenue. He liked looking at all those packages of cigars, especially since each one bore a picture of his mug on the front.

Frankie was also instrumental in helping along Al Capone's budding gangster career, hiring Al as a bouncer at a brothel on Coney Island. Capone later returned the favor by hiring Frankie to kill his enemies in Chicago, Big Jim Colosimo and Dion O'Banion. Yale gunned down O'Banion in a flower shop in one of the more famous mob shootings of the 1920s. O'Banion's funeral cost thousands and was so impressive that Frankie told friends he wanted something similar for himself.

Capone, eventually angry at Yale for hijacking his liquor trucks, did everything he could to help him get it. In 1928, Al paid four men to murder Frankie as he drove through Brooklyn in his new Lincoln. They shot Frankie seconds before he crashed into the stoop of 923 44th Street and ran over the tulips in Sol and Bertha Kaufman's garden.

Frankie's death was a sad moment for his family, including the two women who claimed to be Mrs. Yale. No expense was spared for his funeral, which started out at St. Rosalia's Church (still at 6301 14th Avenue) and ended several miles away at Holy Cross Cemetery. The nickel and silver casket cost $15,000 and was trailed to the grave by 38 carloads of flowers and 250 cars. The $37,000 floral display was especially impressive, particularly the huge clock made of blue and white violets. The flowery hands were set at 4:10 P.M., the moment at which Frankie became plant food.

It was just as Frankie would have wanted it. Too bad he couldn't have been there. Even the *Daily News* boasted that the funeral was "a better one than that given Dion O'Banion."

Palm Sunday Massacre
1080 Liberty Avenue, East New York

The apartment looked like a wax museum. The victims, eight of them children, had been cut down in mid-motion. A woman seated on a living room couch held a pudding dish in one hand, a spoon in the other. Blood trickled down the center of her forehead.

The Palm Sunday massacre of April 15, 1984, was one of the most gruesome anyone in the city could remember. Ten people, all of them between the ages of 3 and 24, were shot dead in a two-story house at 1080 Liberty Avenue.

The house was owned by Enrique Bermudez, a convicted drug dealer, who was not home when the attack occurred. Bermudez and a neighborhood baker, Carmine Rossi, found the bodies, most of them draped over couches and chairs in the living room in front of a flickering television set.

Among the dead was Bermudez's girlfriend, a 24-year-old who was six months pregnant. The only survivor was an 11-month-old baby who Rossi found crying and crawling among the dead.

Detectives discovered drug paraphernalia in the apartment and immediately suspected a revenge attack against Bermudez by a past drug partner. Two months later, Christopher Thomas, 34, of the Bronx, was arrested for the murders, but the police said drugs were not the motive. Thomas, the cops claimed, suspected that Bermudez was having an affair with his wife. Thomas was found guilty the following year.

13

Yusuf Hawkins
2007 Bay Ridge Avenue, Bensonhurst

They traveled to Bensonhurst to shop for a used car, four black teenagers from East New York stepping over the line into a white neighborhood. It was a risk 16-year-old Yusuf Hawkins wouldn't survive, not in the racially divided New York of 1989. Hawkins was surrounded by a mob of angry whites and shot twice in the chest simply because he was black.

Hawkins' death was the city's shame, provoking angry marches by thousands of blacks through Bensonhurst, with whites from the neighborhood responding by waving watermelons and shouting, "Nigger, go home!"

Yusuf's East New York, once the neighborhood of poor Jews and Italians, had become by the 1980s the tattered turf of poor blacks, crowded into sagging tenements, public housing, and crumbling public schools. Many youngsters turned to the big-money business of drug dealing, but not Yusuf, an honors student in junior high who had plans of becoming an engineer.

On the night of August 23, 1989, Yusuf and several friends watched *Mississippi Burning,* a film about the racist South of the 1960s that features scenes of blacks being lynched by the Ku Klux Klan. Afterward, Troy Banner suggested they check out a used car for sale in Bensonhurst, ten miles away. Everyone agreed, including Yusuf and Luther Sylvester, who happened to be related to one of the blacks who was with Michael Griffith the night in 1986 when he was beaten and killed by a mob of whites in Howard Beach.

As Yusuf and his friends rode the N train from East New York, a gang of whites assembled in front of 6801 20th Avenue, near 68th Street in Bensonhurst, where middle-class Italians lived in neatly kept brick-faced homes, the entrances decorated with foot-high religious statues. The neighborhood was also known for housing its share of middle-level Mafia soldiers. A store on 18th Avenue called itself "Wiseguys Formal Wear."

The white gang was a tough-talking crowd, foul-mouthed, muscled, and wearing short haircuts. One, Keith Mondello, 18, spoke angrily about a 20th Avenue girl who had rejected him for a black man. Gina Feliciano, celebrating her 18th birthday that night, had warned Keith several hours earlier that her new boyfriend was coming to the neighborhood to beat him up. Keith and ten to twenty friends were ready, some of them carrying baseball bats and golf clubs. One of those tagging along, Joey Fama, 18, who has the IQ of a fifth-grader, was holding a gun.

Just before 9:20 P.M., the gang spotted Yusuf and his friends walking south along 20th Avenue, heading for 1965 Bay Ridge Avenue, the home of the man who advertised the used $900 blue Pontiac. The whites were certain these were the blacks they were waiting for. Someone in the gang, according to the police, was overheard saying, "Let's club the fucking nigger." Another said, "No, let's not club, let's shoot one."

Yusuf and his friends were surrounded in front of 2007 Bay Ridge Avenue. Suddenly, a blue flash lit the night and Yusuf was on his back, a half-eaten Snickers bar in his hand, two bullet holes in his chest. He died shortly afterward at Maimonides Hospital. Within hours, the police had grabbed four of the gang, including Mondello; Pasquale Raucci, 19; Steven Curreri, 18; Charles Stressler, 21; and James Patino, 24. A week later, the alleged triggerman, Joey Fama, surrendered at a police station in Oneonta, New York.

Hawkins' death occurred at the tail end of the 1989 mayoral campaign and is widely seen as the final nail in Ed Koch's political coffin. Within twenty-four hours of the shooting, David Dinkins, a black mayoral candidate, called the murder a "lynching" and said "the tone and climate of the city does get set at City Hall." Candidate Dinkins said: "This could happen to any person of color. Even me."

Politics spilled over to Hawkins' funeral, held at the Glover Memorial Baptist Church on Dean Street. The service was attended by Spike Lee, the Rev. Louis Farrakhan, and the Rev. Al Sharpton, as well as Governor Mario Cuomo, Koch, Dinkins, and several other candidates running for mayor, including Rudolph Giuliani. The pols, with the exception of Dinkins, were booed and taunted by the crowds outside. "I don't know who shot Yusuf, but the system loaded the gun," Sharpton said before Hawkins was buried at Evergreen Cemetery.

Ten months later, following a bitter trial, Fama and Mondello were convicted of murder and inciting to riot, respectively. Both got maximum prison terms: Fama, thirty-two years; Mondello, a minimum of five. Many blacks felt Mondello got off easy, considering that he boasted—but later denied—that he was the leader of the gang. After the Mondello verdict, hundreds of blacks marched through Brooklyn, some throwing rocks, others chanting, "Burn Bensonhurst."

In time, the rage quieted, but not before more blood was shed, the victim this time being none other than Sharpton. The Reverend was stabbed January 12, 1991, by an unemployed construction worker in the playground of PS 205 at 70th Street and 20th Avenue, just before he was to lead his twenty-ninth protest march past the spot where Hawkins was slain. It was the same playground where the police found the baseball bats swung by the Mondello gang.

Sharpton's supporters, including Yusuf's father, Moses, screamed as Sharpton sank to his knees, bleeding from the stab wound next to his donut-sized medallion of Martin Luther King Jr. Sharpton rode in a friend's car to Coney Island Hospital, where doctors stitched up the wound. The next morning, after a visit by Mayor Dinkins and Jesse Jackson, Sharpton tried a new tack: he issued an appeal for calm.

14

Dog Day Afternoon: The Robbery
450 Avenue P, Bensonhurst

Movies and television may be the way most Americans stay entertained. New Yorkers just walk outside.

Those in the vicinity of 450 Avenue P one summer afternoon in 1972 were treated to a fourteen-hour drama that featured a gunman seizing eight hostages in a desperate plot to raise money to pay for a sex-change operation for his male lover.

Bravo! cheered the three thousand spectators camped outside. They were particularly entertained when the gunman, John Wojtowicz, 28 years old, ordered pizza and tossed dozens of dollar bills at the delivery man. Not so happy were the cops and FBI, holed up in a barbershop across the street that featured a phone with a sign: MAYOR'S HOT LINE.

Wojtowicz, a former Chase bankteller, lived in Greenwich Village, at 250 West 10th Street, a boarding house frequented by gays and known as "Boys Town." He was estranged from his wife and two children, but in love with a man named Ernest, whom he had married in a Village bar. John's friends told reporters during the holdup that Ernest had worn a wedding dress to the ceremony. Two months later, though, they had split up. Now, John hoped to win Ernest back by paying for a sex change.

John and Sal, a petty thief, burst into the bank at 2:50 P.M. and, with their guns drawn, ordered a teller to load up a bag with cash. The duo was just about to leave with $29,000 in bills and $175,170 in traveler's checks when they noticed a police car outside. Suddenly, their plans changed.

They sealed off the bank and announced that no one, not any of the seven women or one man still inside, could leave. The hostages were allowed to use the bathroom and telephone whenever they wanted. At one point, John left five of the women alone with a shotgun, but none grabbed it because, they admitted later, they didn't know how to shoot. All in all, it wasn't so bad. One hostage later told a reporter, "It was like a party."

The crowd outside the bank included Wojtowicz's mother, his shrink, and several male friends who were escorted to the bank's door, where they hugged and kissed John to the cheers of the crowd. John made himself available for telephone interviews with several reporters, telling one that the Supreme Court was "stupid" for overturning the death penalty because it might have dissuaded him from holding up the bank. He also said, "I'm more nervous than the hostages."

The gunman and the police struck a deal. Wojtowicz agreed to give up the hostages in exchange for an airplane. He would not say where he planned to fly. It didn't matter. The FBI wasn't going to let him get off the ground.

Long past midnight, nearly fourteen hours after the siege began, police sharpshooters wearing bulletproof vests took their places on the rooftops and started moving in on the entrance to the bank. Finally, at ten minutes of four, John, Sal, and the hostages emerged from the bank and everyone climbed into a van. Before leaving, John released one more hostage who wasn't feeling well. An FBI agent, frisked before he climbed behind the wheel, drove them to Kennedy Airport.

The agent stopped on runway 22-R, where a two-engine Hansa jet was waiting. As John and the hostages climbed out, the agent grabbed a pistol from a secret compartment, spun around, and shot Sal in the chest. Wojtowicz immediately surrendered.

John was charged with bank robbery, armed robbery, and abduction. He was freed from a Connecticut prison in 1979 after serving less than half of his twenty-year sentence. He collected $7,500 from the makers of the film *Dog Day Afternoon*, $2,500 of which he gave to Ernest for her operation. Elizabeth Debbie Eden, formerly Ernest Aaron, died of AIDS in a Rochester hospital in 1987.

15

Last Supper for Joe the Boss
2715 West 15th Street, Coney Island

The alibi has always been essential to mob life. Listen to Al Capone, for example, the day after his men pulled off the St. Valentine's Day massacre, perhaps the bloodiest hit in mob history: "What do I know?" a suntanned Al shrugged to the cops. "I was in Florida."

Our favorite alibi was delivered by the gangster Lucky Luciano, after the police asked him if he had anything to do with the slaying of Joe "The Boss" Masseria. It was a reasonable question since Lucky was dining with Joe when he was blown away.

Well, not exactly, claimed the Luck, who was one of Joe's top aides. "I was in the can taking a leak," Luciano told the cops. "I always take a long leak."

Luciano and Joe the Boss had been eating with Masseria at Nuova Villa Tammaro, at 2715 West 15th Street in Coney Island. Masseria was the biggest mobster in the city at the time, a bootlegger who drove a steel-plated bulletproof limo with windows one-inch thick.

Joe needed all the protection he could get. In 1922, a gunman chased Joe into a flower shop at 82 Second Avenue and fired three shots, each one

missing Joe as he tiptoed through the tulips. Masseria emerged from the
shooting with two holes in his straw hat and a reputation for dodging bullets.

Most bullets, that is.

Luciano was not happy being Joe's assistant, especially since he considered Masseria to be an idiot. Joe didn't think it was right, for example,
for Italian mobsters to mix with Jews or to bribe politicians—acts Joe
described as "sleeping with the enemy."

Luciano invited Joe for a lunch at Nuova Villa Tammaro on April 15,
1931. The men ordered the rub-out special—fish and pasta—and drank
Chianti. They played cards after the meal, while the restaurant's owner,
Gerardo Scarpato, decided it was time to take a walk.

At 3:30 P.M., Lucky said he had to go to the bathroom. In the next
instant, four men with machine guns—Joe Adonis, Vito Genovese, Albert
Anastasia, and Bugsy Siegel—walked into the restaurant and began firing
at Joe's back. Joe was splattered over the table, all flesh and blood and
wine. A reporter at the time noted that Joe the Boss was left "with five
bullets in his back and an ace of diamonds in his hand" (actually, judging
from the photograph, it was an ace of spades, but who's counting).

Immediately after the killing, Gerardo Scarpato asked police detectives
to take his fingerprints so that if anything happened to him they could
identify his corpse. "Take them for your books; you will need them,"
Gerardo said. "I may be next."

The cops thought Gerardo was paranoid, but eighteen months later
they found his body sewn into a burlap sack in the backseat of a car in
front of 216 Windsor Place. Freshly tattooed on his shoulder was *Scarpato*. Nuova Villa Tammaro is now the General Iron Corporation, but the
owner, a guy named Mario, has preserved the original exterior of Scarpato's restaurant—a tan stone Florentine look with triple arched windows—and pasted it on to a drab modern-day factory.

16

Last Night at the Half Moon Hotel
29th Street on the Boardwalk, Coney Island

Somewhere over Brooklyn flies the spirit of Abe "Kid Twist" Reles, a gangster turned to stardust, mocking every cop or prosecutor who ever thought they had a case.

Kid Twist is floating above Coney Island and Brownsville and East New York, the mobster with the fat lips, the original stool pigeon, the mad gunner for Murder Inc. who once compared a career devoted to the disposal of men to that of being an attorney.

"You get used to it," Reles said.

The prosecutors hoisted Abe like a trophy in 1940. He was the first great rat, a Joe Valachi or Henry Hill, with a song to scare every mobster in the land. A year later, the suits were hanging their heads after Abe, under 24-hour police guard, fell or was pushed out of a sixth-floor window at the Half Moon Hotel. It was the thud heard around the mob world, a mystery for the ages, a sweet lullaby for all gangsters to fall asleep by.

Abe with the billy-club fingers and the flat nose was a Brownsville delicacy. He killed anyone, anywhere, at any time. All you had to do was ask. Cash, too, never hurt, because Abe liked to flash his fat roll, the top bill a grand, everything beneath it a single dollar. Little Abe was weaned on the gun, but he learned that the ice pick and gasoline could get the job done, too. "All cops are yellow and I'll fight any single one with guns, knives, or broken glass," he once boasted.

The Murder Inc. gang, so named by journalist Harry Feeney, was a Jewish bunch, the Kosher Nostra, who attended bar mitzvahs, seders, and brisses when they weren't strangling their enemies or setting them on fire. They spent their afternoons and nights at Midnight Rose's, a candy store at the intersection of Saratoga and Livonia, a corner that was then and is now a crossroads of the criminal world.

Here among the egg creams and twisted pretzels, Abe and the boys would wait for the call, orders from mob bosses sequestered in fancier apartments high above Manhattan. The top dogs themselves never telephoned, but they would send the message out, and sooner or later the bell would ring at Midnight Rose's.

Maybe they would ask for Dasher Abbandando, his legs spinning like windmills, or Happy Maione, his mug so mean that people pulled down the shades or looked the other way when he walked by. Often they would call on Pittsburgh Phil with his two-tone shoes, the gang's most prolific and eager killer. Phil, whose real name was Harry Strauss, stabbed Whitey Rudnick sixty-three times in the chest and neck before he got around to strangulation. "Like a ballplayer, that's me," Phil said at the beginning of his career. "I figure I get seasoning doing these jobs here, somebody from one of the big mobs spots me, then, up to the big leagues."

For ten years they ruled Brownsville and earned wads of dough carrying out murder contracts, maybe as many as two hundred across the country. They were true Brooklyn boys, Abe living at 427 Van Siclen Avenue, Pittsburgh Phil at 574 Vermont, and Dasher over at 2050 Fulton Street.

The 1930s belonged to Abe and the boys, until District Attorney William O'Dwyer and the cops began hauling them in on suspicion of murder. Reles felt the law closing in, as did his pregnant wife, who screamed that he wouldn't be around to meet his newborn. Abe decided it was time to save his hide and have a chat with the district attorney.

O'Dywer put Reles on the stand and, as prosecutor Burton Turkus wrote in *Murder Inc.*, he became a "Victrola with kinky hair." The newspapers noted that Abe said "dese" and "dose" when he meant "these" and "those," and that one afternoon on the stand, he smiled and slipped his hand around his own throat to answer a judge's question about how he killed a man. The evidence was damning enough to send Lepke and Happy Maione and Dasher and Pittsburgh Phil to the chair. Phil, of course, tried to find a way out, at one point feigning insanity by chewing on his lawyer's briefcase.

The prosecutors had everyone they wanted, everyone except Albert Anastasia, who was seen as Murder Inc.'s overlord. Pending Abe's testimony against Anastasia, they locked Reles up at the Half Moon Hotel in Coney Island, a resort for working stiffs who couldn't afford Atlantic City or the Catskills or Miami Beach. A squadron of cops sealed off a wing of the sixth floor with steel doors. A detective was supposed to sleep in a chair a few feet from the Kid while he snored in room 623. Five more cops were supposed to be in the next room.

On the morning of November 12, 1941, a detective said he awakened to find Abe's bed empty. He looked out the window and saw the dead songbird forty feet below. A white sheet wrapped around a wire dangled from the window. Abe's fleshy face looked like a badly folded napkin, all creases and puffiness and blood. The cops were demoted, the prosecutors shamed. Anastasia was a free man, and for years senators and congressman and other good citizens held hearings and issued subpeonas but still could not figure out how Abe Reles ended up the canary who could sing but not fly.

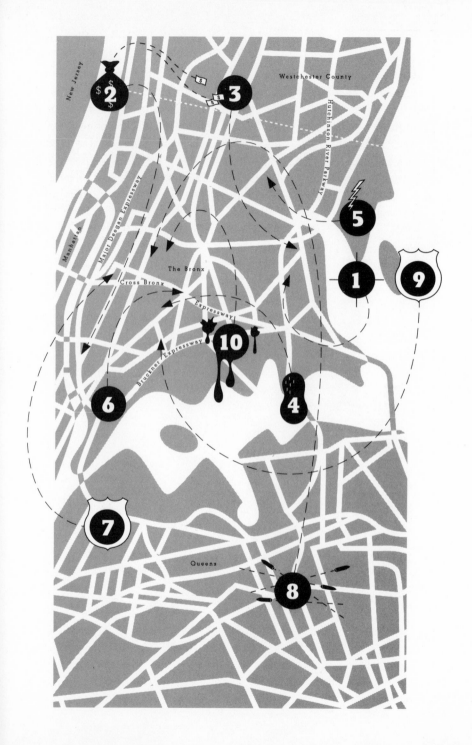

11

The Bang-Bang Borough

The Bronx

SHHH. RESIDENTS OF THE BRONX ARE very sensitive about their borough's murderous reputation. They think of the Bronx as a peaceful hamlet, just north of Manhattan. That's fine, but let us mention one fact at this juncture:

Son of Sam got his start here.

Yes, we know, one serial killer a borough does not make, but consider this: we once saw a group of children playing soccer on a Bronx street, only that was no ball they were kicking around.

It was a human skull.

Did someone say *hamlet?* Did someone say *peaceful?*

Welcome to the Bronx, the bang-bang borough, the borough that never sleeps —because it's too frightened.

Son of Sam: The Tour
2860 Buhre Avenue

California may have Charles Manson, and New England the Boston Strangler, but when it comes to serial killers, New York can compete with the best of them.

Son of Sam. Need we say more?

David Berkowitz, a 24-year-old bar mitzvah boy from Yonkers, liked to shoot pretty young women with long hair. He said a 6,000-year-old demon named Sam told him to. Sam, David insisted, spoke to him through a variety of barking black dogs.

Over the course of a year, Berkowitz killed six people, five of them women, and wounded seven others. He struck eight times in three different boroughs, first in the Bronx, then in Queens, and last in Brooklyn.

New Yorkers were terrified. Parents wouldn't allow their daughters to leave home on weekend nights, Berkowitz's favorite time to attack. Some women wore their hair up or hidden beneath hats. Others simply decided the time was right for a short haircut. Newspaper circulations skyrocketed, as Berkowitz wrote letters to columnists and cops, one of which he signed, "Yours In Murder, Mr. Monster."

Berkowitz was born in Brooklyn in 1953, the illegitimate son of a woman who—clearly no fool—immediately put him up for adoption. David grew up in Yonkers and, after serving in the Army Reserve, committed his first felony. On Christmas Eve 1975, he stabbed a woman in the back with a hunting knife at Co-op City in the Bronx, a crime for which he was never caught. "I wasn't going to rob her," David explained later. "I just wanted to kill her."

Of course.

Berkowitz's Son of Sam spree began in the Bronx on July 29, 1976, when he killed Donna Lauria, 18, and injured Jody Valenti as the two girls sat in Jody's car in front of a six-story beige-brick apartment house at 2860 Buhre Avenue. The police didn't think much of the shooting, but investigators did note that the bullets came from a .44-caliber gun.

Several months later, a man and his girlfriend were ambushed as they also sat in a car, at 159th Street and 33rd Avenue in the Flushing section of Queens. Six weeks after that, on November 27, 1976, two more women were shot—seriously, but not fatally—on the porch of a house at 83–21 262nd Street in Bellerose, Queens.

But Berkowitz didn't become a serial star until he struck in affluent Forest Hills, first on January 30, 1977, and again two months later. Two women died in the attacks, victims of those same killer bullets. Finally, the police got wise. The media had a new phenom: the .44-Caliber Killer.

Berkowitz attacked for the sixth time in April, this time returning to the Bronx. It was a typical ambush: a couple sitting in a car were shot dead as they embraced outside her apartment building at 1950 Hutchinson River Parkway. But now there was an added detail: Berkowitz introduced himself to the world as Son of Sam in a letter found in the street near the car. The letter was addressed to the detective leading the case, Joseph Borelli. Berkowitz, it seemed, was "deeply hurt" that Borelli had called him a "woman hater."

"I am the Monster—Beelzebub—the chubby behemouth (sic)," Berkowitz scrawled. "I love to hunt. Prowling the streets looking for fair game—tasty meat. The women of Queens are prettyist (sic) of all."

Berkowitz attacked for the seventh time in Bayside, Queens, outside a disco, and within a few blocks of the 111th Precinct stationhouse (known to police officers as Fort Azalea, a humorous reference to the usual serenity of the neighborhood).

He took aim for the last time on July 31, 1977. Stacy Moskowitz, a platinum blonde, and her date, Bobby Violante, were about to get out of his Buick and stroll on Shore Road at Bay 17th Street in Bath Beach. It was 2:30 A.M. and Stacy was scared. "What if Son of Sam is hiding there?" she asked. "Are you kidding?" Bobby replied. "This is Brooklyn, not Queens." In seconds, Stacy was dead and Violante blinded. Son of Sam, the tabloids screamed, had struck again.

Berkowitz's final attack was also the beginning of his undoing. Moments after the shooting, a woman noticed a man dashing to an illegally parked car that had just been ticketed by the police. Soon, the cops traced the ticket to Berkowitz. At the same time, Sam Carr, of Yonkers, a former neighbor of Berkowitz's, told his daughter Wheat, a Yonkers police dispatcher, about the strange notes he had received after his black

Labrador, Harvey, was mysteriously wounded with a .44-caliber bullet. Wheat immediately called the police in Brooklyn.

On August 10th, a white-haired detective, John Falotico, led a stakeout of David's apartment at 35 Pine Street in Yonkers. After six hours, David walked out to his car as Falotico and a gang of cops swarmed in for the arrest. Two officers pointed guns at Berkowitz's head.

"Who are you?" Falotico said.

"You know who I am."

"No, tell me who you are," Falotico ordered.

A smile creased David's chubby face. "I'm Son of Sam."

Berkowitz pleaded guilty to six counts of murder, seven of attempted murder, and various lesser charges. He was sentenced to twenty-five years in a maximum-security prison and will be eligible for parole August 5, 2002. He can only be held until 2007, when he will be 54 years old. In the weeks and months after he was jailed, people flocked to 35 Pine Street in Yonkers. Soon, the owners of the site had the address changed to 42 Pine to keep away the curious.

2

How to Succeed in Business the Wedtech Way
595 Gerard Avenue

Sometimes we look at ourselves in the mirror and shake our heads. Where did we go wrong?

Why aren't we getting invitations to the White House or palling around with God-fearing Republicans? How come we're not being indicted for bribing a congressman?

John Mariotta, the mastermind of the $117 million Wedtech scam, did all those things and more. He even went to jail—a real drag, we're sure—but no doubt he appreciated the lengthy write-ups in *Time* and *Newsweek*.

Prior to his trouble with the law, Mariotta was a favorite of Ronald Reagan, who called him a "hero for the 1980s," an example to all small businessmen because he turned his two-bit machine shop at 595 Gerard Avenue into a mega-outlet for Pentagon-ordered weapons.

It was all so inspiring, until the secret to Wedtech's success was revealed and Mariotta became a national disgrace, a businessman whose corrupt fingers had reached all the way to the White House and Congress.

Mariotta learned that it took bribes and lies and friends in high places to make his company grow. Plenty of pols were willing to help—Bronx Congressmen Mario Biaggi and Robert Garcia, and Bronx Borough President Stanley Simon, among them.

Soon, the secrets got out and Wedtech fell on hard times. First there were the strains of the corruption charges, then a declaration of bankruptcy. Finally came four federal trials and plenty of convictions, resignations, and tears of contrition.

Mariotta agreed to plead guilty to some lightened state and federal charges, for which he served time in prison after cooperating in the intricate maze of other Wedtech prosecutions.

Wedtech itself, at 595 Gerard Avenue near Yankee Stadium, is now a vacant, dilapidated warehouse. First pillaged by our respected public servants, this symbol of Horatio Alger–style self-help has now been stripped bare by ordinary vandals.

A Bronx Politician: Mario Biaggi
3255 Westchester Avenue

Here's to the sinners, the politicians who earned their prison stripes in the Bronx. Here's to Mario Biaggi, once described by a prosecutor as a "thug in a congressman's suit."

But no matter what the critics say, no matter what the judges declare, Mario can point to his record—his campaign record, that is. He spent twenty-three years in office, a tenure he definitely prefers talking about more than the twenty-six months he was behind bars.

So what if he received an illegal $1.8 million in cash and stocks from the scandal-tarred Wedtech Corporation. So what if he spent taxpayer money to frolic with a blonde in the Florida sun while his wife was in a hospital fighting cancer.

So what if federal wiretappers once heard a gangster brag about getting Mario's daughter a job.

In the Bronx, Mario could do no wrong. He might have been a crook, but he was the Bronx's crook.

Biaggi knew a lot about crime, having once been a policeman strutting the boulevards with a chest full of medals. Actually, Biaggi now walked with a cane and a limp, but not from chasing the bad guys. He had fallen down and injured himself trying to stop a runaway horse in 1949.

Biaggi won election to Congress in 1965. There were many exciting campaigns after that. Maybe too exciting. In 1974, one of his political workers filed a suit accusing Mario of fathering her child. A family court judge called the charge fabricated.

Onward Mario rolled. He lived like an ordinary guy, in a rented apartment at 100 Moshulu Parkway, and he worked out of a modest one-story brick-face office at 3255 Westchester Avenue. Mario wanted the voters to think he was just like them. Only there were some rather large differences, including a condo in Florida, and $2.5 million in cash and stocks.

He resigned under fire in 1988 after being implicated in the Wedtech scandal. Mario was also convicted in 1987 for taking a bribe—the Florida vacation—from Brooklyn political boss Meade Esposito in exchange for business favors involving government contracts.

A judge sentenced Mario to eight years, but he was let out of jail in 1991 after twenty-six months because of poor health. He returned to his borough a hero, telling reporters he was happy to once again breathe New York City's pollution.

Mario was honored by hundreds of high-powered pals and politicians, including some who referred to his prison term as "a vacation." Mayor Dinkins didn't stay away. "Mario Biaggi is my friend," the mayor maintained, "he has always been my friend."

Promises, Promises: Jimmy Carter Journeys to the Bronx
Charlotte Street

See the mayor shake hands with a wounded war vet, or the congressman give thumbs up to a senior citizen. "We must help the needy," promises the city council president, his arm around a child of the ghetto, his hairpiece blowing in the wind.

Few things are as entertaining as a politician trying to prove he cares about something other than himself. It's enough to make you reach for the voting lever—and kick the clown out of office.

Enter Jimmy Carter, a dentist's dream, not to mention President of the United States. Jimmy put his arm around the South Bronx in October of 1977, just to show he cared about urban wastelands, about the poor and downtrodden, about the "other" America.

The presidential limousine rolled up to rubbled Charlotte Street and out hopped Carter, trailed by dark-suited aides, well-armed Secret Service men, and television cameras. The Prez climbed to the top of a six-foot-high mountain of bricks and mortar, where a tenement once stood, and gazed out at a landscape of abandoned buildings, stray dogs, and emptiness. "Sobering," said the President.

The man could sure sum up a moment.

Quickly, he turned to an aide. "See which areas can still be salvaged," Carter ordered. "Maybe we can create a recreation area and turn it around."

No, nothing was ever done. The Bronx became poorer and the voters gave Carter the boot in 1980. Government bureaucrats couldn't agree on a plan for Charlotte Street—or who would get credit for it.

More than five years later, New York State sponsored a home ownership program and soon there were single-family houses with picket fences up and down what is now known as Charlotte Gardens. It almost looks like Plains, Georgia, Jimmy's hometown, except the people protect themselves with shotguns, iron window gates, and German shepherds.

Baby Lindy
1279 East 222nd Street

Going to the electric chair can be a real bummer, especially if you don't like being the center of attention. Believing that you're innocent also doesn't make it easier. Bruno Hauptmann of the Bronx swore until the moment he sizzled that he didn't kidnap Charles Lindbergh's baby. Evidence even existed to back him up, but the prosecutors, the police, the jury, they didn't care. They threw the switch anyway.

It had been an international spectacle, the 20-month-old dimpled son of an American flying hero snatched from his crib in the middle of the night. Charles Jr. showed up ten weeks later in 1932, buried in a shallow grave on the edge of the Lindberghs' New Jersey estate.

Two years passed without an arrest and the country was getting itchy. A New Jersey cop by the name of H. Norman Schwarzkopf, the father of the boy who grew up to become the Persian Gulf war hero, led the investigation. H. Norman Sr. must have been sweating pretty good as the days and months passed without a collar.

The police moved in on Hauptmann on September 15, 1934, arresting him outside his wood-frame house at 1279 East 222nd Street. Bruno, then 34, insisted he didn't even know where Charles Lindbergh lived, much less who killed his kid.

No matter: the cops found in Bruno's wallet a $20 bill that they claimed had come from the $50,000 ransom Lindbergh handed to a masked man at St. Raymond's Cemetery near Hauptmann's home. The police discovered $14,600 more in the back of Bruno's garage. They also said a ladder used to reach baby Lindbergh's crib was fashioned with a floorboard missing from Bruno's house. It made sense, since Bruno was a carpenter.

All in all, pretty damning stuff, except that there were a few complications. For one, jurors at Bruno's trial—billed by newspapers as "the trial of the century"—were told the kidnapper had worn gloves and that no fingerprints were found on the first ransom letters written to Lindbergh.

Wrong.

The truth, as it was revealed decades later in official records, was that fingerprints *were* found, but they weren't Bruno's. In addition, an expert had analyzed Hauptmann's handwriting and concluded that it was nothing like the scrawl found in the ransom note. The jurors, though, were never told.

Historians have argued that Hauptmann's alibi may have been true—that his one-time partner in a fur business, Isidor Fisch, stashed the marked ransom bills in Bruno's closet for safekeeping while he went abroad. Hauptmann didn't know Fisch was a professional confidence man; his swindles were exposed only after his death in Leipzig in 1934.

Nevertheless, on a warm spring day, streetcorner newsboys sang "Bruno Is Dead" just after Hauptmann was buckled into the electric chair and given enough volts to power a trolley car. Lindbergh, embittered and living in England to escape the press, said justice was done. In her small hotel room near the death house, Anna Hauptmann, Bruno's wife, clutched a Bible and knelt by her bed. "Oh, God," she sobbed, "why have you done this to us?"

Anna is still alive and every year writes to New Jersey's governor asking for an executive pardon for her husband. The state's governors have from time to time considered a compromise proclamation admitting that questions remain about Hauptmann's verdict. But none has ever been approved.

The Hauptmanns' two-story mustard-colored house, meanwhile, still stands, although the garage was torn down years ago.

Happy Land
1959 Southern Boulevard

The bodies were found charred and suffocated in a nightclub called Happy Land. Some were frozen in embrace, others sprawled on the dance floor. They had drinks in their hands and lovers on their arms, a snapshot of a Saturday night tossed into a murderous fire.

Eighty-seven men and women died that March 25th night in 1990 because one drunken man, a 36-year-old factory worker with drooping eyelids and a crooked jaw, was angry at his ex-girlfriend. Four people, including the ex-girlfriend, survived.

Julio Gonzalez's rage cost New York City its worst toll of fire deaths since the Triangle Shirtwaist factory blaze of March 25, 1911, exactly seventy-nine years earlier to the day.

A pall hung over the city for days as families lined up to identify the dead; victims with names like Isabel and Betsabe and Omar were mourned at services punctuated by the moans and shrieks of the grief-stricken. The fire left sixty men and women widows and widowers, and 106 children orphans.

The fire also provoked a crackdown on hundreds of other illegal social clubs in the city's poorer neighborhoods, nightspots without fire exits or liquor licenses where immigrants danced to reggae and salsa under swirling beads of colored lights every Saturday night.

Gonzalez had gone to Happy Land, a red two-story building marked by graffiti and a smile face on its sign, to see Lydia Feliciano, a ticket-taker at the club. Julio had lived with Lydia for eight years. They broke up five weeks before the fire, after she threw him out because he was making advances on her adolescent niece.

At Happy Land, Julio demanded that Lydia take him back, but she refused. They yelled at each other and then a bouncer told Julio to leave. "I'll be back," Julio screamed as the bouncer shoved him toward the door. Gonzalez stumbled across the street to a gas station, where he gave the attendant a dollar for a canister of gasoline. He returned to the club, at 1959 Southern Boulevard, walking just inside the entrance and spilling the accelerant on the floor.

Julio struck two matches and started a fire, with vengeful consequences beyond his wildest imagination. "*Fuego! Fuego!*" the doorman yelled, warning of the spreading fire. But the sweaty throngs kept dancing until they began to drop. Most could not escape through the choking black smoke and flames.

Within hours, Julio was arrested and branded the nation's worst mass murderer. He was taken by radio car to the 48th Precinct in the Bronx in a bulletproof vest. Many New Yorkers at the time would have loved to have had Julio Gonzalez alone in a room for five minutes, not to mention the building's lessee, Jay Weiss, the husband of sultry movie star Kathleen

Turner. The relatives of the dead sued the landlord for $5 billion in civil damages.

Seventeen months after the fire, relatives gathered in the Bronx criminal courthouse for Gonzalez's trial, their tears still not dry. "I keep telling myself that justice here might fail," said one relative of a dead Salvadoran. "But God's justice never fails."

Gonzalez was convicted of 176 counts of murder, arson, and assault. It took the jury foreman five minutes to say "guilty" 176 times, but the families of the Happy Land victims were more than willing to listen for as long as it took him to finish.

Afterward, they traveled to Happy Land and dropped flowers on the doorstep. The outside of the building has been turned into a makeshift shrine, the happy face replaced by a tablet with the names of all 106 victims and the words, in English and Spanish, *May they rest in peace.*

The Death of Eleanor Bumpers
1551 University Avenue

It started out all wrong, the day six police officers, one of them carrying a shotgun, were sent to evict a grandmother of thirteen from her public housing apartment. Eleanor Bumpers, 67, was emotionally disturbed and four months behind on her $96.85-a-month rent. Welfare workers had failed to send in emergency checks on her behalf.

Somewhere along the chain of command, police heard that Eleanor was dangerous. She had once thrown lye in the face of a policeman, or so it was said.

The cops were prepared.

They wore riot helmets and gas masks when they arrived at Bumpers' door on October 29, 1984, at the housing project at 1551 University Avenue. Officer Stephen Sullivan was ready with a 12-gauge shotgun.

Waiting outside apartment 4A, the door slightly ajar, the cops could see Bumpers in the middle of the living room clutching a ten-inch kitchen knife. The officers burst inside. Bumpers, they said, lunged at one of the cops with the knife raised.

Officer Sullivan aimed his shotgun and fired at the grandmother, who weighed 260 pounds. The first bullet blew off two of the fingers on the hand holding the knife, but it didn't stop her from advancing. Sullivan squeezed the trigger again and shot her in the chest. Within thirty seconds of the cops entering the apartment, Eleanor Bumpers was dead.

The case tore the city apart, with blacks calling the shooting "genocide" and the police claiming self-defense. Sullivan was indicted for manslaughter as thousands of cops protested outside the office of then–Bronx District Attorney Mario Merola. Two years later, Sullivan was cleared by a Bronx Supreme Court judge, who said there was no evidence he was doing anything but protecting a fellow officer from a crazy old lady.

"If the situation was still threatening, if I still feared for the other fellow's life, I'd do the same thing again," Sullivan proclaimed afterward. "The whole thing happened in thirty seconds. I wasn't even sure she was black, pink, white, or whatever."

The police department issued tougher guidelines for handling people classified as emotionally disturbed. The new regulations stressed the use of non-lethal weapons and rubber bullets and mandated that a precinct commander or duty captain be on the scene to give the orders.

Bumpers' family sued the city and won a $200,000 out-of-court settlement.

8

The Dude Who Eludes
365 East 183d Street

Heroism in New York City is never as simple as rescuing a cat from a tree. Larry Davis, for example, shot and wounded six police officers and disappeared for seventeen days in 1986. When he surrendered at a housing project, hundreds cheered him as he was led away in handcuffs.

"Lar-ry!" the crowd chanted. "Lar-ry!"

Davis was an avenging angel to New Yorkers fed up with a police department and a court system that they claimed brutalized poor blacks and Hispanics. To the police, Davis was a scourge, a cop-shooter who, they charged, had murdered four drug dealers. But all Davis ever went to jail for was weapons possession.

More than twenty cops had hunted him down at his sister's apartment at 1231 Fulton Avenue near 168th Street. Shots were fired on that November 19, 1986, and Davis came out blazing. Before long, six police officers were down and Davis was gone. A massive police hunt followed, during which the cops traveled nationwide.

The hunt ended at the Twin Parks housing project at 365 East 183rd Street after an informant said Davis was hiding in a second-floor apartment. After the police surrounded the building, Davis ran up to the 14th floor and burst into apartment 14EB. For six hours, he held two women, a man, and three children hostage. More than a hundred cops waited outside until Davis, convinced there was no place to run, walked out shirtless, his hands raised.

Larry emptied his pants pockets, from which Tootsie Rolls fell. Some children in the hall grabbed them, telling reporters they hoped the candy would become souvenirs. Davis was convicted of illegal weapons possession but was acquitted of attempted murder charges in the shootout with the police and of the murders of two drug dealers. In 1991, Davis was convicted of murdering another drug dealer as well as kidnapping and assault.

9

Fort Apache
1086 Simpson Street

The 41st Precinct in the Bronx, otherwise known as Fort Apache, has been the target of many a citizens' revolt. During the 1970s, angry mobs, fed up with a neighborhood of killers and drug addicts, routinely stormed the precinct's front door demanding better protection from a police squad they believed was sleeping on the job.

Sometimes, residents took the law into their own hands, like the night a man shot a drug dealer in the heart with a bow and arrow. The cops arrested the shooter, prompting a mob to storm the precinct demanding his release. The police countered with baseball bats and fired their guns into the air until the attackers retreated.

During the battle, a desk sergeant screamed into a telephone, "This is Fort Apache!"

Violence is certainly a horrible thing, but it can also be quite profitable: "Fort Apache" T-shirts soon followed, as did a Hollywood film about the precinct starring Paul Newman and Ed Asner. The battle scenes were, of course, filmed on location.

The precinct house still exists, but its law-and-order denizens now call it the "Little House on the Prairie." The crime rate has dropped as the neighborhood's population has plummeted and some new, powder-blue low-income homes have gone up along Simpson Street. Time for a new location: the 41st Precinct is moving to modern digs at Southern Boulevard and Longwood Avenue.

Art Imitates Death, or the Jackson Pollock School
of Murder
2380 Arthur Avenue

Bullet-riddled mobster Frank Scalise lay in a mess of tomatoes, green peppers, and peaches, blood dripping from his cheek, larynx, right shoulder, and neck.

Frank was no pretty picture, although we're quite sure that Jackson Pollock, the painter, would have found the splash and chaos inspiring.

Or perhaps literary critics could read meaning into Frank's death, which occurred in 1957 at a fruit stand at 2380 Arthur Avenue. He was shot just after handing Enrico Mazzaro 90 cents for a couple of peaches.

Sound familiar? Like the way a certain fictional Don Corleone got shot up in Mario Puzo's *The Godfather?*

Don Corleone, of course, made it to the next chapter. Frank Scalise, gunned down for selling not-for-sale mob memberships for $50,000 apiece, didn't fare so well. He went to Woodlawn Cemetery in the Bronx.

A fruit stand still operates at the address, although a different family runs the business. They know the whole story and have seen the movie as well.

12

Where Crime Is King

Queens

QUEENS MAY BE THE LARGEST LAND mass in New York (121 square miles), but when it comes to the city's famous murder rate, the borough just doesn't pull its weight. In one recent year, a mere 312 of the city's 2,245 slayings occurred in Queens.

The borough is mostly famous for hosting the Mets, the airports, and the World's Fair. Residents like to think of Queens as a slice of suburbia in the middle of the city. They take pride in their detached homes, patches of grass, and clean sidewalks. Some even call Queens a bedroom community.

Still, there may be reason to suspect that Queens residents are daydreaming. For one thing, the borough is home to more than a dozen graveyards, including the sprawling Cyprus Hills Cemetery. For another, John Gotti and his family are Queens residents. No one has yet linked the two, but this should be chilling enough to keep anyone from thinking that the royal borough is too prim and proper, too classy, for the rest of New York City.

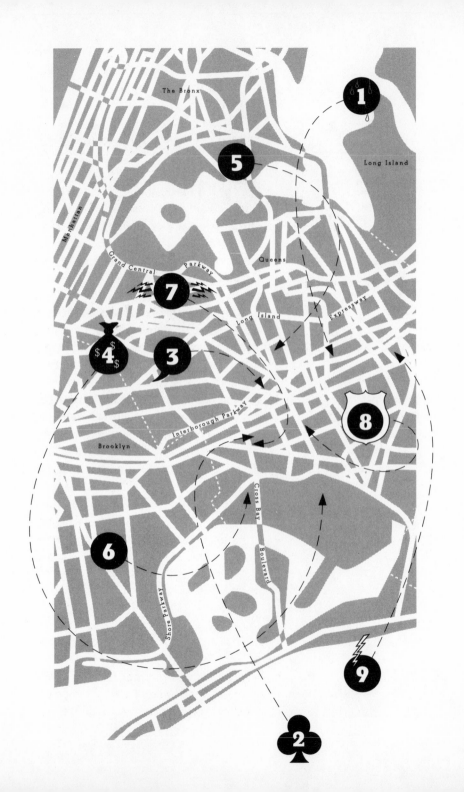

1

The King of Queens
80–65 Chevy Chase Street, Jamaica Estates

Crooked politicians are tough to spot, but here's one telltale sign: they tend to sweat in the middle of winter. We're not talking about a mild Nixonian sweat, a few beads of perspiration on the upper lip. We're talking about the wet look, the August-in-December look. The Donald Manes look.

Everywhere Donald traveled in January of 1986, the so-called King of Queens, friend to mayors and governors and presidents, looked as if he had just walked out of a sauna. In fact, Manes was feeling the torrid heat of a federal investigation that was about to brand him a racketeer. Within three months, he would commit suicide in the kitchen of his Jamaica Estates home.

It was the city's most volcanic corruption scandal in a century, and before it was over, a bevy of public officials were parading off to prison for taking bribes. In one scheme, Bronx political boss Stanley Friedman, acting in partnership with Manes, lobbied the city to pay $22.7 million for new computer technology. Only one problem: the company manufacturing the new technology didn't exist.

At the center of the scandal was Manes, a Boss Tweed with a smile, a backslapper who patronized prostitutes and greasy spoons, a money grubber who enjoyed passing bundles of cash in brown paper bags. Manes had a troubled past (his father committed suicide), but he never seemed gloomy. Perhaps it was his success at the polls. Manes was elected borough president of Queens four consecutive times, inheriting the post of county leader in 1971 from a man who was jailed for tax evasion. Manes was hailed by Governor Mario Cuomo, Mayor Ed Koch, and even President Jimmy Carter, who, visiting Queens on a campaign tour, threw his arm around Manes and called him "Donny."

Manes seemed at the apex of his power until, on the night of January 9, 1986, two days after he was sworn in for a fourth term, two police officers spotted him weaving in and out of traffic on the Grand Central

Parkway. They pulled him over at the 126th Street exit, near Northern Boulevard and Shea Stadium. Donald was bleeding from the left wrist and ankle. On the floor of the car, the cops found a bloodstained kitchen knife and Donald's gold watch.

For twelve days, Manes, who nearly died from loss of blood, claimed he had been robbed by two men. But the police were unable to confirm his story. Finally Donald confessed from his hospital bed that he had tried to kill himself. He didn't bother explaining that he could be indicted at any moment. After the press conference, Manes managed a wan smile and waved goodbye to reporters from his bed.

Manes was released from the hospital in a matter of weeks and sent home, where he was supposed to recuperate and receive psychiatric attention. His condition did not improve. On March 12, 1986, while speaking to his shrink on the telephone in his kitchen, Manes stuck a kitchen knife into his heart. His daughter Lauren, 25, was in the room at the time.

Fittingly enough, Manes's funeral was held at the Schwartz Brother Funeral Home. It was here only a few years before that Manes, in whispered conversations during services for a friend, had set up the bribe-collection network that would eventually bring him down.

Six hundred mourners attended services for Manes, including Mayor Koch, who brought along a portable microphone stand for a press conference outside. Governor Cuomo showed up, along with then–Borough President David Dinkins, and former mayor Abe Beame. "The evil that men do lives after them, and the good is buried with their bones," one mourner told a reporter. "So it was with Caesar. So it is with Manes."

God-Father of Our County
Bergin Hunt and Fish Club, 98–08 101st Avenue,
Ozone Park

To the FBI and the New York City Police Department, he is a thief, a murderer, and someone Boy Scouts should scorn. But to thousands of

Queens residents, John Gotti is a celebrity, a hometown hero, a gangster the whole neighborhood can feel proud of.

"John Gotti?" they say adoringly after he beats yet another round of assault or racketeering charges. "Fuhgedaboudit!" (That's "Forget about it"—or "He's a terrific fellow, really he is" for those needing subtitles.)

Perhaps Johnny-boy's popularity can be attributed to his movie star good looks, that dashing smile, the way his perfectly coiffed hair frames his head like a halo. Or maybe it's his civic pride, his undying loyalty to Queens. For years, Gotti has lived in Howard Beach, not far from his clubhouse, a brick-faced storefront in Ozone Park called the Bergin Hunt and Fish Club, where the walls are lined with framed color photographs of His Dapperness.

It is here that Gotti and his gang host an annual—and highly illegal—July Fourth fireworks show. Gotti has been throwing the party for more than twenty years, but it didn't become a regular stop on our tour until John became the Dapper Don, the Teflon Don, the reputed-then-convicted Boss-of-Bosses who rubbed out Paul Castellano in 1985.

Every year, the police talk tough: no more fireworks. Every year, the skies over the Bergin Hunt and Fish Club light up with red and blue and orange explosions as hundreds of people in the street cheer for a smiling Johnny-boy (the show goes on even when he's in prison).

Gotti was tossed in jail for murder and racketeering in April of 1992, which meant missing Easter at his family's modest two-story home at 160–11 85th Street in Howard Beach. It's the house with the huge satellite dish on the roof, the always drawn curtains, and the security camera out front. Perfect for a guy who claims he's a plumbing salesman. The house is not very attractive, but we wouldn't ring the doorbell and tell the Gottis that. The family is not known for taking criticism well.

Indeed, not everyone survives living near the Gottis. John Favara resided around the corner from the family—that is, until 1980, when he accidentally ran over and killed John's 12-year-old son, Frank. Soon after, Victoria Gotti attacked Favara with a baseball bat.

Several months later, witnesses at a Queens diner saw two men shove Favara into the backseat of a car in the parking lot. He was never seen again. The police figure Gotti was behind Favara's vanishing act, but they could never prove it. At the time, John and Victoria were vacationing in Florida.

Civic Shame: The Murder of Kitty Genovese
82–70 Austin Street

New Yorkers don't usually know their neighbors. Catherine Genovese of Kew Gardens, Queens, was different. A night bar manager, she had days free and ran into the same faces at the bookstore or the super-market. She always smiled and said hello. Her neighbors knew her as Kitty. A lot of good it did her.

Kitty was attacked in front of her building by a knife-wielding stranger on a chilly morning in 1964. She screamed, "Please help me!" but none of her neighbors responded. They simply shut their windows or switched off their table lamps. Their silence—even more than the murder itself—became one of the most shameful and telling moments in New York's bloody history, a graphic testament to the chilly alienation of big-city living.

Genovese lived in a row of two-story, fake-Tudor-front houses in Kew Gardens, a neighborhood of old Sycamore trees and small shops where a woman could feel safe walking alone at night. Back from work at 3:20 A.M. that March 13th, she steered her compact red Fiat into a parking space at the Long Island Railroad station adjacent to her home. Kitty's doorway, at 82–70 Austin Street, was a dozen yards away.

Closing the car door, she noticed a man standing under a street lamp. Concerned, if not quite afraid, she decided to avoid him by walking up Austin Street toward Lefferts Boulevard. If worse came to worse, she knew there was a police call box on Lefferts that she could use, and there were still occasional cars passing. The stranger stalked her, at-tacking her as she reached a darkened bookstore on Austin. She twirled but felt his knife in her stomach. "Oh, my God," she shrieked, collapsing, "he stabbed me! Please help me! Please help me!"

Across the street, lamps lighted and windows opened in the ten-story apartment house at 82–67 Austin Street. A man looking down from an upper floor yelled, "Let that girl alone!" The attacker lowered the knife and walked back down Austin to his car.

Genovese staggered bleeding toward her apartment, but her attacker returned a few minutes later to stab her again. Once more she pleaded, "I'm dying, I'm dying," and again came the lights, the opening of windows, the frightened sets of eyes peering down. The man with the knife again paused, returned to his car, and drove away.

Still alone, Kitty finally reached the entrance to her building, crawling on hands and knees. The killer, who had simply driven around the block, found his quarry struggling to climb up the stairs. With no one watching, he finished what he had started. Kitty Genovese was dead at age 28.

Over the next few weeks, detectives knocked on doors and learned that thirty-eight neighbors had witnessed the crime, but no one had called the police until 3:50 A.M., a half-hour after Kitty's first screams for help. The man who placed the call didn't simply dial an operator and ask for police. Instead, he first phoned a friend for advice, left his apartment, crossed over the roof, and asked to use his neighbor's telephone. "I didn't want to get involved," he would explain later. A woman said, "I thought it was a lovers' quarrel." An older man waved his hand at the cops. "I was tired," he snapped.

Kitty's killer, Winston Moseley, a 29-year-old keypunch machine operator with a wife, two kids, and a mortgage in South Ozone Park, was sentenced to the electric chair after confessing to her murder, as well as the murders of a 15-year-old girl and a housewife from Queens. Mosely escaped from prison in 1968 and committed a rape before being recaptured.

4

Thank You for Fleecing Lufthansa
Building 261, Kennedy Airport Freight Terminal

They have a talent for murder, but magic is definitely the mob's forte. Cash and human beings seem to vanish whenever they're around. Take the $6 million Lufthansa Airlines heist at Kennedy Airport in 1978, for example. It was the biggest theft in American history, but even more amazing was the eventual disappearance of thirteen wise guys connected to the crime.

Disfigured bodies showed up all over the city, everywhere from an unmade bed in Ozone Park to the front seat of a Buick in Canarsie, to a meat hook in a refrigeration truck in Gravesend Bay. Being dead, the men didn't have much to talk about. Neither did the living, particularly the alleged brains behind the heist, Jimmy "The Gent" Burke, a bookmaker and loanshark. Burke made only one mistake, not stuffing a goodfella by the name of Henry Hill into his body bag of tricks.

The boys pulled off the armed robbery at 3:12 A.M. on December 11, 1978. The gangsters were thoroughly prepped for their job by a Lufthansa freight supervisor, Louis Werner, who hoped to clear his debts to mob bookies by funneling inside information to them about the cargo operation. Because of Werner, Burke's gang knew the layout of the freight rooms, who worked where, and when. They also knew that the silent wall alarm inside the safe would activate if touched.

The heist went off without an alarm, or a bullet. In sixty-four minutes the men were gone, on their way to fame and white Cadillacs and fox furs for their mistresses. The heist was the stuff of international headlines as hundreds of city and federal investigators hit the streets. But as the witnesses vanished one by one, the good guys started sweating. True, they had wiretaps of Burke toasting the robbery, and they even put Werner away. But three years after the crime, they were unable to implicate any members of the gang.

Enter Henry Hill, who figured he was next on Burke's hit list. To save his skin, Henry grew a beard and entered the federal witness protection program. He gave prosecutors more than enough testimony to send Burke to prison for life for two of the murders. A much-feared mob underboss, Paul Vario, was sent away for six years for helping plan the robbery. Burke was never charged for the heist, but in 1985 he was jailed for life for murdering a con man.

Hill's story became the material for *Wiseguy,* a best-selling book that became the smash movie *Goodfellas.* Everyone was very entertained— everyone, that is, except the people of Lufthansa and their insurers. Despite all the embarassing attention the case received, the missing cash and jewels were never recovered.

5

Mother Murder
150–22 72nd Drive

She was beautiful, long-legged, and had a gorgeous head of red hair. Alice Crimmins might have been a movie star, a model, or even a terrific mother. If only her children hadn't turned up dead in the summer of 1965.

Her daughter, Missy, a flaxen-haired four-year-old with blue eyes, was found on July 15, 1965, lying in an empty sandlot a half-mile from Alice's apartment at 150–22 72nd Drive. The little girl had been strangled with her pajamas.

Four days later, Edmund Crimmins, five years old, was discovered dead about a mile in the opposite direction, near the 1964 World's Fair grounds. His body, swaddled in his blue-and-yellow plaid blanket, was too decomposed for the coroner to determine the cause of death.

At the children's funerals, 26-year-old Alice Crimmins cried a river.

It was all very touching and, for a while anyway, the police believed Alice's story: the children had vanished, probably out the first-floor window after she tucked them in and locked the bedroom door to keep them there. When she went to check on them in the morning, Alice said, they were gone.

But detectives grew suspicious when they found a notepad listing the names of twenty-five of Alice's boyfriends. A nosy neighbor told of seeing a man and a woman leaving Crimmins' apartment the night the little girl disappeared. The couple was carrying a bundle. They drove away in a car, Mrs. Sophie Earomirski said. Then Alice and the man returned. Alone.

Alice, who was estranged from her husband, hired the best attorneys she could find. Two murder trials later, during which Alice's lovers were paraded with damning testimony before a jury of twelve married men, she was convicted of murder. Prosecutors charged that she had killed her daughter out of anger and that a boyfriend's pal murdered her son to make it seem like a twisted stranger had done the deed in the middle of the night.

"I didn't kill my children," Alice wept as she heard the sentence—a minimum of twenty-five years at an upstate women's prison. The verdict was thrown out on appeal by a judge who ordered yet another trial, in which Alice was convicted only of the death of her daughter. She served nearly five years before being freed on parole in September 1977, then married one of her ex-lovers and moved to the suburbs of New York City.

Howard Beach
156–71 Cross Bay Boulevard

Howard Beach is no longer a neighborhood. It's an incident—vile and sordid—in which a black man was killed after being chased by a gang of whites because they didn't like the color of his skin.

Michael Griffith, the 23-year-old son of Caribbean-born parents, who lived in Brooklyn, hadn't planned on being in Howard Beach that December night in 1986. But the Buick in which Griffith was riding broke down on an isolated marsh-lined stretch of Cross Bay Boulevard at 12:40 A.M. The driver stayed with the car while Griffith and his two companions, also black, walked north on the boulevard looking for a pay phone and a mechanic. They were headed for the heart of Howard Beach.

The men stopped at New Park Pizza that December 20th, a shack of a restaurant at 156–71 Cross Bay Boulevard, but were told by the man behind the counter that no phone was available for them to use. Hungry, they ordered slices and sat. Two cops walked in to check out an anonymous 911 complaint about "three suspicious black males."

After the officers departed, Griffith and his companions walked outside, where they were accosted by a dozen white men. "Niggers, you don't belong here!" the gang shouted, beating them with bats and fists. The gang had just come from a party in the neighborhood, where 17-year-old Jon Lester had told them, "There are niggers on the boulevard.

Let's go kill them." After he was arrested later that night, Lester told the police that his dream was to join the Mafia.

Somehow, Griffith and his cousin, Cedric Sandiford, 36, managed to escape the beating outside the pizza parlor. They ran north and then west. The gang caught them at the edge of the Belt Parkway. "God, don't kill me," Sandiford cried as the blows kept raining. The two pulled back and squeezed through a three-foot hole in the parkway fence where they split up, Sandiford running west along the parkway, Griffith east. Sandiford got away, but as he tried to cross the Belt, Griffith was struck and killed under the wheels of a passing car.

Racial rage exploded throughout the city. Mayor Ed Koch, a one-time civil rights lawyer, compared the mob attack to a lynching and offered a $10,000 reward for information leading to a quick arrest. The locals, who wanted to be left alone, shouted racial slurs as the Rev. Al Sharpton rolled in with five thousand marchers chanting, "Howard Beach, have you heard, this is not Johannesburg!" Sharpton, with his taste for symbols, bought a slice from New Park Pizza. One 17-year-old, apparently summing up the sentiment abounding in Howard Beach toward the victims, told a reporter, "Aw, they deserved it."

A year later, Lester and two other members of the Howard Beach 12 were convicted of manslaughter and assault, receiving prison terms with maximums ranging from fifteen to thirty years. Three other defendants were acquitted. A seventh turned state's witness and spent half a year behind bars. Two others were ordered to perform two hundred hours of community service.

The books were finally closed in 1990 when Judge Thomas Demakos sentenced the last three young thugs to community service, prompting one to salute the judge. "Four years after the incident," Demakos said plaintively, "these defendants do not comprehend the evil they did that night, or appreciate the harm they did to the entire city."

7

Stun Gun Scandal
106th Precinct

The headline in the community paper read: DRUG BUSTERS HONORED. Below was an account of a small group of police officers named "Cops of the Month" by the 106th Precinct on April 10, 1985. The presiding lieutenant described the work of Sergeant Richard Pike and his crackerjack narcotics unit, mentioning scores of drug arrests, the shutdown of illegal smoke shops, the reclaiming of schoolyards from junkies.

"Outstanding," said their superior officer.

The residents of Ozone Park and Howard Beach, the neighborhoods covered by the 106th, were proud of their officers.

The feeling lasted exactly eight days, until it was announced that Pike was at the center of one of the worst cases of police brutality in the city's history. Pike's success, the department discovered, depended on the torturing of drug suspects with what they called a "stun gun," a weapon that can fire up to 40,000 volts of electricity.

The cops began investigating Pike after Mark Davidson, a drug suspect, told prosecutors he had been punched in the face, whacked in the head, thrown on a table, and finally tortured with a stun gun, all following his arrest on a $10 pot-selling charge.

Davidson claimed the cops drank beer, threw jagged "kung fu stars" around the station house, and drove 80 miles per hour to his booking so they could be back before a party ended at the precinct. The 106th station house became known as "the torture precinct," and Benjamin Ward, the police commissioner at the time, called Pike and his men "cowards." Ward approved of their criminal indictments and forced five top commanders responsible for the shamed narcotics unit to retire.

Pike, his law enforcement career in shreds, served three years of a maximum six-year sentence for convictions on assault and other allegations. Two other members of his unit were also convicted. A fourth officer's charges were quietly dismissed in 1991 after six years of legal wrangling. The cop was broke and his marriage was in disarray. Prosecutors figured that was punishment enough.

8

Death of a Rookie Cop
Inwood Street and 107th Avenue

George Bush keeps a police officer's shield on his desk in the Oval Office. Badge no. 14072 belonged to Eddie Byrne, the rookie cop from a Queens precinct whose bloody death helped turn the city's crack epidemic into a national cause.

Byrne, four days past his 22nd birthday, began his last shift at 12:15 A.M. He sat alone in his radio car, guarding the home of a man whose house was fire-bombed after he complained to the police about crack dealers. It was frigid that night, February 26, 1988, in the eerily silent, forsaken neighborhood of South Jamaica. But primarily it was boring, consumingly so. By 3 A.M., as Byrne waited for his relief to show up, his eyelids drooped. He didn't notice a run-down yellow Dodge rolling by his post at Inwood Street and 107th Avenue.

Suddenly, a crackhead's face flashed in Byrne's passenger window, a decoy wearing a hood. "Agghh!" the decoy screamed. Byrne's eyes blinked wide open. His hand reached for his holster. Just then, a man clutching a .38-caliber gun approached the driver's side of the car. The rookie behind the wheel was just turning to his left when a bullet exploded through his side window and pierced his head. Four more shots followed and Police Officer Eddie Byrne was a martyr.

Now the crack problem was everybody's problem. More than a thousand cops probed the tattered corners of Queens in search of Byrne's executioners. City Hall posted a $10,000 reward. A newspaper matched it. At the cop's wake, his father, Matthew, called his son's killers "scum." His teeth gritted, he also said New York City was going the way of Beirut and Bogota.

"None of us is safe," the father said.

The cops arrested four men who worked in Howard "Pappy" Mason's multimillion-dollar crack ring. Mason had ordered Byrne's hit to flex his muscle on the street and intimidate the police. In the summer of 1989, the triggerman, David McClary, 23, became the last of the four sent away for a minimum of twenty-five years. One hundred cops in the Queens courtroom cheered. McClary grinned, spun around, and blew a kiss to his mother.

But the prized conviction came in time for Christmas 1989, when Mason, 27, was found guilty. Pappy, his face expressing no emotion, watched the jury foreman's announcement from his holding cell on closed-circuit television. Matthew Byrne cried on his way out of the courthouse, slumping over his open car door.

The house that Eddie Byrne was guarding when he died was supposed to be turned into an after-school learning center for neighborhood youngsters, but money couldn't be raised and soon the property was so badly vandalized that the city had it demolished. The street outside Byrne's 103rd Precinct station house, 91st Avenue between 168th and 169th streets, was renamed "P.O. Edward R. Byrne Avenue."

9

Fatal Distraction
93–27 22nd Street

No one can say that Queens has never had pioneers. Ruth Snyder, for one, was among the first women ever sent to the electric chair, a fate she earned by killing her husband in 1928.

Needless to say, Snyder, in her twenties, was not a happy wife. She was bored with her husband, Albert, thirteen years her senior, quiet, and hard of hearing. The Snyders had little in common, even keeping separate bedrooms in their Queens home.

Sometimes, Ruth tried to liven things up by poisoning Albert. Nine times she tried. Nine times she failed. It wasn't that she lacked creativity—she once fed him mercury tablets for a cough. Albert swallowed the pills, but he only felt better afterward.

Bosomy Ruth had affairs with as many married men as possible and liked one in particular, Judd Gray, a girdle salesman from New Jersey. Ruth and Judd would rendezvous for afternoons of lacey amour at the Waldorf Astoria. Everything was ducky until March 20, 1927. Albert Snyder, an art editor at *Motor Boating,* turned up dead in bed in the couple's Queens Village home at 93–27 222nd Street. His nostrils were stuffed with chloroform-soaked cotton, his throat in a garrote of picture wire.

Ruth was distraught, having been found by her nine-year-old daughter bound and gagged on the hallway floor outside the bedroom. Ruth told the police that one man, "apparently a foreigner," broke into the house to steal money and jewelry. It was something awful, she said.

The detectives were suitably impressed by Ruth's tears, but they did have their doubts. For one thing, there was no sign of forced entry. For another, they found Ruth's jewelry—supposedly stolen—underneath her bed. They were also interested to note that Mr. Snyder was the owner of a $96,000 life insurance policy that was of value only if he died a violent death.

Soon enough, the police discovered Judd Gray, Ruth's 34-year-old boyfriend. Judd, the detectives told Ruth, had confessed to teaming up with her to kill Snyder. "That low, cringing jackal," Ruth blurted out. "I'll tell you what really happened." So much for grace under pressure.

Ruth claimed that it was Gray who murdered her husband, but Judd stuck to his story, saying he had drunk half a bottle of whiskey while hiding in Albert's bedroom closet, awaiting the couple's return home. Gray said he jumped out and whacked Ruth's husband over the head with a window sash weight, and she then finished him off.

The Snyder-Gray trial was among the most sensational of its time, drawing dozens of journalists, writers, and playwrights, along with thousands of spectators. Newsman Damon Runyon calling the slaying "The Dumbbell Murder" because, he said, "it was that dumb." Of Ruth he wrote that she was a "chilly looking blonde with frosty eyes and one of those bet-you-will chins." Of her relationship to Gray, Runyon wrote: "They were redhot lovers when they first met, but they are strangers now."

Both were sentenced to die at Sing Sing, an execution the *Daily News* captured on film when a photographer tied a hidden mini-camera to his ankle. Ruth Snyder, 32, appeared on the newspaper's front page the next day, January 12, 1928, hooded and strapped into an electric chair, her final moment frozen forever.

The headline screamed: DEAD!

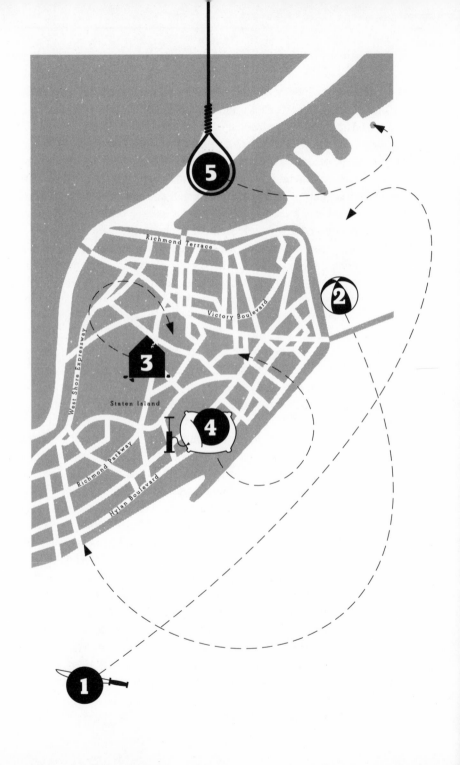

13

Continental Drift

Staten Island

EVERY SO OFTEN THE PEOPLE OF STATEN Island stand up and threaten to secede from New York City.

Promises, promises.

The way we figure it, one less borough, one less headache.

Most people travel to Staten Island for the ferry ride or the view of Wall Street and the Statue of Liberty. That's fine with the locals, as long as visitors don't stay too long. A whiff of the city's garbage dump, located on the Island in a place called Fresh Kills, is enough to send most people packing soon after they arrive.

Fourteen miles long and seven miles wide, Staten Island hosts the highest point on the eastern seaboard, Todt Hill, which was also where a certain mob chief lived before he made Sparks Steak House famous and took his bellyful of hot lead to the Moravian Cemetery, down the street from his home. Plenty of gangsters have resided on the Island (they like safe neighborhoods just like the next guy), but mostly it's inhabited by the likes of cops and firemen, not to mention a large contingent of card-carrying members of the National Rifle Association.

Staten Islanders are proud of their life on the water, far from the ever-menacing Manhattan isle most refer to as "the City." Island residents are forever complaining about unfriendly mayors raising the ferry fare or dumping homeless shelters and prisons in their midst. New Yorkers elsewhere, hard-pressed themselves, show little sympathy, suggesting

that if it can't take the heat, perhaps Staten Island should get out
of the city.

All Aboard! (Except You with the Sword!)
Staten Island Ferry

Ride the Staten Island Ferry and here's what you see: the towered tip
of Manhattan, the World Trade Center, the Statue of Liberty. It's the
city's best bargain, all for just 50 cents.

You could even be murdered while on board.

If death isn't what you had in mind, we offer the following advice:
before buying a ticket, make sure no one on line is carrying a two-foot-
long sword. The last and only time that happened, July 7, 1986, a madman
stabbed two passengers and injured nine others.

Juan Gonzalez, a 43-year-old refugee, bought the sword in the criminal
consumption mecca of the world, Times Square. He wrapped it in newspaper and boarded the 8:45 A.M. *Samuel I. Newhouse* ferry, packed with
five hundred commuters and sightseers.

Only a week before, Gonzalez had been living in a homeless shelter
in Upper Manhattan. One night, he was heard screaming, "I'm going to
kill! God told me so!" The police sent him to nearby Columbia Presby-
terian Hospital, where he was examined and released after promising—
scout's honor—to seek psychiatric help.

As the ferry left the dock, Juan sat on the first deck, his newspaper
package on his lap. He was quite familiar with boat rides, having arrived
in the United States nine years earlier with thousands of Cuban refugees
on the Mariel boatlift (another criminally distinguished Mariel alum was
Julio Gonzalez—no relation to the sword carrier—who torched the Happy
Land social club in 1990).

The boat was nearing the Statue of Liberty as Gonzalez unwrapped
his sword. Without warning, he stood up and began slashing a gruesome
swath through the horrified crowd. He killed Jordon Walker, a 61-year-
old security guard, and Rose Cammarota, a 71-year-old church volunteer
on her way to serve lunch at a Staten Island nursing home. The injured

included a professor, a bank president, and a middle-aged tourist from Austria. One of the wounded said the blade's slashing his back had felt like fire.

Gonzalez was attacking a woman when a retired cop on board, Edward del Pino, interrupted by firing a gun in the air. Del Pino, a 24-year police veteran, aimed the pistol at Gonzalez's face and shouted, "You move and I'll kill you." After he was arrested, Gonzalez told the cops that God was responsible for his rampage. He was found unfit for trial and was packed off to a state psychiatric ward.

2

Getting Lucky
Huguenot Beach

So you wanna be a gangster.

It takes more than a gun, a well-polished wingtip, and an especially troubled childhood. It takes a quality nickname, something catchy, something that sells newspapers, something related to body parts, food, geography, or state of mind.

We're talking about Scarface, Pittsburgh Phil, or The Lord High Executioner; Legs, Joe the Boss, or Crazy Joe.

It also helps to have biographers who'll make up a good story to go with the name.

Lucky Luciano was said to have gotten his nickname after some gangsters took him for a ride to Huguenot Beach on Staten Island and he survived. A "ride" in gangland isn't a quick trip to the local shopping mall—unless, of course, it's under construction and the mob decides the concrete foundation needs a human touch.

In *The Last Testament of Lucky Luciano,* a book supposedly based on interviews with the gangster himself, the authors claim Luciano returned from the October 17, 1929, ride known as "Lucky." Terrific tale, except that the newspapers, including the *New York Times,* called him Lucky the next day, suggesting that Luciano had already been given the name.

Lucky had been picked up earlier that night at 50th Street and Sixth Avenue by gangsters cruising in a limousine with curtains drawn over the windows. Luciano told the police that when he woke up on the beach, he "thought he was dreaming," the *Times* reported. But he wasn't too sleepy to offer a police officer $50 to get him a cab back to Manhattan.

Before being released by the cops, the *Times* said, Luciano "wearily insisted that he had no enemies."

3

Where Geraldo Made the Grade
Willowbrook

The atrocities of the Willowbrook mental institution were shocking when they were revealed in 1972, but at least the state-run facility eventually closed down.

We can't say the same for Geraldo Rivera, who snuck a camera crew inside the school and told a story of children living in filth and feces.

The story had already been reported by newspapers, but Geraldo, at the tender age of 29, made a big splash. The public called for politicians' heads, and for more TV spots featuring the handsome newsman with the mustache.

Of course, Willowbrook, now a college campus in the making, was only the beginning for Geraldo. Soon television announcers nationwide were teasing viewers with promises like "Topless donut shops of Colorado—next on 'Geraldo'!"

But no one can forget when Geraldo broke into Al Capone's secret vault in Chicago on national television and found nothing but some dust and old bottles. He now claims he did much better with Bette Midler, Margaret Trudeau, and Chris Evert, among the many beauties he claims he took to bed.

"With great practice I became an expert at juggling several relationships at a time," Geraldo wrote in his autobiography, *Exposing Myself*.

How impressive.

Paul Castellano's White House
177 Benedict Road

Mob bosses are known for their share of slinky mistresses, but most are good enough to stow them a safe distance from their wives.

Not Paul Castellano.

He kept his wife and girlfriend under the same roof, the Castellano mansion in well-to-do Todt Hill.

Gosh, how considerate.

It wasn't difficult since the "other woman" was the Castellanos' Spanish-speaking servant, Gloria Olarte.

Space certainly wasn't a problem. Paul and his two women had seventeen rooms in which to float, and his Doberman had plenty of growling space in the professionally manicured yard. Paul called his home the "White House" and had it custom built in the 1970s. Lots of marble, mirrors, and inlaid wood. There was a swimming pool and bocce court out back, two pillars in front, and a glassed-in porch.

Castellano showered Gloria with many gifts, including a bright red Datsun 280-Z. While Mrs. Castellano was upstairs, Paul and his honey hugged and kissed in the kitchen. "What about Mrs. Castellano?" the petite Gloria would ask. Big Paul didn't care. He was the boss. The boss of bosses, even in the kitchen.

For all his underworld muscle, though, Castellano couldn't please his mistress with much more than a few pecks on the lips. He had this problem, you see, with his manhood. No need to get graphic about the surgical procedure he underwent, but let's just say that afterward Paul liked to compare his private parts to a gooseneck lamp. Or a periscope. Laugh all you want, but we hear Paul died a fairly happy man, even though it was on the wrong end of a gun.

As for Big Paul's house, no need to worry—it's safe to visit. His daughter, Connie, put it up for sale in the spring of 1992 for a reported $5 million.

5

Before Miss Liberty
Liberty Island

Don't even think about missing the Statue of Liberty. Go there for the memory of Albert Hicks, an axe murderer who was hanged in front of ten thousand cheering New Yorkers long before Bedloes Island became home to Miss Liberty and her freedom torch.

Albert was a felonious phenom, crook of the year in 1860, his name chanted by crowds outside the Tombs jailhouse, his face immortalized in a plaster cast by circus master P. T. Barnum.

All because he murdered four men at sea.

The trouble began after Hicks was whacked on the head one night and hauled aboard a merchant ship skippered by four men. It was not entirely unusual at the time for short-handed crews to employ such methods of recruitment, or so said Herbert Asbury in his 1927 classic, *The Gangs of New York*. Albert learned when he awoke that he was headed for Virginia to pick up a cargo of oysters. He was not pleased. Albert became very angry when he was not pleased.

Five days later, the empty boat was found drifting off Staten Island. The police discovered puddles of blood on the floor and walls of the boat's cabin. They also found four fingers and a thumb on the deck. A few feet away was a bloodstained axe.

The following day, Hicks' neighbors at 129 Cedar Street in Manhattan told the police that Albert had come home one night with a bag of cash, packed up his wife and child, and taken off for Providence, Rhode Island. Hicks was arrested and charged with piracy and murder after the cops found a watch and picture he had lifted off the dead crew members. It took seven minutes for a jury to convict him and a judge to sentence him to death.

A few days later, Albert took it upon himself to confess to all the murders. He told of how "the devil took possession of me" and how he decapitated one boatman, while cutting off the fingers of another who was hanging by the railing off the side of the boat. Albert made sure that all the bodies, living and dead, ended up in the deep blue sea.

Prison guards at the Tombs on Centre Street put Albert in a special metal cage and thousands of New Yorkers lined up to get a look at him. P. T. Barnum was among those who visited, and he convinced Albert to pose for a craftsman designing a plaster mold of his face. In exchange, P. T. gave Albert $25, a suit, and a couple of boxes of cigars, which Hicks returned to Barnum for display in the showman's famous museum before he went to his execution.

It was a momentous day, that July 13th. Hicks and his chaperone marshals bowed to the thousands rooting for the hanging and the brass bands playing outside the Tombs. Albert was handcuffed, his legs were shackled, and he was placed in the cage on a steamship called the *Red Jacket*. The boat was crammed with people who wanted to see Albert die.

He was shipped to Bedloes Island, where the city maintained a gallows. Hundreds of boats, some decorated with flags and bunting, crowded the water. Everyone craned their necks to get a view of Albert as the marshals slipped the noose around his neck. It wasn't too hard to see; the marshals built thirty-foot-high scaffolding for spectators a few yards from the water's edge.

It took Albert three minutes to die, but no one missed a second of it, not if they could help it. He was buried in Calvary Cemetery. Days later, his corpse was dug up by thieves.

ACKNOWLEDGMENTS

A THOUSAND AND ONE JOURNALISTS WERE GENEROUS ENOUGH TO STOP MOV-ING for a half-second to recall some particularly salacious murder or scandal they thought should be included in *New York Notorious*. Among them were Mike Pearl, Pete Hamill, Bill Bastone, Marsha Kranes, Mel Juffe, Brad Hamilton, Dave Lewis, Eddie Borges, and Michael Shain. Special thanks to Barbara Glauber for the maps, to former *Post* editor Jerry Nachman and *News* editor and publisher Jim Willse for permission to use the photos, and to *Post* headline writer extraordinaire Jimmy Lynch for the title.

Thanks also to Municipal Archives director Ken Cobbs, and Faigi Rosenthal and Merrill Sherr, the head librarians at the *Daily News* and *New York Post*, respectively. David Hacker, an assistant librarian at the *Post*, took time out to lead us through the paper's sprawling library. Perhaps no clip was more helpful than a story by former *News* reporter Mike Santangelo, recounting the entrees, appetizers, and desserts that were the last supper of a certain overweight gangster.

Other friends, family, and colleagues provided a good deal of support, both moral and otherwise, sometimes without even knowing it. Cheers to Mark Kriegel, Mike McAlary, Charlie Sennott, Michael Powell, Alex Polner and Margret R. Saraco, Michael and Lisa Weiss Schwartzman, Stevie McFadden, Peter Mones, Zoe Vander Weile, Richard Gooding, Charlie Carillo, Kevin Davitt, Joel Siegel, Seth Kaufman, Jason and Laura Shearer Schwartzman, Beth Polner Abrahams and Mark Abrahams, Lyle Harris, Dave Seifman, Mark Mooney, Richie Steier, Rita Delfiner, Nick Balaban, Betsy Causey, Steve Miller, Joel Roberts, Mike Babcock, Dave Hallinan, and Antony Fine. We're also grateful to Katie the Cat and Jack the Dog, who were good enough not to eat the manuscript.

Monica McIntyre and Laurie Merrill were insightful and kind and pulled us through. Special thanks to David Vigliano, our agent, for taking a chance, and Jane Meara, our editor at Crown, who was patient, encouraging, and always good enough to laugh at the jokes.

P.S. and R.P.
New York City

INDEX

Duringer, Rudolph "Tough Guy," 38–39
Dworkin, Andrea, 130–131

Earomirski, Sophie, 223
East New York, 191
East Third Street Pier, 138
East Village, 134–140
Ebbets Field, 181–182
Eden, Elizabeth Debbie, 195
Egan, Eddie, 11
Eisenhower, Dwight D., 152
Elliot, Mr. and Mrs. Osborn, 23–24
Emerson, William, 133
Empire Boulevard, 187–188
Empire State Building, 105–106
Entratta, Charlie, 96
Esposito, Meade, 206
Executioner's Song, The (Mailer), 137
Exposing Myself (Rivera), 234

Factory, 118
F.A.L.N., 170–171
Falotico, John, 204
Fama, Joey, 192–193
Farace, Gus, 24–25
Favara, John, 219
Featherstone, Mickey, 101–102
Federal Witness Protection Program, 102
Feegal, Thomas, 151
Feeney, Harry, 197
Feffer, Gerald, 75
Felder, Raoul, 8
Feliciano, Gina, 192
Feliciano, Lydia, 210
Fisch, Isidor, 209
Five Points, 148–149
Floater, the, 59
Flynn, Elizabeth Gurley, 130
Fonda, Jane, 151–152
Fonda, Vanessa, 151–152
Fort Apache, 213–214
Franconeri, Peter, 13–14
Fraunces Tavern, 170–171

"French Connection, The," 11
Friedman, Stanley, 217
F.T.S., 100

Gabel, Hortense, 8, 9
Gabel, Sukhreet, 7–9
Galante, Carmine "The Cigar," 116–117, 183–184
Gallagher, Charles, 55
Gallo, "Crazy" Joe, 97–98, 144–146
Gallucio, Frankie, 177
Gambino, Carlo, 86, 98, 183
Game of Death, The (movie), 94
Gangs of New York, The (Asbury), 149, 236
Garcia, Robert, 205
Garfield, Bea, 130
Garofalo, Eddie, 95
General Slocum, 138–139
Genovese, Catherine "Kitty," 220–221
Genovese, Vito, 83, 117, 146, 147, 183, 196
Gerney, Brigitte, 27
Gigante, Louis, 146
Gigante, Vincent "The Chin," 34, 146
Gilmore, Gary, 137
Giuliani, Rudolph, 47
Goetz, Bernhard, 164–165
Gold, Grace, 45
Goldfus, Emil R., 182
Gonzalez, Juan, 232–233
Gonzalez, Julio, 210–211, 232
Goodfellas (movie), 222
Gotbaum, Betsy, 59
Gotti, Frank, 219
Gotti, John, 72–73, 95, 143–144, 146, 215, 219, 220
Gotti, Pete, 143
Gotti, Victoria, 219, 220
Gracie, Archibald, 14
Gracie Mansion, 14–15
Grant, Hugh, 162
Gray, Judd, 228–229